# Praise for *The Light*

*"My life is dedicated to that which motivates, educates, inspires and uplifts humanity.* The Light *does exactly that—it empowers people to find their greatness and serves to make this world a brighter place for us all."*
**Jack Canfield,** originator of the *Chicken Soup for the Soul* series, featured teacher in *The Secret* and author of the bestseller, *The Success Principles*

"The Light *is a treasure chest of wisdom offering the reader both physical and spiritual guidance. It will certainly help both men and women come to a place of deeper understanding about the Ultimate relationship—understanding who we are and how best we can shine—and I am all for that!"*
**Dr. John Gray,** international bestselling author of the *Mars Venus* book series

"The Light *has been created out of the generosity of its contributors and is offered in service to humantiy. How refreshing! Each chapter is an invitation and opportunity to break through all of the baggage of past conditioning and to transform your life from the ordinary to the extraordinary. You, my brothers and sisters, are destined to live in that Possibility."*
**Lisa Nichols,** featured teacher in *The Secret* and international bestselling author of *No Matter What!*

"The Light *is a shining reflection of the five principles I hold dear to my heart. It is written with integrity to empower the reader to find that place within of love and truth. It is offered without agenda and communicates a message of hope and transformation. The contributors have each given their best and they invite you to be still, to listen, to have discrimination and to be guided by the innate wisdom that is our birthright."*
**Don Miguel Ruiz,** author of the bestselling books *The Four Agreements* and *The Fifth Agreement*

*"The practice of working with the "Light" has been central to my work of Soul Transcendence for the past forty years. I have termed it Living In God's Holy Thought and its presence is a source of transformation and goodness. In using the Light it's best to remain neutral and detached. No push. No force. You just let your Light shine and those who can see it will know its truth. I am delighted to see Keidi Keating's excellent book available to many as a way of spreading the Light and sharing the knowledge that it is available to all of us to be used for the highest good of all concerned. The many contributors openly share their way of spreading their Light and their message of upliftment. In the testing times we live in Keidi's* The Light *is available as a beacon and source of hope, comfort and strength."*

**John-Roger,** D.S.S., founder and spiritual advisor to the Movement of Spiritual Inner Awareness (MSIA)

*"Imagine a book with some of the most powerful healers, psychics and masters in the world all sharing their secrets in one place. Impossible? Yet here it is!* The Light *is a magical journey of enlightenment."*
**Jacky Newcomb**, bestselling author of *An Angel Saved My Life*

*"Reading* The Light *is a transformational experience resulting in increased joy, more love, freedom, inner peace and an undeniable sense of bliss."*
**Steve G Jones**, clinical hypnotherapist

*"*The Light *is a magical journey into the lives of people who reach out to other realms. It will help you to take steps to uncover the real value of creation and indeed yourself. As an international author I highly recommend* The Light; *a masterpiece and a must-read for all."*
**Joseph Alexander**, international bestselling author of books including *My Life with Spirit, Talking with Spirit, My Life Between Two Worlds* and *The Life of the Great Masters*

*"*The Light *is a book that will ignite your spark and can be used as a guide to help make your dreams become reality—a subject very close to my heart. Never has it been so important to shine, and as we attain our full potential it will be good news for you and great news for the world."*
**Marcia Wieder**, Founder and CEO of Dream University

# The Light

## A Book of Wisdom

# KEIDI KEATING
*...with 21 luminaries*

***The Light***
by Keidi Keating

Published 2012 by The Light Network
Copyright © Keidi Keating

Printed in the UK by CPI Group (UK) Ltd, Croydon, CR0 4YY

*Cover design by Tri Widyatmaka*

*Interior layout by Christi Koehl*

*Edited by Richard Laws and Julie Chimes*

*Editors Note: As this book is internationally available, we decided to include Americanisms.*

ISBN: 978-0-9571596-0-0

We offer this book and all it represents at the feet of the Masters of Light.

For everyone
who wants to see
the Light, feel
the Light, be the
Light and spread
the Light, this
book is for you.
Our intention is
to enhance the
world's beauty by
working together
as One Light.

*There is a Light that shines beyond all things on earth, beyond us all, beyond the heavens, beyond the highest, beyond the very highest heavens. This is the Light that shines in our heart.*

**Chandogya Upanishad**

# Contents

# Contents

# Light

A sincere spiritual seeker threw himself at the feet of an enlightened master begging to have a direct experience of the mysterious inner Light. The master smiled and then playfully slapped his follower on the back of the head. Within seconds the man was writhing on the floor and begging for the experience to stop. The master roared with laughter and gently touched his arm and calmed him. Taking hold of the devotee's trembling hand he explained, "In order to know the Light, you have to prepare yourself. Would you put high voltage through faulty wiring or pour precious water through a hose that was full of holes?"

Out of their compassion, the mystics, teachers, saints and sages of all traditions have given us practices to perform, which systematically purify and strengthen our physical, mental and subtle systems. They tell us that if we follow these teachings and apply the practices with diligence, combined with a heartfelt longing to know the Truth of who we really are, we attract the omniscient Grace of God. Gradually the heavy burden of our self-opinionated, self-righteous, rigid ego diminishes and our flexibility and humour increases. We begin to shine. Becoming perfect in these practices is not the goal, although many do get lost in believing this to be the case. No, these techniques are simply getting us ready; preparing us for the greatest gift a human can receive.

Sacred architecture around the world, from remote Himalayan temples to South American pyramids, serves as a physical reminder of this ancient promise of a gift for humanity. They are also representative of the human form. As we enter these monumental buildings, according to our worthiness and preparedness, we are allowed to penetrate deeper and deeper until ultimately we reach the *Sanctum Sanctorum*, the holiest of holies, the inner chamber where the treasures and secrets are kept safe. Traditions explain it could take a lifetime to be deemed worthy of entering this hallowed place and many lifetimes to be ready to receive the highest teachings held therein. And where in the human body is this chamber? And what are these secrets that have been guarded for centuries? The ecstatic mystic and poet Rumi gave us a clue when he wrote: "Only from the heart can you touch the sky."

Within the *Sanctum Sanctorum* a small light glows, representative of the Divine Spark flickering within our own hearts. The awakening of this spark into its full potential is considered to be the most sacred and glorious of initiations. *Shaktipat*, which in Sanskrit literally means the *descent of Divine energy*, can be transmitted by the look, thought or touch of an enlightened being, either living or in spirit. It can be given in dreams or meditation, sometimes the whispering of ancient mantras, whose vibration is the key to opening the locked inner doors of our hearts and minds. Time and space are irrelevant as *Shaktipat* transcends all restrictions of an earthly nature. It cannot be forced and will never be given on demand. Once received, that tiny spark is ignited, exploding into Light; a Light that transforms a person's life from the ordinary to the extraordinary; a Light which contains everything. When this Light is revealed, the mysteries of life and death become apparent and how to live becomes intuitively obvious. There is no more fear, only a deep desire to serve, a feeling of eternal gratitude, a compassionate heart and a marvelous sense of joy and laughter, knowing the sublime truth, that we are all One.

The Christian mystic Saint Augustine wrote of this moment in his work Confessions, Book VII:

> **I entered and beheld with the eye of my soul (whatever that is), the Unchangeable Light beyond my ordinary vision and above my mind.**

*This was no ordinary light, which all humanity may gaze upon, nor was it a greater form of the common light, as though the light of the day should be made brighter, until it floods all space. I should be saying too little if I only said this. No, this was not the common, earthly light, but something other, far from these. Nor was it above my mind, as oil sits above water, or yet as heaven is above earth: it enveloped me and transcended all descriptions. It was the Light that made me. He that knows the Truth, knows what that Light is; and he that knows It, knows Eternity.*

May everyone who reads this book be still and know...

*The Light*

*See it, feel it, be it.*

# About Keidi Keating, Creator of *The Light*

Keidi experienced a sudden spiritual awakening at the age of thirty after a series of transformational healing sessions. The mystical chain of events that followed sparked a yearning to learn about the Soul and continue her spiritual journey.

As a result she grew increasingly intuitive and joyful. This led to the compilation and launch of *The Light* with the goal of raising money for seven charities.

Keidi now edits, writes and publishes books and products, which empower people to reawaken their Light within. She is currently writing her next book, *Teachings from the Light*.

For more information about Keidi, log onto
**www.keidikeating.com.**

# Seeing the Light

*By Keidi Keating*

*I will love the light, for it shows me the way. Yet I will
endure the darkness for it shows me the stars.*
~ **Og Mandino**

There is a Light shining inside all of us. It is a beautiful sphere of radiance and it lives in our spiritual Heart. Some of us may have allowed it to dim over the years until it is no more than a vague glow. Others know of its presence and might tap into it on occasion, but fail to harness its amazing power permanently. This book gives you the tools to take back that power and shine once again.

The world is changing. As individuals we are experiencing difficult times due to the shift in energy which is occurring on the planet. And there are larger changes too—from governments, to systems, to an increased flurry of natural disasters. Amidst this turmoil it is time for everyone to reawaken their inner Light and remember that we are all One. We may look different on the outside and each have unique personalities, but inside we are the same. By loving, forgiving, meditating daily and brightening this inner Light, our lives will flow with the changes. Then we will be in a stronger position to help our fellow man, to help those souls who have not yet transitioned into the Light and to help our Mother Earth to heal. However, we will never reawaken our Light if we continue seeking solutions outside of ourselves. The awakening must come from within. And this book is here to empower us to do that.

**An introduction to my story**

In this chapter I am going to tell the story of how I

discovered my own Light, which led to the birth of this book. It is a very personal tale that directed me to plant an idea *seed* into the *ethereal soil*. This seed soon began to thrive and the universe brought the right people and circumstances my way to enable *The Light* to spill its rays over the world. That seed has transformed into a magnificent tree complete with branches, leaves, blossom and the most succulent fruit one has ever tasted. It is no coincidence that this book has found its way into your hands. Throughout my journey during the last few years I have learnt that everything, yes *everything*, happens for a reason.

## Hitting my lowest point

In late 2009 I felt completely lost and my Light was very dim. I had lived on the Costa del Sol, in Spain, for five years and the expatriate magazine I had started back then had grown into a huge success. My sister and brother-in-law took over the day-to-day running of the magazine in 2006 and I looked for something else to occupy my time. Three years had passed yet I felt more lost than ever. I had no idea who I was, what I was doing, where I was going or even where I wanted to go. And to make matters worse I had just been diagnosed with an overactive thyroid. In my mind things could not get much worse. Every morning when my alarm clock sounded I struggled to find the motivation to drag myself out of bed. What was the point anyway? It seemed like my life had no purpose and I wondered why I had agreed to come to earth in the first place. Often I would curl up on the sofa and cry for hours on end, feeling weak, stuck and useless.

Anyone looking at my life from the outside probably assumed I had every reason to be happy. I lived in Spain where the weather was hot and sunny for at least seven months of the year. I owned my own apartment across the road from a beautiful beach. I had a loving boyfriend.

I owned a magazine business. My first book had been published. All of this meant I should have been happy and overjoyed 24/7, right? Wrong!

My depressive feelings could not sink any lower. I had reached the bottom of a pit. After spending weeks, perhaps even months feeling trapped, a pivotal moment occurred. In a state of exhaustion I asked the right question. I simply looked up and with total presence I said, "Whoever is listening up there; angels, granddad, God, please help me. Let me know my purpose in life and help me to feel happy again." When nothing instantaneous occured I curled back into the foetal position and the tears continued to flow. However, even though it seemed as if nothing had happened, my emotionally-fuelled intention shot into the stars and the cogs of the universe began to turn.

**Following the signs**

A few days later I was flicking through a magazine and noticed an advert called the Mind Body and Spirit Festival in Marbella. I could not stop staring at this advert and *knew* I had to go there. Back then my confidence and self-esteem were so low that I did not even have the courage to attend the exhibition alone. I persuaded my boyfriend, who had no interest in spiritual subjects, to come with me. While he popped to the bathroom I passed a stand focusing on *cellular healing* and feeling drawn to it I picked up a leaflet. It described a process helping to clear people's emotional issues via healing at a cellular level. I felt the words resonate at a profound level of my being.

"Can I help you," said a male voice. I looked up to see a friendly, almost familiar face peering back at me. "Do I know you from somewhere?" he continued, scanning me intently. The ensuing conversation revealed that we lived in totally different areas and there were no rational explanations for the feeling of familiarity. I took one of his leaflets home, knowing that I would book a session with him when the time felt right. Two months later, just after Christmas, that time arrived. The thought of continuing in a state of depression for any longer was unbearable.

We scheduled an appointment for a fortnight later. The night before the session I did not sleep at all and in the morning I felt sick and anxious. I called the healer to cancel, but he reassured me that many people experience similar pre-session feelings, so I took a deep breath and battled through my body's resistance. In the healing room I sat on a chair and the healer sat opposite. It took just one question and perhaps five seconds before I burst out crying, unleashing what felt like years of trapped, pent-up emotions. Snivelling and wiping my eyes, the questions continued coming and I continued answering, feeling that my soul was being stripped practically naked as I shared my deepest secrets with a stranger.

After a while I laid on the bed and the healer led me through a deep breathing exercise. My body trembled violently, releasing trauma that had been stored in my cells for years. The two hours felt incredibly powerful and I knew that I had made the right decision to show up. By the end of the session my hands tingled, my body ached and my head was so light that I no longer felt earthbound. I headed home and, despite the fact it was only midday, fell straight into bed. A few hours later I awoke with a jump at the sound of my name whispered in my ear. I shrugged the incident off and muddled through the rest of the day feeling tender and emotionally raw.

**Seeing the Light**

That night I went to bed as usual and in the early hours I awoke to see a haze of light hovering in my bedroom doorway, which I instinctively knew was the energy field of a man. He spoke, but his voice sounded muffled as if

I was not accurately tuned into his frequency. After a few minutes the Light-being backed away before vanishing into thin air. I lay awake in bed for half an hour or so wanting to comprehend what I had experienced.

And that was just the beginning. In the days that followed a stream of other mystical events occurred. A digital photo frame turned itself on in the night; I grew increasingly psychic and I had a series of incredibly vivid and lucid dreams. Then early one morning my spirit, soul, Light body (or whatever you want to call it) left my physical body and traveled to a different dimension. It began with a high-pitched buzzing sensation, which started in my head then moved throughout my entire body. Physically I was paralyzed and then I felt *myself* sinking down into the bed, feeling the density of the mattress and then the wooden bed all around. A split second thought that I would prefer to be moving upwards instantly manifested and I shot up through a kaleidoscopic display of colors and patterns, which appeared so beautiful I did not want them to end. I *landed* in a different dimensional reality to the earth plane where I met and spoke to other beings before finding myself back in my body, which was still lying on the bed. The out of body experiences continued and involved extra-terrestrial entities, the downloading of a long, complicated code into my being and a trail of past lives—and the feelings associated with them—sliding across my consciousness. These incidents sparked a yearning to discover more about who we really are and how we can live our full potential during our time on earth.

**More awakening experiences**

One day, during my afternoon meditation and having recently purchased a rare crystal called moldavite, which I set on my third eye, I was asked by an anonymous voice to write down my name. I remember the feel of the pen in my hand and observed the letters as they were written. M…E…S…S…I…A…H. Five seconds later my head pushed into the scene and I thought, "That's not my name. My name's Keidi!" Now I am not claiming that I really am a Messiah figure who is here to change the world! When I went inside to discover why this had happened I realized it was to make me aware that every single one of us is the God energy. We are all One.

Another day I was walking along the beach contemplating my purpose in life. I was busy putting *The Light* together at the time and for a fleeting moment wondered whether I was doing the right thing. At that moment I glanced ahead and saw a large white feather lying amongst the pebbles. My initial thought was "Thank you angels. That's a sign." But as my mind sprinted away I decided it was not too weird to see a white feather on the beach above which hundreds of seagulls fly all day long. After my walk I returned to my apartment and as it was a warm day I opened my balcony door a few inches. Imagine my surprise when a white feather blew straight through the small gap and landed in the middle of my living room floor! I had that door open everyday, certainly during the summer months and in eight years of living there nothing had *ever* blown in. I was sure the angels were saying, "You were right the first time. We are here and you are on track with *The Light*!" I could not help but laugh. This white feather was smaller than the one I saw on the beach earlier but it was such a pure white that it practically glowed with gorgeousness. I picked it up and slipped it between the arms of a Buddha ornament on my mantelpiece. It is still there now!

### Discovering my purpose

These unexplainable, irrational, unjustified happenings, which I describe as "my wake-up call" led me to learn that the physical and external is only a part—a small and relatively trivial part—of our life experience. The inner experiences involving the Soul or the Higher Self are what really matter. When we connect with this part of ourselves miracles happen, magic occurs and lives unfold naturally and beautifully. We begin to awaken to who we are and why we are really here.

And that is exactly how it happened for me. One evening, in my new blissfully happy State of Being, I was eating dinner when an idea literally *landed* in my head. I even felt the impact as it touched down in my brain; a string of words which read: "Include those who have helped you find your own Light in one book." And that was it. That was all I had to go by. I vowed to take immediate action and two years later the book was fully compiled and ready for launch. The title eventually came to me in a mysterious way. One day I drove along the coast to see a very special, gifted man, who sees spirits on a daily basis. As I sat on the sofa in his living room he spoke to my spirit guides and my deceased relatives and he passed me some truly inspirational messages. Then one night this man appeared in a dream. At first I was unaware of him as all I noticed was a green hill in the middle of a field and crowds of people clambering to the top where the skies had parted to reveal the most splendid Light. Everyone on the hill reached their hands up to touch those rays of golden Light. Then I became aware that I was watching this on a cinema screen and the man who sees spirits was sitting next to me. He turned to me and said, "I told you one of your books would be made into a film. Congratulations on *The Light*!" Then I woke up.

Despite receiving such a clear and obvious message, I sought further clarification about the title. At the time I was halfway through reading *Autobiography of a Yogi* so I closed my eyes, pictured Paramahansa Yogananda in my mind's eye and said to myself, "Give me a sign about the title of my book. I'm going to open your book and the first word I see will be that sign." The first word my eyes fell on was *Light*.

Some people would call these events coincidences, but so far as I have learnt there is no such thing as a coincidence, only signs.

Eternally grateful to the universe for leading me along this path of self-discovery, I began to seek other teachers who could help to reawaken even more of my Light. I soon attracted an inspirational group of people who empowered me to make this dream a reality.

Then, by a heavenly dose of magic, this collection of bright sparks united as a Divine team to contribute chapters to this book, creating a Light so bright that the pages sparkle with wisdom, knowledge and insight. Each contributor offers a strand of vibrant color, which has been woven into a magnificent tapestry of Light. You may be attracted to one particular strand which calls to you and you can be assured that is the doorway to your truth. I hope with all my heart that the words, energy and experiential exercises inside this book will lead you to a lifetime of love, joy, peace, truth, beauty and freedom. Every one of us has the natural birthright to *See it, Feel it, Be it* and to remember that it is *we* who are *The Light*.

Love and Light,

Keidi Keating

**I recommend that you read and work through the three sections of this book sequentially in order to enhance your experience of *The Light*.**

 Watch Keidi's latest interviews for *The Light*, plus other relevant press and media information by entering this link into your browser: **www.thelightnetwork.com /thelight/media/press-room.**

# Section 1
# Preparation

*There was once a traveler who was determined to discover the truth of who he was. He was prepared to go to the ends of the earth on his quest.*

*As he was about to begin his journey a radiant woman stood in his path. "Before you begin," she said, "there are certain attributes you must master." She smiled with compassion. "There are many obstacles on your path and you must be prepared."*

# About Ken Lauher

Ken Lauher advises individuals, businesses and organizations how to implement practical *Feng Shui* solutions to help them achieve their goals and live a more fulfilling life.

His inspiring and transformational work with celebrities and business owners also makes him a sought after speaker on *Feng Shui* and life enhancement.

Based in New York City, Ken works with local, national and international clients. For more information log on to **www.kenlauher.com**.

# The Home:
# Our Sanctuary
# of Light

*By Ken Lauher*

*We can't change the direction of the wind, but we can
adjust the sails.*

~ **Indian Proverb**

One day I meditated on the question "Who am I?" After several hours the answer came to me in three simple words: "I am Light."

Light is all around us and it is one of the many forms that energy can take. We are *all* Light because Light *is* energy and we are energy. Everything around us is *also* energy and Light, which means we are One with everything.

When we look at a house, a plot of land or a forest, we will see that some areas have no animals around, the vegetation is dead or dying and it is not very vibrant—that place has a negative flow of Light. Then we go to another area and we see that the grass is green, the trees are growing and the birds are singing—that place has a positive flow of Light.

In the same way, the Light in our homes reflects our inner Light and we create the Light around us based on our thoughts, actions and patterns. We can use the power within us to create everything we desire simply by bringing our own energy—and the energy around us—into better alignment with what we want.

The Light that travels through our home and workplace carries valuable information. If we are attuned to it we can discover amazing things about ourselves. The way Light flows through a space reveals certain patterns and outcomes in our lives. These patterns may serve us, leading us to success, happiness and fulfillment—or they may not.

For instance, if the entryway in a home is extremely bright and welcoming it shows a pattern in the lives of the residents. They are people who welcome opportunities and frequently recognize and take advantage of these opportunities as they appear.

On the other hand, if a home's entryway is dark and uninviting the residents may perceive themselves as unlucky. However, in reality the Light which carries opportunity is not attracted to their home. The inhabitants may not be attuned to recognizing good opportunities when they come their way because they are not accustomed to seeing them.

As we get more in touch with our spiritual side we take steps to prepare ourselves for the amazing things to come. Just as we prepare our bodies for the Light to flow through we can use *Feng Shui* to prepare our home.

Once we learn to harness the Light around us so that it flows in alignment with our goals, everything else begins to fall into place. As we *are* Light, when we begin to make changes to our space, we also begin to change.

*In essence Feng Shui is about harnessing the energy of our living environment, including the way the Light flows and collects in our space, to help us achieve our goals and live a more fulfilling life.*

*Feng Shui* can help us to rediscover our inner Light and return to our true Self. When this happens we feel a sense of peace and calm and we begin taking life's small annoyances in our stride. We start to want to give back to others and, when we do, it feels effortless. Most importantly things will have a sense of natural flow—the energy in our space, the opportunities we have made room for in our life and everything we need and want to fulfill our goals will begin gravitating towards us.

Have you ever been in a space where you felt completely

at peace, creative, mindful and in the moment? Maybe, for you, it is out in nature, perhaps in the master bedroom or the bathroom of your home, or maybe you have a special sanctuary. That space feels right to you because the Light in it is in alignment with your goals and with your true Self. Often, when we feel stuck, we put up blockages in our mind and those blocks manifest in our space. By being on the look-out for these blocks, usually shown by the way Light travels through our home, we can correct them with simple *Feng Shui* adjustments.

### *Feng Shui* your main entrance to welcome opportunities

Start by viewing your space from the outside in, looking for patterns and seeing where you may be blocking the flow of energy and opportunities into your life. When you first consider your home, stand quietly at your doorway or on your front lawn and listen to your inner voice. What does your intuition tell you about the space? Quietly observe the Light and life energy of your environment—are plants, trees and even living animals in good health? Is the property filled with happily singing birds or does the environment seem *dead* to you? Is water on the property flowing in a healthy way, or is it stagnant?

What about the neighborhood and surrounding houses? Overall, is there a positive sense of life and energy in the environment? On some level, you may have chosen this particular space and this neighborhood because it was in alignment with your goals and your focus. If not, if the space feels dead and uninspiring to you, you may have chosen that (or created it) because you were feeling blocked in your life at the time too.

Pay close attention to the path to your front door. Is anything blocking that pathway, such as large trees, building pillars, or broken pavement? Your home's front entry, both inside and out, is one of the most important areas; a space that reflects how you are viewed by the outside world, how you view yourself and your willingness to allow opportunities into your life. It is also the primary means by which Light flows in and out of your home.

Once inside your home the front entry or foyer should be well-lit, spacious, open and immediately make you and visitors feel comfortable and at peace. The door should be able to be opened a full ninety degrees with nothing behind to block it from opening. Walking into your home after a long day you should immediately smile, knowing you are in a space that is in alignment with your true Self. Here are some simple *Feng Shui* changes you can make to your front entrance.

☼ Add plants to introduce life energy.

☼ Paint the foyer beige, light blue or light green to open the space and create a sense of brightness.

☼ Add lights on timers so you come home to a well-lit space for a feeling of comfort and security.

☼ Place a mirror on the wall, especially if you face a wall when you enter your home. Make sure you can see your entire face in the mirror. A mirror reflects light to create a brighter space and can also boost your confidence as you leave your home to interact with the world.

### *Feng Shui* in the master bedroom

Not only do simple adjustments to the Light in your environment help opportunities, income, health and happiness flow more easily, but these changes also serve as constant, subconscious reminders of your true intentions as the Light in your environment shifts to match your goals.

The bedroom plays a significant role in your self-confidence, health and happiness. It should be a private retreat where you feel nurtured and comfortable in order to get a good night's sleep and awaken feeling well-rested and refreshed in order to pursue your goals.

Set your intention to make the bedroom a nurturing space, even if you just make small, inexpensive changes. As you begin to love your bedroom, you will find your energy levels and your confidence increasing. These are two major components to happiness and success. When you are well-rested you will find it so much easier to find happiness.

☼ Place your bed in the command position for a good night's sleep. When your bed is in the command position, you have a clear view of the door to your bedroom, but you are not directly in line with the door.

☼ Create a sense of balance in the bedroom by placing your bed so there is room to walk around it on both sides, with matching nightstands.

☼ Your headboard should be solid and firmly attached to the bed.

☼ A queen size bed is the best size. A twin or full size bed is too small and does not leave you room to grow emotionally or spiritually. It also does not leave room for a partner in your life. A king size bed, which often has two foundations or box springs, can split your energy.

☼ Do not store anything other than soft linens or blankets under the bed—nothing sharp or metal, no paperwork, no photos, no mementos from past loves or experiences.

☼ Do not place family photos (other than pictures of you and your significant other) in the bedroom.

### *Feng Shui* in the kitchen

For most people, money, career success and recognition are at least small parts of their quest for happiness. Career success helps attract income that lets us buy the things we need and want for comfort and enjoyment.

In *Feng Shui*, the kitchen plays an integral role in our status; how we are viewed by others and in our career success, which often leads to greater income. Follow these tips to *Feng Shui* your kitchen.

☼ Do not cook with your back to the kitchen entry. If your stove faces the wall place a mirror in front of it so you can see people enter and leave the kitchen.

☼ Additional mirrors to the side of your stove, reflecting the burners, will symbolically double your wealth.

☼ Keep your stove clean and make sure all burners work properly as the stove represents how you are viewed by others. Use the stove every day and use each burner regularly.

### *Feng Shui* in the living room

As one of the rooms where we spend the most time with friends and family, engaged in activities or hobbies that bring us happiness, the flow of Light in our living room tells us a lot about the patterns of our lives. Look around your living room or family room and decide what stories it tells about the life you are living right now. Is it in alignment with what you want, with your own true purpose and inner Light? If not, you can make changes to the space that will improve the flow of Light and provide everyday reminders of your life's goals, helping you stay on track to achieve them.

☼ Clear clutter from this room to create a stress-free environment where you can relax and entertain.

☼ Furniture should be placed to encourage the flow of Light and avoid dark corners. If people cannot navigate a space easily, neither can the Light.

☼ The best colors for a living room are yellow, beige or tan, green or blue. Energize the Light in a living room by adding a variety of brighter colors, shapes, shades and patterns.

☼ Add live plants to the living room to introduce more life *chi* into the space, especially if you have a corner that tends to attract clutter and stagnant energy.

### *Feng Shui* in the bathroom: creating your private spa sanctuary

One place where you can really nurture yourself is in the bathroom. Many people neglect their bathroom not realizing how this space is tied into self-confidence, sense of self and success. Your bathroom should provide the lift in confidence that you need to go after your goals without fear or hesitation. More so than any other room in your house, it should make you feel like your best self before you step out to meet the world. Self-confidence, after all, is a key component to success and happiness.

What stories is your bathroom telling about you? What would you like it to say, instead? A bathroom that is neglected may be saying your confidence and finances require attention. Constantly dripping water not only wastes water and raises your water bill, it creates a sense of neglect in the bathroom. When water escapes down the drain, positive energy, good fortune and opportunities go with it.

Like the bedroom, the bathroom is a private place you can stock with all the things that raise your confidence and help you to feel pampered. If you have a make-up or perfume collection you treasure, showcase it on shelves or your bathroom counter. Stow electrical items like hair straighteners, curling irons and hair dryers neatly. Getting ready in the morning and winding down at night should be an effortless experience that makes you feel good—almost like going to a spa and having someone else take care of all your needs.

When you decorate your bathroom pay attention to all of your five senses. For instance, luxurious towels—the kind you would find at a five-star hotel—can make you feel pampered right out of the shower or bath. Here are some more easy changes you can make in your bathroom:

☼ Make sure your bathroom offers proper ventilation. This prevents unhealthy mold and mildew from sprouting, improves the air quality and ensures the plants and people in your home will thrive.

☼ Keep the toilet seat down before you flush and when it is not in use. This prevents wealth and opportunities (in the form of *chi*) from being flushed down the drain and it also keeps bacteria out of the air.

☼ Add task lighting for personal grooming tasks like shaving or putting on make-up and lights on dimmers to create a luxurious sanctuary at bath time and in the evening before bed.

☼ Your bathroom mirror should permit you to see your entire face comfortably. Mirrors that cut off the top of your head or any part of your face can symbolically hurt your self-esteem and prevent you from living up to your true potential.

☼ Add live plants or fresh herbs such as wheat grass, rosemary, lavender or mint to the bathroom to introduce living *chi* and infuse the air with fresh scents. Avoid artificial air fresheners.

**Creating a private sanctuary for meditation**

It is important to stay attuned to our inner Light as much as possible and one way to do this is through meditation. While we can meditate nearly anywhere and at any time, building a meditation room or sanctuary within our home is one way to make meditation and spirituality a focal point in our life. A meditation space does not have to be large, expensive, or ornate. In fact, the simpler the better.

☼ A meditation room should be decorated in pleasing, sedate *Feng Shui* colors, with no patterns to create a busy environment. Consider colors such as earthy green, light blue, or colors designed to enhance spirituality, such as black. Muted reds and yellows can also work.

☼ A water element can be a pleasing addition to a meditation room. The soft lull of the fountain adds to the calming and peaceful environment.

☼ Lighting should be soft, low-key and pleasing. Himalayan salt lamps have cleansing properties and emit a soft glow that is ideal for a sanctuary or meditation room. This room will exemplify the way you have used *Feng Shui* in your home.

Adopting *Feng Shui* measures in our home and our lives creates new pathways for the Light to flow. As a result of some simple changes, you will be more connected to Source than ever before.

Add a little *Feng Shui* to *The Light* by printing out and focusing on our visualizations, which includes a check to Charity from *The Light* for one million dollars. This can be downloaded from our Lightbox via this link: **www.spreadthelightcampaign/thelightcheck.**

# About Taran Cameron Macdonald-Parker

Taran is a highly qualified physical fitness trainer who combines her love of dance, yoga and eastern martial arts with an extensive knowledge of healing therapies. Having owned her own health club in Portugal, she has worked throughout Europe as a dancer, choreographer, model and fitness trainer for international competitions. Taran now specializes as a *Kundalini Yoga* Aquarian Teacher and Gong Practitioner, healing through sound.

She is also an acclaimed international artist whose creative talent was spotted and polished by Disney. She has created her own unique style of spiritual tribal fusion art, which led her to expressing these ancient sacred symbols onto silk and skin through her UK based Skin Art studio, Kiss my Ink. Her inspired illustrations are about to reach a younger audience in *The Wish-Fulfilling Tree,* a spiritual adventure story written by Julie Chimes.

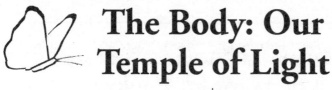

# The Body: Our Temple of Light

☼

*By Taran Cameron Macdonald-Parker*

*Do you not know that your body is the temple of The Spirit of Holiness who dwells within you, whom you have received from God?*
~ **Corinthians 6:19**

Yoga is a profound Sanskrit word, which has many layers of meaning. Often these sacred words get overused and misunderstood when they enter the western world, losing their essence and potency. The word *yoga* probably invokes stereotype images of designer clad ladies clutching their colorful mats or eastern ascetics sitting in the perfect lotus posture. Whilst both hold a part truth, neither image reflects the whole truth. In a mundane sense yoga means the yoking together of horses or oxen to pull a cart. Yoga is also a series of proven techniques applied to bodies, minds and spirits enabling us to expand our awareness and explore our multi-dimensional depth, in order to reveal our true nature and potential as human beings. In the deeper sense it describes the joining together and the uniting of the individual with the universal. In other words yoga is the union of the individual's consciousness with the Infinite consciousness and this is the ultimate relationship and goal of all spiritual practices.

Preparing the physical body is the first facet of yoga we must master and understand, as the body is our vehicle with which we travel through this life. The inner workings of our physical body are very complicated yet it is also a subtle system and an amazing design. The body has glands, blood, circulation, skin, bones, organs, breathing apparatus, heartbeat, pulsation, a brain, a sensory system and a complex nervous system. It is an extraordinary gift that needs to be treasured.

***This body is the only one we get and it needs cleaning, nurturing and regular tuning.***

The normal everyday use of our body creates wear and misalignment. Our physical body should be strong and in balance; a sturdy yet flexible spine constitutes a robust and healthy nervous system. The particular branch of yoga I specialize in is called *Kundalini Yoga*. Initially it teaches us how to gain a strong nervous system, good circulation and an awareness of the impact of our habits. This gives us a firm foundation and releases energy, allowing us to deal with the mental and spiritual aspects of our lives. *Kundalini* can be described as a dormant spiritual energy that exists in all of us. Her awakening is one of the marvels of human life and transforms us from ordinary to extraordinary beings.

These days there are very many ways to keep fit, from weight training, running, *boxercise,* to *zumba* and all manner of sport, the list is almost endless! However, none of these combine the profound mastery of body and mind in the same way yoga does. The mind is the second facet of yoga we have to study. In our human life the mind guides our actions and consequently, without discipline it will control our emotions.

**My story**

Since I can remember, going back to the age of five and six, I was extremely active and simply loved sport. I would win everything especially on sports day. After leaving school all my friends were drinking and smoking but I just couldn't join in so instead I would go out dancing! I loved (and still love) dancing! I suppose it was another form of exercise, a letting go and feel good sport. By the time I was twenty-one

I part owned a health club in Portugal. I was teaching weight training, step aerobics, stretching and dance. I ran on the beach for relaxation! I was physically fit and loved it; loved feeling fit, loved looking fit, loved teaching being fit, but I did ask myself, "Where is all this going?" Even back then I knew something was missing and my quest to discover something deeper began.

It took a few years, a lot of synchronistic meetings and a return to the UK, but gradually that longing for understanding blossomed into two passions: art and yoga. I discovered that the practice of *Kundalini Yoga* filled in everything that I had been missing. As well as mastery of our physical bodies it is also the yoga of awareness and a science and technology to heal the Soul. I know that my yoga practice has helped in achieving all the things that my heart desired. I now feel I have received so much that I can also help and serve others to claim their happy, healthy, birthright, so they too can shine their Light and become a beacon of hope in this world.

**How does Yoga work?**

Yoga predominately works the spine as it helps to have supple back and good core strength. The spinal column is connected to the central nervous system and nerve signals in this system cause the brain consciously or unconsciously to sense something and send a response. Yoga increases the energy moving through particular nerve pathways. The techniques are known as *Breath of Fire*, intensifying this movement. *Breath of Fire* is a fundamental breath technique that accompanies many postures and has numerous beneficial effects, such as boosting the immune system and helping to prevent *dis-ease*. It also strengthens the nervous system to help resist stress, aids in physical and mental healing and much more.

Stress is our modern day *dis-ease*, which if not dealt with will gradually put all of our physical and subtle systems out of balance, resulting in all manner of health and emotional problems. I see that even children as young as four or five are becoming stressed, having to deal with divorced parents, step families and siblings, school, peer pressure and a sense that the world is in chaos. This results in a lack of security, which only adds to their stresses. The media has a significant role to play, constantly bombarding our youngsters and teenagers with superficial values, distorting their young and easily influenced bodies and minds, making them become dissatisfied with what they have, especially physically! When we can learn how to overcome stress, then a level of contentment and deep relaxation can be achieved even in restless and irritable teenagers.

## Why do any physical spiritual practice?

Our bodies have been perfectly designed to carry us through our lives and we can heal and evolve the body and mind with simple yoga techniques. We do not have to be super strong or super flexible, yoga is for everyone and that is its beauty.

*It is our highest duty to respect and care for our body and mind.*

There are many bad habits that cause us to neglect the body. There are those who think it unimportant to obtain spiritual understanding but that limited view is nonsense! We can only attain the higher states of awareness when we bring balance to the body and the mind. The ultimate spiritual awakening happens when the thousands of energy channels in us, known in Sanskrit as *nadis*, allow the unrestricted flow of the life breath, the *prana*. Without effort to get spiritually fit, we will not get very far!

The benefits of practicing yoga are a stronger and more flexible body and mind. Age can be measured by the flexibility of our spine, so exercises that work the spine help us to stay young and healthy. Yoga dissolves stress, resulting in less greying of our hair and boosts immune and glandular systems so our skin glows and we look younger. Even on a mundane level yoga generally makes us look and feel great!

There are many different branches and styles of yogic practice and there is evidence that spiritual teachers have been mastering these techniques for centuries. In 1939 Peter Kelder published a small book, which created quite a stir in the western world. It contained a series of exercises known as *The Five Tibetans*, reported to be over 2500 years old. Also known as the five rites of rejuvenation, these simple exercises systematically re-align and balance the energy centers and stimulate the circulation of essential life energy throughout the body. Readers who began doing them found that in only a few weeks they were looking younger, sleeping soundly and waking up feeling refreshed and energetic. They also found that serious medical problems were healed. Other positive side-effects were reported, such as relief from painful joints and arthritis, weight loss and many participants even lost the need for glasses! Of course these improvements are great, however they are not the goal, rather they are an indication we are ready to begin the journey that is our birthright. Before we embark on this great adventure it is important to understand what lies within and the workings of our subtle body.

**The chakras and *Kundalini***

Our bodies contain major subtle energy centers, known as the *chakras* or wheels of energy. They begin at the root of the spine and continue up along the spine to the crown of the head. Each energy center needs to be balanced and energized so that they spin in a way that creates the correct vortexes of energy to allow the sacred and mysterious *Kundalini* to begin Her holy work. Through yogic exercises and breathing techniques and if it is the right moment in our destiny, we can come into alignment with each center, so the flow of the purifying *Kundalini* energy travels unrestricted on the way to

Her final destination. The actual process allows our *prana*/life force (breath) to merge with the *apana* (eliminating energy) and a subtle pressure is created, drawing the *Kundalini* upwards. When the chakras come into balance, concentration of the scattered mind can be achieved. Although there are many ways in which this one-pointedness can be attained, the underlying principles are the same. If the mind is focused then it is easier to deal with the negativity and delusions that create the obstacles in our path. When *Kundalini* passes through the central nerve known as the *sushumna* and reaches the highest chakras, we are truly blessed.

Each of the centers in our bodies contains different qualities both positive and negative. My teacher Yogi Bhajan explained this process saying, "Men of great knowledge actually found out about the chakras, their workings, their petals, their sounds, their infinity, their co-relationship and their powers. They found that the life of a human is totally based on these chakras. They developed into a whole science. This total science gave birth to *Kundalini Yoga*."

Negativity is stored in the first, second and third energy centers, such as fear, depression, anxiety, anger, shame, despair, guilt and irresponsible relationships. Whether we are aware or not, our lives generally revolve around these and we can become imprisoned by them and addicted to our negativity and a life of shallow values.

***If these centers remain blocked, it keeps us in the dark making it is impossible for our Light to shine.***

Spiritually based exercise stimulates these centers, shifting negativity; opening up our perception, feelings and choices; allowing a flow of fresh and positive energy to sweep through our lives and uplift our thoughts.

We can become addicted to depression, anger and negativity issues, even though that is hard to believe. Most people think addiction is predominately alcohol or drug based but this is only a part of the problem. We can also be addicted to harmful relationships and all these ultimately cause problems, illness, dis-ease, dis-contentment and unhappiness within our being. How do we get free from these limiting beliefs? We begin by exercising the body. Simple spine exercises can balance and energize these centers in a way that can release all the dark and negative qualities to reveal a more grounded, creative, contented and secure Self. We become a positive person. The optimum human being is designed to allow a flowing sacred energy, creating exquisite patterns visible to a trained eye: energy flowing through the spine, the energy centers and the body and limbs.

The chakra system is composed of eight subtle energy centers, seven in the body and one in the aura, or *magnetic field* as it is sometimes known. A whole chapter could be dedicated to each chakra, but here is a brief description of each and how they influence our lives.

### The first chakra - *Muladhara* (Earth)

Sometimes known as the root chakra, it is located at the end of the spine between the anus and the sexual organs and connected to the organs of elimination. Here it is said the sacred *Kundalini* energy lies sleeping, waiting for the Divine moment in our destiny when She is called to awaken. This first chakra is concerned with the basic questions of security and survival and is the arena of our sense of individuality, selfishness and early life. It also contains the qualities of the earth, strength and steadfastness and is linked to the sense of smell.

### The second chakra - *Svadisthana* (Water)

Located in the sex organs, this chakra rules our sexuality, sensuality and is also linked to the taste buds. This is the arena of burning desire, lust, clinging, false projection and delusions. It takes great discipline and grace to quieten the raging passions found within the second energy wheel. This is where the guidance of a teacher and adherence to the practices are invaluable because when we overcome the lure of this chakra, we can have the sublime experience of cosmic bliss.

### The third chakra - *Manipura* (Fire)

Located at the navel point, *manipura* signifies luster and is sometimes called the jewel in the body. Here is the center of fire, burning away impurities and blazing enough light to power our ability to see. This is the seat of treachery, sadness and shame—we often say we "have a gut feeling" that something is wrong. The will of the spiritual warrior is awakened here, determined to transform negative qualities into positive attributes, essential for the continuation of the spiritual quest.

### The fourth chakra - *Anahata* (Air)

This is one of the key subtle centers, located in the region of the heart. Here positive traits emerge out of the negativity in the lower chakras as kindness and compassion awaken. We develop the power to discriminate and discern what supports our spiritual growth. In the heart we are invited to go beyond the sense of *I, me and mine* and experience a deeper sense of brotherhood and universality. This is the location of the inner temple where the sages have glimpsed the wonder of the Light of their own soul. The opening of the heart is an actual experience drawing us into the subtle realms.

### The fifth chakra - *Vishuddha* (Ether)

Located in the region of the throat, this is the center of communication where one experiences the vibration of sound and the power of the word. This chakra relates to hearing and in the ethers we begin to hear subtle and celestial sounds. We also learn to listen to what is behind words and develop clairaudience. The melodramas of the lower chakras are behind us as we stand at the gateway to liberation.

## The sixth chakra - *Ajna*

Located between the eyebrows and often called the third eye, this is where we leave the elements of the physical world behind. It is the still point, where the mind ends its relentless chatter, becoming single-pointed and focused on the inner realms. However, before we can enter into the highest experiences we have to have mastered seeing the unity and connectedness of the world and we also assess the long range effects of our actions. We begin to perceive Light in all things as well as ourselves.

## The seventh chakra - *Sahasrara*

Located at the top of the head and known as the crown chakra, here we arrive at the final destination. Since time began, the experiences and states of bliss attained when this chakra is fully awakened have been known, recorded and guarded as the most precious secret. When the Divine Mystery is revealed we experience the Infinity of the Self and we become enlightened.

There is also an eighth chakra, which is the aura. This is located in the magnetic that surrounds us at a distance of up to nine feet in each direction. The quality of the aura reveals the personality and reflects our radiance. When we are at a certain level of purification, seeing and reading auras becomes the most obvious way of *knowing* each other.

Most people believe that enlightenment is for great masters and yogis on a strict yogic path. It is an interesting fact that the true meaning of the word *guru* means from darkness (*gu*) to light (*ru*) and a true *guru* knows the secrets of guiding us to enlightenment. Fortunately, because of their compassion, we do not have to run off to live in a cave in the Himalayas. They have given both written and oral guidance on how to lift ourselves out of our ignorance into the Light.

They tell us it can be achieved through the practicing of yoga and meditation but always advise us to have the guidance of qualified teachers.

A person with a well prepared body and mind shines incredibly and becomes a magnet to others. We become a human lighthouse, a beacon for all living things that are attracted and uplifted by the warmth we radiate. This warmth is created by unconditional love and it is palpable when in the presence of an enlightened one. Yoga transforms us into beings of Light.

---

### ☼ Light Practice ☼

The following is a fundamental exercise in *Kundalini Yoga* and it is one of the few exercises that is a complete action within itself, known as a *kriya*. It is no ordinary exercise, a *kriya* works on all levels of our being—known and unknown. We might block the more subtle experiences of higher energies by pushing the physical body too much or we may have an experience of higher consciousness but not be able to integrate it into our life because our body is too weak. So we need to prepare ourselves by steady practice. This particular practice is called *Sat Kriya* and it is a highly potent spiritual workout, said to stand alone like a precious gem.

These are some of the benefits attained through the practice of *Sat Kriya:*

☼ Strengthens the entire sexual system and releases phobias about sexuality, allowing us to control the insistent sexual impulse. Sexual energy is re-channeled and transmuted into creative and healing activities in the body.

☼ Stimulates the natural flow of energy resulting in the improvement of our general physical health, as all the internal organs receive a gentle rhythmic massage. The heart gets stronger from the rhythmic up-and-down of blood pressure generated from the pumping motion from the navel point.

☼ People who are severely maladjusted or who have mental problems benefit from this *kriya* since these disturbances are always connected with an imbalance in the energies of the lower three chakras.

☼ This Light Practice works directly on stimulating and channelizing the *kundalini* energy, enabling us to deepen and embody our spiritual experiences.

Begin by sitting on the heels and stretch the arms over the head so that the elbows hug the ears. You can also sit in easy position or on a chair. Interlock all the fingers except the first ones (index) which point straight up. Cross the thumbs: females cross left over right and males cross right over left.

This Light Practice must always be done with the chanting of a *mantra*, a set of sacred and often secret syllables, which set up an intense healing vibration. If you imagine your body as a series of doorways, these sacred mantras are the keys which will open them. The mantra we must use is *Sat Nam, Sat* meaning *Truth* and *Nam* meaning *Identity.* It is important to make the right sound. *Sat* should sound like *sutt* and needs to resonate from the navel point and solar plexus. As you chant *Sat* pull the umbilicus all the way in toward the spine. *Nam* is chanted almost like a sigh and with a long *a*, so it sounds like *naam.* On chanting *Nam* relax the belly and release the lock. Begin to chant *Sat Nam* emphatically in a constant rhythm about eight times every ten seconds.

The eyes should be slightly open (one tenth of the way) staring at the tip of the nose. This puts pressure on the frontal lobe at the pituitary gland and aids the brain.

Continue chanting for at least three minutes. The hips and lumbar spine should not rotate or flex. Your spine should be straight as your arms stretch slightly up and down with each *Sat Nam* as your chest lifts. Inhale and squeeze the muscles tightly from the buttocks all the way up the back, past the shoulders. Mentally visualize energy waves flowing out through the top of the skull.

To end, inhale and stretch upwards. Hold the breath and squeeze the anal, sexual and navel muscles. These represent the first three energy centers and the position is known as *Mulhabandh*. Hold for ten seconds then release and repeat twice more. Do not try to force *Mulhabandh*—it happens automatically if the navel is pulled inwards. You may build the time of the *kriya* up to sixty-two minutes but remember to relax immediately afterwards. Ideally, you should relax for twice the length of time that the *kriya* was practiced. A good way to build up the time is to do the *kriya* for three minutes, then rest for two minutes. Repeat this cycle until you have completed fifteen minutes of *Sat Kriya* and ten minutes of rest. Finish the relaxation by resting for an additional twenty minutes. Respect the inherent power of the technique. Deep relaxation after this *kriya* is essential and nearly as important as the initial effort. The body's systems need time to regenerate and reconstitute themselves.

Even if you have time for nothing else, make this *kriya* part of your everyday exercise.

We believe that "it's time to shine!" Read our Mission Statement for The Light Network via this link: **www.thelightnetwork.com/about-us/the-company**.

# About Dr. Sadeghi

Habib Sadeghi, D.O, is the founder of Be Hive of Healing, an integrative health center based in Los Angeles. With more than fifteen years of direct patient care, he provides a comprehensive knowledge of revolutionary healing protocols in integrative, osteopathic, anthroposophical, environmental and family medicine, as well as clinical pharmacology. Through a unique and individualized approach to healthcare that includes evidence-based, western medical interventions and intuitive eastern healing modalities, Dr. Sadeghi has successfully integrated eastern and western healing practices earning him a respected reputation and a patient base that reaches around the world.

Dr. Sadeghi is also an on-air expert for health issues for *FOX News* and *Geraldo at Large*. He is regularly sought after as an expert in the fields of dietary supplementation, detoxification and holistic interventions for chronic conditions and venues around the world.

For more information about Dr. Sadeghi, go to
***www.behiveofhealing.com.***

# Spiritual
# Nutrition

*By Dr Habib Sadeghi*

*You already have the precious mixture
that will make you well. Use it.*

~ **Rumi (13th Century)**

Food is simple. At least, it used to be. Knowing what to eat and whether it was healthy and healing for us was clear. It was instinctual. We did not have to think about food. We just ate it. Today, food has become complicated. As humans normally do with most issues, we over think them, relying too much on our intellect instead of intuition. At a time when we have countless scientific studies telling us this is good or that is bad, it seems that identifying what food really is would become easier. It has not. How many times have you watched the evening news cite a recent study that declares eggs, red meat or any other food is bad for you in some way? How long did it take before the same programs reported on a newer study praising the virtues of these same foods? It is no wonder we are confused about what food is and whether it is good for us. Adding more complication are labels like *all natural, vitamin-fortified, organic,* and so on. Who knows what to eat anymore? The good news is that food is still simple if you trust yourself and know what to look for.

## Food versus *phood*

As whole beings, our mind, body and spirit are inseparable. An imbalance in one leads to problems in the other. We cannot be fully conscious or spiritual if our bodies are in an unhealthy state. Real food is simple and identifiable. Fake food-like substances, or *phood* as I call it, has always undergone some type of processing where elements are either added or taken away. Food is complete. *Phood* is always changed in some way. The more processing a food undergoes, the closer it gets to becoming *phood*. A good rule of thumb to use is that if something comes in a can, box or bag, it has probably undergone a high amount of processing and therefore is no longer food. The more processing food goes through, whether it is high heat sterilization, added preservatives, or emulsification, the more it becomes denatured. These processes destroy the fragile vitamins, minerals and enzymes that our bodies need to function properly. That is why you often see food labels that read "Fortified with Vitamin X." This is because the initial processing methods the food went through destroyed its original vitamins, so they had to be added back in at the end of the assembly line. By that time, your body cannot absorb these *tacked on* vitamins because their co-factors have been destroyed as well. Certain vitamins and minerals work in tandem in our bodies and are known as co-factors. We cannot absorb one without the help of the other, so arbitrarily adding single vitamins and minerals after processing does little to no good.

We are gradually becoming more familiar with the dangers of *phood*, such as produce from genetically modified organisms (GMO), pesticides, chemical colors and flavorings. Even so, it is not always easy to tell the difference between food and *phood*. It is obvious that a frozen pizza is processed food, but what about something like a jar of organic apple juice? No one would argue the benefits of apple juice, but remember real food is simple. If we have an apple and peel it, we have taken it one step away from its original form. We then cut it, remove its pulp, pasteurize the juice with high heat then store it in an anaerobic, oxygen-deficient environment like a jar. We have now added four more steps of processing. The end product is a denatured substance that is not even close to its original form. It has become *phood* and that is not organic. Think about it. The universe gave us apple trees. Have you ever seen an apple juice tree? This is the Divine's way of telling us that food is to be eaten in the form in which it is presented to us. You could certainly juice your own organic apples and that would preserve the vitamins, but the loss of the skin and pulp would allow the sugar to be absorbed far too quickly into your bloodstream, causing a spike in insulin among other problems.

An apple is a complete food because it has all the proper nutrients we need, provided to us in a way that allows them to be introduced to our bodies in an ideal, time-released fashion. Juice has a place in our diets, particularly when we are recovering from sickness. Even so, if you have a choice between apple juice and an apple, always go for the apple. Although we can consider ourselves educated about healthy food, it is easy to misunderstand that processing means more than added chemicals. As such, we can find ourselves making choices we think are healthy and end up eating *phood* instead.

When choosing real food, ask yourself how many steps a particular item had to go through to get to its current state. Does it appear in nature in this condition? Ask yourself, "If a prehistoric caveman were holding this item, would he be able to recognize it as food? Would he instinctually know what to do with it?" If the answer is "No," it is not food. Whole food is always presented to us in exactly the way it came from nature with little to no processing, providing the highest nutritional density. Nutrition and processing are inversely proportional. The less processing food has, the higher its nutritional content will be and vice versa.

### Light or lite foods

In regard to food labels, I find it best to choose items that have five or less ingredients. If it has too many, or something

I cannot pronounce, it is not real food. If you can afford it, always choose organic produce. Today, food travels long distances and can be stored for extended periods of time. Once a fruit or vegetable is separated from its root source, it starts to breakdown, slowly losing its nutritional value. This is why it is important to choose produce that is grown locally and sold at a neighborhood farmer's market. The shorter the distance and amount of time it takes for your food to get to you, the more nutrient dense it will be.

Nature made fruits and vegetables colorful for a reason. They are supposed to catch our eye and let us know that they are good to eat. Subliminally, we know that color means nutrition and flavor. We are drawn to it. Be sure the color is bright, the odor is strong and the flavor intense. These attributes are also nature's way of signaling to us that these foods are full of powerful antioxidants.

When food fills our senses like this, we feel connected to it. It is a kind of rush, an energy exchange that makes us feel the food is alive. That is because it is. What we sense in the moment, when we take in the sharp, zesty scent of a lemon, is its life force energy. Every living thing emits this same energy to greater or lesser degrees. The Hindus call it *prana*. The Chinese call it *chi*. There are many names for it, but it is the energetic vibration emitted by everything that is alive. For thousands of years, this idea was looked upon as strictly spiritual philosophy, but today we can prove this vital life energy exists through Kirlian photography. The process involves placing an object on a photographic plate that is connected to an electrical source. The electrical energy field of the object will interact with the electrical current in the photographic plate and become visible. A fresh, raw piece of broccoli will reveal a bright, vibrant energy encircling it much like sun rays or strands of lightening extending outward. Interestingly, a piece of cooked broccoli is surrounded in darkness and emanates no energy.

Life is energy and energy is health. The more energy we

have, the healthier we will be. It only makes sense that if we want to stay healthy and full of life, we need to eat foods that are alive, as well. The closer food is to its raw, natural and unprocessed form, the more life it has to give us. Every food choice we make is either giving its energy to us or taking ours away.

**Enzyme issues**

In addition to vitamins and minerals, unprocessed foods offer us another invaluable resource: enzymes. The digestive process requires more energy than almost any other system in the body. Think about the amount of work required to break down a T-bone steak into invisible energy that you can use. It takes a huge amount of resources. Because nature gives us complete food, not only do we have all the necessary vitamins, minerals and fiber in each offering, but we have the perfect amount of enzymes to digest it. Different food components require different enzymes for digestion. Protease digests protein while lipase helps break down fats and so on. When food is processed or cooked at high temperatures, not only are the vitamins destroyed, but the enzymes too. It has been found that once food reaches 119 degrees, the enzyme content begins to decline.

Without its natural enzymes, the body needs to get the tools to break down the food we eat. Our bodies have their own store of metabolic enzymes. Unlike digestive enzymes, we are born with a finite amount of these helpers that operate every single function of our bodies. From blinking an eye to walking or even breathing, every bodily action requires enzymes to execute it. When we eat processed or cooked food, it contains no enzymes. As a result, our bodies must take from their own metabolic enzyme reserves to create the digestive enzymes necessary to break down our food. When our metabolic enzyme reserves are depleted, our bodies cannot carry out their necessary functions and we die. This is why you feel such an energy drain after eating Thanksgiving dinner. With zero enzymes to work with, the body is pulling heavily from your metabolic storehouse just to process it, leaving you with less energy to do other things.

The key to having more energy is to eat more food in its raw, unprocessed form. The digestive enzymes in the food will do the work so your body will not have to. This does not mean you need to avoid cooked food all together. I suggest eating as much raw food as you can and taking digestive enzyme supplements with each cooked meal. Take them thirty minutes before and immediately after.

I also highly recommend lacto-fermented foods. They have extremely high amounts of probiotics (good bacteria) and enzymes. These foods help promote digestive health and boost immunity. They are also extremely easy for our bodies to process because the probiotic cultures have pre-digested them for us, making their nutrients immediately accessible. Every cooked meal should have some kind of lacto-fermented food served to aid in its digestion. The Korean diet, normally high in cooked meat, is always served with kim chi, a side of lacto-fermented vegetables similar to sauerkraut. There are many lacto-fermented foods you already know like yogurt, kefir and properly prepared sourdough bread. Beet kvass; an effervescent enzyme rich drink originating in Russia and kombucha; a cleansing tea made from mushrooms, are excellent choices too.

**What your food eats**

Some say we are what we eat. Others say we are what we absorb. I see healthy food choices a bit differently. Assuming our digestion is good, we are absorbing properly and eating real food, there is one link missing in this chain to support great health.

The food chain is a circle and we are part of it. That means whatever our food source eats, we eat too. My mantra is: "you are what you eat, eats." You can buy a dozen free-range organic eggs, but the odds are that a large portion of their vegetarian diet is feed made from soy beans. Soy is not a part of a chicken's natural diet. If it is eating it, however, soy will be found in every part of the chicken, including its meat and eggs. I am not a proponent of soy because the high level of anti-nutrients far outweighs any benefit it could provide. It should be avoided, especially by men because of the high amount of phyto-estrogens it contains.

The same goes for beef. Set a cow loose in the wild and he is not going to search out the nearest cornfield. He is going to find the first open plain and start grazing. Cows are fed corn to fatten up quickly. Corn is very high in Omega 6 fatty acids. As a result, the beef is extremely high in Omega 6 as well. There are different kinds of fatty acids necessary for health, but they must be in the proper proportion to each other to be effective. If we consume significantly more of one than another, serious problems can occur. Is it any wonder that a diet high in red meat has been singled out as a risk factor for cancer and heart disease? The problem is not the meat itself. It is what the cows are eating that ends up in the meat we eventually eat. You may have noticed that processed food companies are now advertising added Omega 3 fatty acids to their products. This is an attempt to balance out the terribly high Omega 6 level in the population because corn is in virtually all processed and factory farmed food.

The same goes for fruits and vegetables. It is great that organic farmers do not use pesticides, but if the soil they are growing in is depleted from over-farming, the produce can be both pesticide and nutrient-free. Sustainable farmers understand how to rotate crops so soil does not become depleted. I like to say that if it is not in the soil, it is not in the food.

Becoming a little savvier about where your food comes from and how it is raised, instead of simply looking for the organic seal, can go a long way to eliminating hidden toxins in your healthy food choices. Organic, soy-free eggs are now available, as is grass-fed beef.

**Brain drain**

Now you can see how the US has become one of the most well-fed but malnourished nations on earth. Without proper nutrition, our bodies cannot function optimally and neither can our minds. How many people do you know who have concentration problems, brain fog, adult attention deficit disorder, or memory issues?

I am convinced this phenomenon is due to nutritional deficiencies. If the body is lucky enough to get half the amount of nutrients it needs and to decide whether it is going to use the bulk of them to keep your heart beating or remind you to call your best friend back, which do you think it is going to choose? When we are malnourished, our concentration suffers and a strong spiritual practice takes focus. We cannot meditate properly or keep an intention in mind when we are mentally fatigued or scattered. The best way to stay clear-headed is to eat clean, real food.

**To each his own**

The biggest mistake those in the healing food movement make is to assume that their way is the only way. Someone will experience a dramatic healing then write a book about it and insist that everyone should be eating the way they do. This only creates more confusion. Just as there are many paths to God, I believe there are many paths to healing. As a physician I have seen two people create the same condition in their bodies but for very different reasons, so naturally the route to healing for both is different. The same goes for food. While one person may have healed from something with a raw vegan diet, another can regain wellness using macrobiotics or by consuming red meat. Having experienced a healing of my own, I can sincerely tell you that diet, although an extremely important part of any healing plan, is only one part.

In Ayurvedic traditions, the body has three humor centers that balance energy and wellness. These are called the doshas.

When one is too dominant or weak, illness can occur. Ayurvedic medicine treats illness with nutrition among other interventions. Each *dosha* has specific characteristics. *Vatta* (air/ether) represents elements that are dry, light, cold and clear. *Pitta* (fire/water) carries qualities that are sharp, hot and liquid. While *Kapha* (earth/water) represents things that are heavy, slow, oily and dense. Depending on the illness, patients are given foods with these various qualities to correct the imbalance. While one person may need something hot and spicy to aid healing, another may need something bitter and bland. Food is literally used as medicine, therefore a prescription that is good for one person would never be right for another with a completely different condition. Would you take a blood pressure pill to ease back pain?

I encourage everyone to explore, so long as their diet is based on whole, real food.

**Taking the garbage out**

One of the biggest mistakes I see people make is when they confuse cleansing diets with sustaining diets. Someone may experience dramatic results on a raw vegan diet and then assume that because it has brought their desired results, it is a sign that they are supposed to eat that way for the rest of their lives. I believe there are diets that are optimal for cleansing and healing, but that does not mean our bodies are designed to sustain themselves on those diets. Just because someone achieves great results from a juice fast does not mean they are supposed to drink only juice for the rest of their lives. To remain on a healing diet for too long, the body is denied specific nutrients that it needs and invites additional health problems later on.

The body is either cleansing or building at any one time, but it cannot do both simultaneously. That is why we have no appetite when we are sick. Our body does not want food because it knows it has to redirect its energy normally used for digestion and building toward cleansing and healing. Once the healing is done, however, it needs to rebuild. That is why you are usually very hungry after recovering from a long illness. If we remain on a cleansing diet indefinitely, we become deficient and our bodies never get a chance to fully recover. In a state of good health, a diet should be balanced by including a wide variety of foods. I feel animal products in moderation are very important to good health because they provide nutrients we cannot get anywhere else in nature. In 10,000 BCE prehistoric cavemen were not getting their B12 supplements at a vitamin store. Taking our cue from nature, our diets should be balanced and simple. I suggest eating real food, some animal products, mostly plants, as raw as possible, in moderate amounts.

You should plan on doing at least two major digestive cleanses or fasts per year. There are many great programs available you can do at home. Most include detoxifying herbs, an intestinal bulking agent to help move waste out and a natural laxative herbal tea. To be effective, a cleanse needs to last between four and seven days. If you can have a couple of colonic irrigations during the process, it is even better. On an occasional weekend throughout the year, it is a good idea to give your digestive system a rest. This includes not taking supplements.

While a good fast can eliminate most harmful toxins, I strongly recommend that everyone is tested for heavy metals such as lead, arsenic and mercury. These metals are quarantined by the body because they are so toxic and difficult to remove through standard cleansing. The proper removal process is not difficult but it needs to be done by a physician. Heavy metals hiding in the body can easily undermine the best of health programs.

### The spirit of food

No matter what we eat or how we eat it, we must remember that food is alive and just like any other sentient being it has consciousness and a spirit. When we are grateful, we offer a very powerful energy that affects everything in our immediate sphere. Because everything is energy, we affect the quality and energetic composition of our food when we say grace and are truly thankful for it. Do not just be thankful for the food, but thank the food itself, especially if it contains meat from animals who gave their lives to provide you with nutrients and energy. Japanese researcher, Masaru Emoto, has done some dramatic research showing the powerful effects of energy and our attitude on food.

He took two canning jars, filled them with cooked white rice and screwed the lids on. After placing them on a shelf in an elementary school classroom, he gave the children specific instructions. Each morning they were to say, "Thank you" and "I love you" several times to one jar of rice. They were to tell the other, "I hate you" and speak unkindly to it. Ordinarily, cooked rice will breakdown, mold and decompose like any other cooked food in a matter of weeks. Amazingly, the rice in the jar the children were yelling at started to decompose much faster than usual. In a matter of days it was already discolored. A week later, it was a black, decayed, gelatinous mass. The rice they thanked every day remained completely white. It looked like it had just come out of the serving pot minutes ago, after months of being in the jar. Even after one year, the rice that was being shown gratitude and love by the children stayed pure white.

Our thoughts, either positive or negative, generate energy that is transmitted like a vibration through water. Sound vibrations move through water four times faster than through the air. Water is in everything that is alive, including you and your food. Feelings of gratitude and respect for your food create vibrations in the water that change its energetic structure. Your body is over seventy percent water, so how are the vibrations from your thoughts affecting you?

Your body is listening to you while you eat, so be sure to remain in a calm, grateful mindset during meals. Sit, do not stand when eating and direct as much of your attention to the meal as possible. No reading, watching TV, or doing work. Any additional activity creates a diversion of energy that must be directed toward digestion. Eat with love and gratitude, but remember to prepare food for others with the same amount of love. We put our energy into everything we do. We change its vibration just by being involved with it, including food. If we love making a special dinner for someone, our love goes directly into the food and changes its energetic vibration. As a result, that person receives our love and it becomes part of the energy they emanate and affects their whole mind and body. Because food is a form of endearment in many cultures, the most important ingredient we can include in its preparation is our love. When we feed others in this way, we allow everyone to be nourished in the Light we all share.

Feed your mind and soul with a delicious series of Light-based affirmations. Go to **www.thelightnetwork.com/thelight/ affirmations.**

# About Richard Waterborn

Richard Waterborn developed an early interest in healing due to the near death of his mother who sought help from many of the healers of the time.

In his twenties he moved to Ireland where an intense journey of personal healing and transformation began, leading to profound spiritual experiences and a life changing connection to the Ascended Master, Hedekhan Babaji.

In 1994, he met and studied with Drunvalo Melchizedec and became a certified facilitator of the *Flower of Life*. Since, he has combined a busy healing practice, teaching metaphysical and spiritual wisdom and leading sacred journeys of remembering to locations such as Egypt, Peru, Mexico and the ancient sites of Ireland and England.

Richard divides his healing and teaching work between Ireland and Spain. For more information log on to ***www.richardwaterborn.com***.

# Healing the Past

☼

*By Richard Waterborn*

*To return to the place from which we
started and to know it for the first time.*

~ **TS Elliot**

However much we might like to believe that the past is the past and its memories and experiences no longer affect us, we are destined to repeat it until we heal the past. While we may aspire to live in the present, to be in the moment, the majority of our mental and emotional activity is locked into past experiences projecting them into not just the present but also the future, thereby ensuring that it turns out much like the past! The point of power is in the present moment yet that is the one place we rarely find ourselves despite our best intentions.

***In order to be truly in the present, to create a
genuinely new future we must first heal the past.***

Like an iceberg, most of whose bulk is below the waterline, ninety percent or more of our mind operates below the conscious threshold. In any one waking moment we only pay attention to a tiny fraction of the total information we are receiving from all of our senses, both external and internal, and other inputs of conscious activity like information processing, planning, routine activities and memory. So a major function of the conscious mind is to filter out all information which is not relevant to the immediate task in hand and consign it to the subconscious repository. It is in this subconscious realm that all our deepest memories are recorded.

## Cellular memory: we remember everything!

How far back in your life can you remember? Take a moment to close your eyes and think back to childhood. What is the earliest event or experience you can clearly remember? Personally I can recall some isolated events from around the age of three or thereabouts: a sunny summer's afternoon on the beach exploring rock pools, a painful fall on my face, the death of a pet cat. Some of you may be able to remember even further back, though that is relatively rare. Quite commonly people cannot reach back beyond the age of five or six and sometimes virtually the whole of childhood is a sealed book which cannot be opened. Yet whatever our conscious recall span might be, the truth is that we have always stored absolutely everything of significance, which has happened to us from the beginning of our lives and even before. This cellular memory is part of our fundamental biology and something we share with all life forms.

A common houseplant was connected via electrodes to a polygraph, (a machine used in lie-detector tests) which measures changes in electrical conductivity across the skin. When we tell a lie we increase our level of stress causing a change in the conductivity of the skin, which is registered on a moving graph. The experimenter then attempted to stress the plant by taking droplets of stagnant water teeming with microbiological life and dropping them into a beaker of boiling water. Each time he did so the plant registered a spike on the graph—it had *felt* the microbial annihilation and responded to it! Even more extraordinary events were to follow. The trial over, the experimenter left the laboratory leaving the plant still connected to the polygraph. Sometime later he re-entered to dismantle the apparatus, whereupon the plant immediately produced another spike on the graph! It had no specialized nervous system yet this common house plant not only registered an act of microbiological mass murder with which it had *no* physical contact, but it also *remembered* the perpetrator.

Recent advances in heart-transplant surgery have revealed fascinating glimpses of such cellular memories in human beings. In one documented case a female transplant recipient was given a heart from a young man who had been violently murdered. Not long afterwards she began to have disturbing nightmares and waking flashbacks of being attacked. The visions became more and more graphic until she realized that she was reliving the murder of the donor. Not only had a heart been transplanted, but the memories of its original owner's death had been implanted as well!

The existence of such a profound and universal memory system is hard to understand from a purely physical point of view. How can a plant react to an event in which it is not physically involved? How can a person share in such vivid detail the experience of another, separated as they were not just by space and time, but by death as well? A purely mechanical view of life cannot provide answers and we need to embrace a new paradigm of reality in order to understand the workings of cellular memory. Einstein's Theory of Relativity demonstrates that the universe and everything in it is really energy and forms an interconnected matrix known as the *Universal Energy Field*. Whilst this energy can neither be lost or destroyed, it can be transformed into matter and vice versa. In this extraordinary world of quantum reality thoughts and emotions can become molecules and affect the way cells function and communicate. In addition, this universal energy is not just neutral, but intelligent conscious energy and constitutes an Intelligent Energy Field (IEF), which encompasses and interconnects all life forms. Events that threaten or compromise our physical, emotional and mental survival and well-being produce modulations or distortions in our individual IEF, which persist as cellular memory until the original event is healed and the shock and trauma released.

## Patterns from the past

In this way significant events of our lives from the very beginning are implanted as cellular memories within our subconscious mind, our energy system and our physical bodies. Painful, distressing and frightening experiences, too intense or overwhelming to be understood or dealt with and integrated at the time, remain with us as energetic imprints. Areas of our energy field which are disturbed or distorted by the wounding experience form a distinctive pattern, out of balance and harmony with the rest of the energy body. In many cases such events often occur early in life when we are at our most vulnerable and it is not uncommon for traumas experienced in adulthood to be similarly buried and repressed.

Such patterns from the past are not lessened or erased by the passage of time. They remain with us; continually emitting distress signals, calling for attention and healing. If unanswered the calls become louder and stronger until eventually they cannot be ignored. Often this breakthrough into awareness of something buried from the past is some form of repetition or re-enactment of the original event, causing the same emotions and attitudes to be re-experienced. The past does not begin or end at birth. As babies developing in the womb—especially in the last months of pregnancy—we are extremely sensitive to what is happening around us. It is now known that the pre and peri-natal stage of development, along with the birth experience itself are when we are at our most impressionable. And it may not even stop there. In my own professional experience cellular imprints are also carried from experiences in previous lifetimes!

There is a natural and inescapable law which states that whatever we have not healed we are bound to repeat. Ultimately this is so that we not only heal whatever baggage we are carrying from the past, but also learn and grow stronger and wiser from the experience. In many cases these messages of unhealed trauma can be quite literal, often involving the same part of the physical or emotional anatomy which was originally impacted.

A few years ago I met an old friend with whom I had lost contact. He shared that he had recently suffered a heart attack. Since he was always a very health-conscious man who had looked after himself this had come as a great shock. As we talked it emerged that for many years prior to the attack and at the same time of year, he had suffered intense chest pains over a period of a few days, which had grown progressively stronger until eventually he had a full-blown heart attack. When I asked him if the date had any special significance he thought hard for a while then exclaimed, "My God, that's when my father died—suddenly—when I was a boy! My family was so devastated and I was so shocked, that I never really grieved his death." My friend's heart, sorely wounded by the premature loss of his father, had been signaling its need for attention and healing for years and years, eventually provoking a crisis, which could not be ignored.

**Healing is natural!**

When you cut your finger, what happens? Immediately it bleeds as the body's first aid system goes into action, flooding the wounded area with all the materials necessary to repair the damage. After a while the bleeding stops, the blood congeals and forms a protective scab. A few days later, when the skin has knitted back together, the scab falls off leaving a faint scar, which eventually disappears and your finger is as good as new. This amazing miracle happens without any conscious action on your or anyone else's part. You may have cleaned the cut and put a dressing over it to protect it, but these are measures which simply optimize the conditions for healing to take place. The healing itself is natural. My job as a healer is to create the optimum conditions for healing to occur and to facilitate the removing of whatever defensive blocks are getting in the way of full and complete healing. Just as in the example of a cut finger, every one of us carries the power and ability to heal on all levels within ourselves. And once again, it is the heart (guided by the mind) which does the healing, in its capacity for unconditional love and compassion, which are the real healers.

## Lost memories and the etheric record-keeper

When the memory of something which has had a lasting negative affect on us is close to the surface and the associated feelings are already activated, then healing can be achieved by following the emotional trail back to its point of origin. However, where traumatic memories are so deeply and successfully buried that there is no conscious recollection of them whatsoever, a more subtle approach is necessary. There are many different ways to enter the subconscious mind and access the cellular memories it holds, but in my experience the most direct and accurate reference point is the etheric body.

We are much more than just our physical bodies being made up of no less than seven distinct layers or bodies, all nesting within each other like Russian dolls. Of these seven, only the innermost one, our physical body, is material in nature. The remaining six layers are metaphysical, becoming increasingly subtle moving outwards. Next to the physical body and extending an inch or so beyond it, is the etheric body, also known as the physical template since it contains all the information of our physical body, in the form of energy instead of matter. It is the inner layer of the aura and, with a little practice, can be seen by most people.

All the imprints from past traumatic experiences are recorded in the etheric body as patterns from the past, localized disturbances in the energy field. This personal *road-map* of our past can be read using a simple technique of hand-scanning. With a little training and sensitizing one can feel the irregularities in the field caused by the imprint from the past. Once the position and nature of a pattern has been identified, it is possible to trace it to the point of origin to find out what caused it.

The accuracy and reliability of this etheric guide was vividly proved to me in a rather amusing way. Some years ago, at an exhibition of healing arts, I was introducing people to my approach to healing and offering etheric scanning sessions. A young couple approached me and the woman requested an etheric scanning. Her husband was obviously very skeptical about the whole idea and asked me to scan him in order to prove to his wife that it was a "load of nonsense." When I had finished I shared the patterns that had shown up whilst enquiring as to possible causes. He kept shaking his head in dismissal until I came to the last pattern. It was in a very unusual place, high up on the inside of his left thigh. I asked him if he had ever had an injury there and his eyes opened wide in surprise. Quite shaken up, he recalled that in his childhood he had been involved in a serious accident on his bicycle, which resulted in a long deep gash to his thigh in the exact place where I had detected the disturbance in his etheric field. The injury had required intensive emergency treatment in hospital and the incident had been extremely shocking and upsetting for him. He had grown up and forgotten all about it, but his etheric body had clearly remembered the trauma!

## Entering the subconscious mind

Connecting to our subconscious or cellular mind is neither as difficult nor as perilous as we may have been led to believe. Since Freud first coined the phrase, the subconscious has had something of a bad rap; the proverbial cupboard in which all our skeletons are buried! In actual fact it can be accessed relatively easily and in a safe and emotionally manageable way. Stepping into the subconscious mind we enter an infinitely large parallel reality. Not only is everything which has ever happened to us of any significance recorded here in a vast virtual archive, but entire realms of more subtle spiritual experience filtered out by the conscious mind are also accessible and self-evident. Direct connection to these levels can provide invaluable insight, strength and support as we undertake this inner journey.

## Complete understanding

Once inside, the etheric patterns can be traced right back to their source, to the events and experiences which caused them. Temporarily suspending the dominance and control of the conscious mind, which functions through logic, rational analysis and deductive reasoning (for example, two plus two equals four) we are able to hear and follow the guidance of our intuition (in-tuition, the inner tutor), which is a clear and direct channel of knowing unlike thinking. From the point of view of our intuition, all information held in the subconscious is immediately and clearly available as all we need to do is ask and the answer appears. With this intuitive faculty engaged, the most deeply buried memories from the past can be recovered and reviewed. Of course, since the reason they are buried in the first place is because the events they record were overwhelming, it is crucially important that in reconnecting to the memories we do not actually re-live them. Fortunately, in this virtual reality we can distance ourselves sufficiently from the remembered experience to fully review it without being re-traumatized by it. Although we are in an altered state of consciousness it is not a hypnotic trance. We are aware of our present time reality and the support and safety provided by the therapist or healer. From this secure vantage point the healing can begin. This involves understanding and integrating the event or experience at the physical, emotional, mental and spiritual levels of our being.

The essential first step to healing the past is to reconnect with the feelings and emotions associated with the wounding event. E-motion is exactly that: life energy (symbolized by the letter E) in motion. When faced with extremely frightening or painful experiences our bodies are flooded with such strong and intense feelings that we are emotionally overloaded and overwhelmed. To survive, we shut down the flow of emotional energy, suppressing it into the physical body; in extreme cases we may leave our body entirely, pulling our point of awareness out to a place which feels safe. This defence mechanism results in a loss of our general life energy (which in extreme cases leads to depression). Reconnecting to the emotional stream in a safe and supportive environment allows life energy to flow once again and to be harnessed as a powerful healing force. Safety is the key here and I have found that the healer's ability to hold a space of profound safety for the client is far more vital than any particular technique in facilitating complete healing.

The importance of reconnecting to the original experience is equally true when dealing with damage or wounding of the physical body, for example in serious accidents, violent attacks, physical and sexual abuse or rape. Unlike the conscious mind, the subconscious has no concept of past or future; there is only the continual present. A traumatic experience may have occurred years, decades, or even lifetimes ago, but if it has not been fully healed and the trauma completely released, the subconscious thinks it is still happening and acts accordingly: protecting the affected parts by shutting down awareness and sensitivity and ringing alarm bells in the brain to warn us of the danger. Although the conscious mind soon learns to filter out these alarm signals, they continue nonetheless. Therefore, whilst the physical damage may have been repaired at the deeper organismic level, the persistent defensive reaction is a source of continual stress and can lead to serious long-term problems.

To release the trauma at this deep level the subconscious mind needs to know that we are safe, that it can relax and disarm its state of defensive alertness. While we may be aware that something bad, frightening, or painful has happened to us, we may be utterly confused or at a loss to understand exactly what happened and—even more importantly— why it happened. This is especially true where the event occurred when we were very young. As children we tend to attribute cause and blame to ourselves, saying inwardly that "this nasty thing happened to me because I am bad or because I deserved it." This becomes a self-fulfilling prophecy causing us to unconsciously recreate the same or similar "bad experience" for the simple reason that it is what we have learned to expect. This is why, for example, a person who has been abused as a child is highly likely to find themselves in an abusive relationship when they grow up. To break this vicious cycle understanding at the mental level is essential; being able to see what happened and why, the part played by others, their responsibility and our own innocence. Assimilating this information means we learn from it and once we have learned the lesson we no longer need to repeat it. We grow wiser and stronger, more confident in our self and our ability to look after our self and we can make new choices which support our well-being and happiness. In the light of this learning we can re-evaluate the negative and self-sabotaging beliefs and expectations and reprogram the subconscious mind accordingly.

### Scars on the soul

The *Veda's*—the ancient spiritual teachings of India— refer to *sanskars*, a Sanskrit word meaning scars or grooves on the soul. These are cellular imprints from previous lifetimes, often involving extremely painful experiences of death and suffering. These memories are so deeply imprinted that they stay with us when we reincarnate setting up a subconscious program, which may have a profound negative influence on our present life. Like old long-playing records when the needle would get stuck in a groove, churning out the same phrase of music over and over again. Being stuck in the groove of a particular unhealed issue means that we continually recreate it in some way, thereby repeating the old familiar negative feelings and behaviors, such as self-sabotage, "hiding our Light" and under achieving. As these *sanskars* exist at the soul level, clearing them involves connecting to the spiritual level of our identity, which in itself is an extremely powerful and illuminating experience and can result in the most profound healing and transformation.

## We are spiritual beings having a human experience

As spiritual beings we are learning and growing, attempting to find our way back to our spiritual source and reuniting with it. On this journey, which we embark on blindfolded from a spiritual point of view, the wounds, problems and traumas we experience are really opportunities for growing and becoming wiser and stronger.

Getting the bigger picture, seeing the issue from the perspective of our spiritual identity and understanding it in the context of our soul's journey is the final stage of complete healing. The healing takes place when all levels of our being: physical, emotional, mental and spiritual line-up in clarity and understanding. From an observer's point of view this is quite visible. The body appears to become almost fluid-like as strong currents of energy begin to flow, opening up new pathways, repairing and renewing physical wounds, dissolving accumulated pathological tissues, releasing blocked emotions and erasing negative beliefs. Though it may take time for this healing impulse to fully integrate on all levels, the process has begun and it then remains for the person to sustain and nurture it through consciously embracing new attitudes and habits of behavior, relationship and thinking.

With determination, patience and courage we can heal the past and embark on a life which is genuinely new, built on a sound foundation. And most importantly, we become more empowered, fulfilled, wiser human beings!

Download and listen to Richard Waterborn's CD *Heal Yourself* for FREE by entering the link below into your browser: **www.thelightnetwork.com/thelight/healyourself**.

# About Vishen Lakhiani

Vishen Lakhiani is the co-founder of the award-winning company MindValley comprising fifty innovators, artists, dreamers and geniuses from twenty countries.

The company's mission is to bring together marketing and technology to help spread enlightened ideas.

MindValley has won the World's Most Democratic Workplace Award for three consecutive years and it is considered one of the top companies in the world to work for.

Vishen has shared the stage with luminaries including Tony Robbins, Sir Richard Branson, His Holiness the Dalai Lama and Noble Prize winner President F.W DeKlerk.

For more information about Vishen log on to
***www.mindvalley.com***.

# Expressing Gratitude

*By Vishen Lakhiani*

*Gratitude unlocks the fullness of life. It turns what
we have into enough and more. It turns denial into
acceptance, chaos to order, confusion to clarity. It can
turn a meal into a feast, a house into a home, a stranger
into a friend. Gratitude makes sense of our past, brings
peace for today and creates a vision for tomorrow.*
~ **Melody Beattie**

Gratitude is the key to happiness. When gratitude is
practiced regularly and from the heart, it leads to a
richer, fuller and more complete life. When I learned about
gratitude, I saw amazingly positive changes take place in
my business and personal life and like me, you too can
use it as a tool to attract your deepest dreams and desires.
People who are grateful have higher levels of well-being
and generally feel happier, less depressed, less stressed and
more satisfied with their lives. They also have more positive
ways of coping with difficulties and are more likely to seek
support from other people and grow from the experience.
As well as all of this, grateful people sleep better, probably
because they think less negative thoughts and more positive
thoughts before going to sleep.

It is impossible to bring more abundance into your life
if you are feeling ungrateful about what you already have.
Why? Because the thoughts and feelings you emit as you
feel ungrateful are negative emotions and they will attract
more of those feelings and events into your life.

I learnt about the art of gratitude from Esther Hicks

when I attended one of her seminars. Esther teaches gratitude a bit differently than many of the other law of attraction gurus, in that she calls it appreciation. She showed me and the rest of the attendees that by doing little mental or written exercises daily you can boost your happiness levels leading to increased appreciation for life.

When I returned from Esther's seminar my business partner, Michael Reining, had been experimenting with gratitude and he came up with the idea of a website called *GratitudeLog.com*. We implemented his idea into my company and my employees began to express gratitude to each other throughout the day to help build and maintain relationships in the workplace. We began to notice that it is much easier to do business in this kind of environment as everyone encourages and supports one another.

I knew about gratitude before I attended Esther's seminar but had never grabbed the real gist of it until hearing her speak. She said that in order for the decisions about your future to fully function it is important to become happy in the now.

Happiness is not dependent on big things. It is true that some people might be grateful for the fact that their business has made a quarter of a million dollars in one day. However, for the majority of people the little things in life are what matter the most and these little things prove far more important than how much money they are able to earn. So simply put, I have found that expressing gratitude works better in small slices.

My theory about how gratitude actually works in the grand scheme of things is to do with Creative Congruence, better known as flow. Flow is dependent on two things:

1) visions / desires
2) being happy and content in the now

Gratitude is a critical aspect of flow. Most people are

constantly waiting to feel happy once they have achieved their goals and desires. They keep putting off being happy, deciding that they will only feel this way once they have the dream job, the dream car, or the six-bedroom house with indoor and outdoor swimming pools. But I am here to inform you that it does not work that way around! Only once people are happy and content are their goals and dreams able to manifest. I call this *The Paradox of Intention.*

Setting visions and goals should be the easiest thing to do, but many people find this hard because they have no idea what they want to be, do or have in their lives. Instead, they sit on the sea of life and get tossed around, rather like a ship on a turbulent ocean with no one at the wheel.

---

### ☼ Light Practice ☼

One of my favorite exercises is to feel gratitude for all the good stuff that is happening in my life for thirty days. Every day I write down five things I am grateful for in my personal life and five things I am grateful for in my business. I do not stop until I have written them on my sheet of paper. Often the personal list is made up of simple things, such as:

*"I'm so happy to have woken up this morning and eaten a tasty bowl of cereal."* Or

*"I'm so happy that it rained this morning and I got to skip through the puddles."* Or

*"I'm so grateful for my beautiful wife and children."*

Try this Light Practice for yourself.

---

The truth is, expressing gratitude is something so simple that people tend to overcomplicate it.

Running a multi-million dollar business with forty-three members of staff can prove frustrating at times, especially when someone does something I am not happy with. It may not even be their fault, but it is human nature to react in an angry or heated way. However, I have learned an important and effective lesson. Rather than complain to my member of staff about their actions, I search my memory bank for things I find wonderful about them. I express heartfelt gratitude for them and acknowledge that they are a valuable member of my team. This changes the energy around the issue instantly. People tend to live up to what you expect of them. When I practice this exercise, the issue is no longer a problem and all stress associated with it is diffused on the spot.

You can do the same with the people in your life. If your partner does something to make you angry, take a deep breath and think of all the things about him or her that you are grateful for. If it helps you can even write a list. Notice how the energy around the problem changes; suddenly you will wake up to the fact that it is not such a big issue anymore. You should feel your anger wane, which is very empowering.

When I write my daily gratitude lists I start by sitting down comfortably and I meditate in the outer level of mind. Then I write down the things I am grateful for about that day. Scientists have revealed that by expressing gratitude for the things you are grateful for every day for thirty days, by the end of that period your happiness level will raise by twenty-five percent.

A good exercise is to think of five things you are grateful for in the last twenty-four hours, five things you are grateful for in the last two weeks and five things you are grateful for in the last four weeks. The key is to keep it simple. You could just be happy and grateful that you are alive in the world today with a roof over your head, given that there are millions of people in third world countries who starve every day and who have no shelter.

You may be happy that you have access to the internet, to water and electricity. Even these basic elements of life are worth expressing gratitude for.

☼ **Light Practice** ☼

Here are five powerful processes that you can begin right now to start feeling grateful and appreciative:

**1. Gratitude journal...**
Purchase an attractive book with blank pages and write *Gratitude Journal* on the front. The left side of the page is for Gratitude Now and the right side of the page is for Gratitude in the Future.

**2. Before you sleep…**
Every night before you fall asleep give heartfelt thanks for the wonderful day you just had, even if it was awful. Think about tomorrow and set the intention that it is going to be wonderful and the best day of your entire life. Recognize that it is going to be filled with love and joy and that all good is coming to you so everything will flow perfectly.

**3. In the morning…**
When you awake declare your intentions for the day again and give deep thanks, as though you have received your every wish. As you do this you will begin to deliberately create your life and you will experience the power within you to create the life you desire.

**4. Think of yourself as a giant magnet...**
Whatever you are feeling creates a resonate magnetic force which draws events, conditions and circumstances to you. Expressing gratitude for these things projects a greater magnetic force that attracts even more things towards you to be grateful for!

**5. Write and deliver a letter of gratitude to someone in your life...**
Or simply think about a living person for whom you

are grateful. Allow yourself to really feel the energy behind this gratitude. We cannot show gratitude without sharing it with someone. Make showing and sharing your gratitude a part of your life. If someone shows you kindness thank that person as soon as possible. For example, you can leave a message on their answering machine saying how much you appreciate their kind words or deeds.

Demonstrate gratitude in your actions every day. Gratitude is more than just a thought process. Make a commitment to show your gratitude by sharing it with others whenever you have the opportunity. When you start looking for ways to show your gratitude you will find more and more to be grateful for.

The Hebrew term for gratitude is *hikarat hatov*, which means *recognizing the good*. Practicing gratitude means recognizing the good that is already yours. If you have lost your job, but you still have your family and health, you have something to be grateful for. If you can only move around in a wheelchair, but your eyesight is perfect, you have something to be grateful for. When you live charged with gratitude, you will give thanks for anything that has benefited you, from the water flowing from the tap, to the air you breathe into your lungs.

If we can be grateful for things such as mountains, clothes, cars and tables just think how grateful we can be towards human beings who help us out of the goodness of their hearts?

The best form of gratitude is independent of situations and circumstances. It is a feeling of gratitude for life itself.

Here are some examples:

**Your life**
**The universe**
**Time and space**

Your problems, challenges and hardships
Your mistakes
Your consciousness
People who treat you unkindly or unfairly
Your thoughts and emotions
Your freedom of choice
Ideas and concepts

This form of gratitude simply means that you are utterly fascinated with the very notion of existence. You become grateful for life itself, including all of its ups and downs and there is no attachment to circumstances, outcomes, fear of loss or change.

When you feel grateful for existence itself, you move from doing grateful to being grateful. At this level you finally activate the Law of Attraction because you broadcast an attitude of gratitude constantly and it becomes part of your identity. You begin to attract circumstances that resonate with who you really are.

Gratitude is one of the keys to having a successful and fulfilling life. Try the Light Practices mentioned in this chapter and recognize the changes which manifest in your life. The Light Practices do not take very long, yet the effects will reap you huge rewards. Even after a very short space of time you will find that you quickly forget that you burnt your finger or missed the train. Instead, you will remember only the good things that happened in your day.

By training yourself to see the positive side of life instead of the negative, opportunities will begin to materialize in your life that you never even knew existed.

Take a look at the Gratitude Page on our website by entering the link below into your browser:
*http://spreadthelightcampaign.com/gratitude.*

# Section 2
## Practices

*The traveler felt pleased with himself. He had accomplished much, as he lay beneath the Banyan tree and began to drift into sleep. "WAKE UP!" she cried. "Your journey has not begun and there is still more to be done. I give you the gift of Practices that are older than time itself. They will protect you, they will guide you, they will heal you. When you have mastered them, I will appear to you again."*

# About Deirdre Hade

Deirdre Hade is a spiritual teacher, master healer, mystic and visionary leader in the ancient arts of the wisdom traditions. She founded her own modality of Light work, Radiance Healing™ and Radiance Meditation™ after a lifetime of studying *A Course in Miracles, Vedic* healing, mystical *Kabbalah*, cranial sacral healing and energy Light work.

She is the creator of the Foundation for Radiance, a philanthropic program whose goal is to deliver the healing properties of Light through hands-on work, spiritual counseling and meditation programs.

Deirdre is currently launching the Radiance University, which will teach her methods of energy healing work and how to be a healer with integrity, virtue and character.

For more information about Deirdre and her Radiance Meditations, log on to ***www.deirdrehade.com***.

# The Power of Meditation

*By Deirdre Hade*

*The moment you go in, all connections with the outside world are broken; all bridges are broken. In fact, the whole world disappears.*

~ Osho

Meditation is as natural to humans as breathing or sleeping. It is part of our basic design; we come into this world perfectly engineered for it. As children we go into a meditative state frequently. We spend minutes gazing at nothing, blissfully tuned out from the world around us with no thoughts filling our minds. These are moments of profound, simple contentment. We feel part of nature and one with the world. As a result we are free of fear and stress.

As adults we tend to call those still moments spacing out or wasting time. We tell our children to snap out of it and pay attention—not realizing they are paying attention to the energy around them—and we feel guilty if we zone out ourselves. Society tells us that being productive and making things happen is what counts and that doing nothing gets you nowhere.

This used not to be the way, of course. For most of human history this quiet-mind state was part of daily adult life. From gazing at the campfire to daily contemplation and prayer, our minds regularly dipped into the alpha-wave state, where active thoughts fall away and a more expansive, silent state of awareness takes over. This supports us in living; it is as important as eating everyday. When the brain is in a meditative state, it recalibrates the body. The heart and all the organs receive the energy they need to heal imbalances. The entire nervous system can push out the stress that otherwise stays stuck inside, accumulating over time. The emotions get a chance to harmonize and anxiety and anger can clear or melt away. From scientific study we now know that meditation gives a deeper level of restoration and healing than sleep. Our DNA has evolved over millions of years and needs this state in order for our cells to keep us healthy.

Today we are experiencing levels of stress unknown in human history. The sacred texts of ancient India called this epoch *kali yuga*, a long era of unrest and fear. We only have to take a look at modern life to see this upheaval; billions of bytes of information are coming at our brains every second, life is getting faster and communities and families are breaking apart. There are natural disasters, the monetary system is in turmoil and wars are raging around the world. The toll of all this on our physical and emotional health is extraordinary. Disease is rampant and we feel mentally unsettled or depressed. As a result our relationships and work suffer because when we are tired and our mind is foggy we fall into blame and resentment instead of insight and understanding. Worse still, without the regular experience of Oneness—that innocent state we enjoyed as children—we may feel profoundly separate from the world, unsafe and deeply alone.

This is why it is now more important than ever to take the time to meditate each day. It does not have to be for hours, minutes will do, but it helps us to operate at a higher level. When things get more unsettled and uncertain outside, as *kali yuga* comes to an end with upheaval and shifting, meditation helps us find stability, peace and confidence on the inside. It gifts us with the ability to have more understanding in a world we otherwise have no control over.

Meditation also leads to profound inner shifts. When you lose stress, gain more energy and feel happier, you change. And when you change everyone around you changes too because their energy is affected by your energy. Over time the deeper shadows—those wounds or traumas in your unconscious from past experiences that cause you pain or suffering—begin to fall away. Once you begin to meditate, it is not just the stresses from today or this week that are released. The stress and trauma from your childhood and your whole life begins to get lifted out of your nervous system where it has been held deep in your physical-electrical system, affecting your psyche and spirit. Even the negative imprints from past lives lift.

Meditation enables you to pour Light into yourself. You find yourself staying positive instead of having self-sabotaging thoughts. You feel serene, knowing that everything is all right no matter what is happening around you. You have more vision, you understand why things are the way they are and you also look brighter and younger. Turning up the Light literally slows down the aging process. The lines on your face begin to disappear and you glow with a refreshed sparkle!

When you meditate regularly you let Light in where there used to be dark and then nothing can remain the same.

## My story: a path to Light

As a child I was sensitive, emotional and extremely creative. Today doctors probably would have said I had Attention Deficit Disorder, as I had a hard time focusing and I could not sit still for long.

When I was around fourteen-years-old my mother was diagnosed with breast cancer. This was almost forty years ago when cancer was not as common and because of this there was no support for her. Cancer patients were shunned. My mother had a mastectomy and afterwards she became very depressed. There was no counseling, therapy, or reconstructive surgery at that time and she had a giant scar across her whole body. The breast cancer soon spread into her bones and the doctors said she would not live for long. My mother was reluctant to leave my younger brothers and I behind. She said she wanted to try and keep herself alive. So as a teenager, I decided to help her.

We began to embark on a spiritual journey together, intent on healing her by any means necessary. We did not know what to do or where to go and we only had a couple of books to help us: *The Tibetan Book of the Dead* and *A Course in Miracles*. Inspired by their teachings, I began to sit with my mother in prayer. Each time I went into an altered state—deeply energized, expanded in my awareness and witnessing Light pouring through me to her. This was my first experience of channeling and using energy to heal.

Mom always looked younger afterwards and said she felt better, so we continued to do this on a regular basis. She lived for fourteen years longer than the doctors predicted. Throughout the last five years of her life, they said, "There's no longer any medical reason for your mother to be alive."

Then one day she said she needed to go. I was not happy, but I knew her time had come. She said she had work to do on the other side, so I stayed with her and helped her pass over. I watched her soul leave her body. In that moment a brilliant Light filled the room; an extraordinary experience. Three days later she appeared to me in spirit and said she was in a world of Light. She thanked me for helping her, sent her love and asked me to tell everyone she loved them, but that she had work to do and then she would return.

During the years I helped to heal my mother, she often spoke to me about energy. She said we were all attached by strings or threads. Once she passed away I felt a great emptiness inside and I searched in earnest to find something to fill it. I dedicated myself to understanding what she meant and to discovering what was on the other side of the material world.

I studied *A Course in Miracles* in depth for some twenty years. I also practiced Transcendental Meditation, from the Indian *Vedic* tradition and I really enjoyed it but I knew there was something more. Thirsty for knowledge I went to India to study energy work. There I had several transformational experiences that expanded my mind and gave me knowledge to pass to others. As a young girl I had often seen angels and I began to work with them giving readings to people based on what their angels wanted them to know. Simultaneously I was given a message to study the *Torah* and the *Kabbalah* mystical teachings of ancient Judaism.

After years and years of study one day I received the message, "It's time for you to teach." I was afraid. I said, "Me? What am I supposed to teach?" The answer was "Radiance." The voice said it would show me how and I began to receive a great quantity of information on energy—how to work with it, how to use Light in the purest form, how to heal people, how to put Light into people and how to pull out disease and negativity. I documented all of this information then I started to teach it and it grew from there.

The practice of Radiance Meditation is a form of energy work born out of the ancient teachings. Their wisdom has been merged and emulsified to create a new kind of meditation built for 21st century living. Most of us do not have the opportunity to live in an ashram for our entire lives and we are unable to practice the strict dictate of the ancient traditions when it comes to spirituality. I knew we must find a way to fit this profound wisdom into modern life. This is what Radiance has become.

**Experiencing the Light**

Healing Light is the highest frequency of life. We are all energy; it is the basis of everything and it is what animates life. Energy causes a seed to grow into a tree and a baby to grow into an adult. It begins to dwindle away as we get older, causing us to tire and age. At its highest frequency, energy becomes pure Light. This is the Divine Light of creation—the white Light that contains all the colors of the spectrum.

By working with this pure Light we can powerfully increase the vibration of energy in our body and amplify our vital essence. This leads to greater vitality, clarity of mind, joy and much more radiance.

Think of the volume control on a stereo. You can turn up the sound and hear the music more loudly. You can even change the equalizer settings and create fine adjustments in the sound's tone. If you can do that with sound waves in electronic equipment, why not do the same with your own energy waves?

## Connecting to the Light of your soul

Most people are confused when they hear the word *soul*. What does it mean? What is a soul? Your soul is your Light, one with *All That Is*. It is unique to you. Picture one facet on a glittering diamond with thousands of facets.

While your body has a biological age and physical matter, your soul is outside of time and form. Most of us are so caught up in the physical and material aspects of ourselves and our lives that we have forgotten to tend to our souls. We are estranged from them and our soul is a stranger to us. But we must explore our soul, tend to it and care for it. Our soul is here to experience and learn what it means to be in this world and that awareness is far bigger than our thinking mind. Through exploring its dimensions, clearing it and strengthening it, we delve into this journey of meaning, experiencing our connection to the Oneness.

If you are disconnected from your soul, you feel lost, without purpose and as if you have no place in this world. You cannot feel the juice of *All That Is*. Being in exile from your soul brings profound grief and despair that you cannot name. Many people experience this in modern life.

Meditation allows you to connect with and converse

with your soul. Ultimately, when you meditate regularly, this is why you feel more integrated, more peaceful, happier and present.

Meditation helps you get to know this dimension of yourself. You discover there is a world of Light not just around you, but also within you. It is like finding a whole dimension you never even knew existed. When you meditate you find there is a beautiful Temple of Light within you. This is where your soul lives, safe and untainted. This temple contains many chambers of exquisite Light, crystal caves filled with fresh water and a Sacred Garden at its center, where the Fountain of Life bubbles over with an infinite flow of energy.

Within this garden stands your Tree of Life, tall and strong; the sacred core of your being where you discover the presence of pure creation, continually creating the fruits of pure thought and Divine love. Meditating guides you into this garden, allowing you to merge with the Tree of Life in a state of Oneness.

Often when we meditate large amounts of negative energy are released. It is like bathing in a wonderful healing Light, immersing in Divine energy and gaining new insights. Many people are illuminated about something they could not see before. Couples on the fast-track to divorce realize the Divine purpose of their union. A son or daughter heal their own wounds, leading their parents to experience relief too.

When we allow Divine energy to run through our body our perspective shifts dramatically. Traumas and stress from the past are what stop us from following our dreams and passions—and this is at odds with what our soul wants, which is to learn, grow and love. Almost everyone has had traumas of some kind and these create an energy template in the body that contains a profound memory of the abuse. Because it is human nature to connect with abuse and re-live it, traumas cling and they have a power that can over-ride the good experiences.

Unless we go deep into the energetics of the trauma and release it, it is like pouring water over concrete—the healing does not seep in! But when we go deep enough within and access the areas of the mind that control and create our world, the Light percolates through the cracks in the concrete and the trauma is effortlessly lifted out. We do not have to re-live anything and after we are free to be who we are supposed to be.

Ultimately each one of us has everything we need to live in peace. With our minds we can shift and transform whatever objects are in our way, even those that may seem insurmountable or agonizing. It is just a matter of using the tools and the Light. We can all continue to thrive, to live more, love more and experience the exquisite presence of the Divine within us, even while we pass through this age of great upheaval. This moment calls for commitment and discipline; taking the time to meditate and connecting to our soul. But if we commit to turning up the Light within ourselves, extraordinarily beautiful things await—for our families, our communities and our planet.

---

## ☼ Light Practice ☼

The seven steps to radiate your Light:

**1. Identify the tension.** Identify the place in your body where there is pain, stress or a twitch. Do this by closing your eyes and scanning the interior of your body. Remember your body is your friend.

**2. Gather the Light.** Draw the white Light from above into your heart and then into your shoulders and then into your hands. Draw the golden Light from below up into your heart, then into your arms and hands. See the brilliant Light in your hands.

---

**3. Wash your body with Light.** Starting at the top of your head, gently brushing downwards over the front of your face and body, the sides of your head and body and then behind you.

**4. Inquiry.** Place your hands on the identified area of stress on the body. Ask the questions:
A. What is your message to me?
B. What are you here to teach me? Listen carefully.
C. Pour the Light from your hands into the area and affirm: "I love you. I accept you." Ask, "What is my healing affirmation?"

**5. Call in the Angel of Light of your affirmation.** Imagine opening your crown chakra on the top most part of your head. An Angel of Light will descend into you, filling you with healing.

**6. Say a prayer of gratitude and thanksgiving.**
Example: "Beloved Presence of Pure Creation, I am grateful for _____, _____, _____ and I want to say thank you for your generous healing of my mind, body and spirit."

**7. Affirm**, "I am safe. I am whole. I am protected."

The Light Experience is a one-day workshop to help awaken your Light within, through various methods including periods of meditation. We are currently arranging to hold The Light Experience in venues across the world. To register your interest please go to ***www.thelightnetwork.com/events*** and submit the online form. Thank you!

# About Mike Robinson

Mike Robinson is a bestselling author who facilitates global one-day and residential workshops challenging people to look within themselves for their own solution to the suffering of humanity. Mike has an extensive repertoire of life experiences to use as examples of dealing with the illusions that exist in relationships to each other. He was raised in a children's home, which was fraught with turbulence and abuse. His passion to find a solution to the human suffering drove him to look deeply at himself through his reactions to life. This led him to become a mirror for others so they could see how their conditioning stopped the flow of love.

Most people describe Mike as a graceful, gentle man, who has touched their life deeply. For further details about Mike, log on to ***www.mikerobinson.eu.com***.

# Flowing with the River of Light

By Mike Robinson

*Do not dwell in the past; do not dream of the future,*
*concentrate the mind on the present moment.*

**~ Buddha**

What do we allow to flow into our life and what do we allow to flow out? Like the ocean, life is a constant movement of ebb and flow, yet we find ourselves often trying to control this movement by rejecting what appears to be difficult and forcing things to happen in order to experience more pleasure. Sometimes we dive into this ocean without waiting to receive the proper equipment to deal with its depth and then we find ourselves drowning and struggling. Yet if we had taken a moment to be aware of the whole situation and listened to ourselves deeply, the struggle would never have occurred.

This impatience and frustration we have against the natural flow of life is evident in most humans. Because of this movement to reject or attract our desires, to reach a state of fulfillment has brought about the suffering of humanity for thousands of years. To answer the cry of poverty, crime, starvation, the death of war and the constant striving to survive, we have created societies with their institutions, religions and systems. None of these have worked, as the suffering of humanity continues; so something bigger than a reform needs to occur. There needs to be a revolution. Not an external revolution of a mass against the government, but an internal revolution in which all the ties that bind us to the restraints of following a corrupt system come to an end. Each one of us is the silent revolution, where we see the suffering within our self. The seeing of it is the understanding of the fundamental cause of all suffering. Once the root is revealed we will know exactly what action to take. Only then will there be an external revolution, which moves with the natural flow of life.

## Complete listening

Before we can even begin to get in touch with the power of this flow of life or intelligence and allow it to move through us unhindered, we have to understand how we became separated from it into a perpetual state of living through pain versus pleasure. When we were born we were empty vessels, innocent and vulnerable to the world. Over time we have been conditioned by our parents, carers and the whole system that is the foundation of society, religion and education. All of this conditioning has a central core belief that we must become something other than who we are, so we are taught to strive, to be continuously better, or to reach some ideal of a perfect Godlike state. This has been deeply embedded within our minds and it has given us a source of great confusion; hence the innocent, vulnerable Self has been put to one side as not being good enough.

We communicate with each other through the five senses and we translate those feelings, sights, tastes, smells and sounds by using words. Over the ages words have become more and more powerful. The internet age, with its roots of communicating by language, is an example of this movement. Therefore, words have become such a powerful medium that we are no longer in touch with our flow of feelings, but instead we allow external words to control and lead our life. We have become a slave to words and we no longer listen for the flow of intelligence.

To build a relationship with this natural flow of life and allow it in every aspect of our life we need to clearly understand what it means to listen. Few people actually listen to each other. We may hear what someone is saying, but we are usually thinking and analyzing what we are going to say once they have finished speaking. For example, I am describing my experience of being in a restaurant and as I am speaking to you my words are triggering your memories, which form a response of pictures and dialogue in your mind. Complete listening has now ended and you are only hearing and thinking.

Focused listening requires you to be attentive with your whole being in that moment. Your whole being as a human is the five senses, so you are able to feel any tension in the body, observe the person and be completely attentive. Inwardly, you will be aware of your mind's reactions and see how your thoughts move from the rear of your mind to the front and disappear. All this requires a level of self-abandonment; complete listening without an agenda. Having the whole of your energy present in the moment is being in this flow of vitality, allowing it to move through you without stopping it with the mind, which wants to fill this moment with the past. This is an act of love, as you feel that there is no barrier between you and the speaker. No resistance just listening and therefore separation ends.

## Seeing as a whole

When we look at something we look with the past, so we do not actually see the object as it is. For example, we watch a beautiful sunrise, but rather than being completely in the moment of the newness of this sunrise where vitality is, we think about the sunrise we saw yesterday or one that we remember as spectacular and we compare the two. We have now moved out of the moment as we think about the differences and a judgment is formed about one being better than the other.

We do this with everything. We compare our children, our cars, our homes, décor, clothes and we feel disappointed if we are shown to be less than the thing we are comparing our self to. At the same time we also feel secretly pleased if we deem our Self to be better. We do not know how to actually observe something without this comparison of the past taking place within our thinking, so we may look, but we do not actually see.

Whole seeing requires that you let go of the past with all of its labels, descriptions, preferences, likes, dislikes and instead just look. For example, when we look at a bird, the mind instantly recognizes the image and labels it "Robin" and from that word comes all the known attributes of the Robin, so you no longer see the bird, you see the past, which is now between you and the bird. To actually see without the past would mean not getting caught up in your train of thoughts, but going back to observing. Like listening, there is an immense vitality present when you observe without filling the space between you and the observed with the past. Separation between you and the bird then ends.

By listening and seeing in this way we can do the same when it comes to the senses of touch, smell and taste. Be with all the five senses without the past infiltrating the moment. This is where the very flow of life exists, in this acute sense of the moment and once it has been felt and allowed entry into your being, life will never be the same again.

**Desire is a barrier to allowing the moment**

One of the major causes of chaos upon this beautiful planet is our confusion about the whole movement of desire. This feeling of wanting to be fulfilled and safe is the driving force behind the whole workings of desire, yet this is also what brings about our suffering. For example, we see a bright red Ferrari and we marvel at its beauty. Immediately we want one and we have visions of driving it and what people will say. Esteem grows and we feel pleasure at owning such a prestigious car. We walk away from the car and decide that having one is a goal to be achieved, so we begin to strive—we work longer hours and no longer take note of the trees, the flowers and the sky. We have one goal and we are filled with only reaching this ultimate pleasure. When we get the car we are fulfilled for a while, until the next thing to achieve is presented to us, so we never feel fully fulfilled.

We usually always desire something that will bring us pleasure and not pain, so we are constantly striving to get pleasure whilst rejecting any pain. They have a symbiotic relationship, so where there is pleasure pain will follow. Underlying any desire is fear; perhaps the fear of not having enough or not being enough, so we are constantly seeking a better life, which also includes a better life after death or a better next life and so on. We are always moving away from the moment to the next thing on our psychological list and we constantly want to change things so they are better and more advanced.

Look at your life and how it currently is. You will immediately react and see things that you like and things you do not like and want to change. Look again with complete surrender and acceptance that everything in your life is as it should be. Now you look without your mind moving to change anything—there is a feeling that comes when you look at something you do not like, so observe and be with that feeling. Observing in this way allows us to have clarity and we may become aware of the unfulfilled desires and harsh judgments against ourselves and our lives. Maybe you allowed it into your life through a desire to be safe or maybe it has pushed its way in during times of great struggle and you cannot get away from it. The struggle to escape is the very thing which you need to feel and let go of as it is this which keeps you striving to reach safe shores.

The natural state for the flow of intelligence, with its ability to support you and show you the right actions to be taken, cannot enter your life if it is already filled with desire. We have allowed desire, with its constant striving of achievement, goals and the fulfillment of self-worth to take the place of innocence, vulnerability and vitality. When there is no striving to become something or be anywhere else and no movement to manipulate the universe or even run away from it, stillness occurs and the universe is allowed to move through us.

The ego, or our personality, which has been formed from our conditioning will find it hard to let go of desire and its drive to control our life. The defensive mechanisms of our personality, such as our reactions, thoughts and feelings from the past believe they know best. The conditioning of what is good and what is bad has been deeply embedded in the psyche through generations of traditions and expectations. When you no longer follow the dictates of desire and when there is no longer anything to become or strive for, in the eyes of society you will be classed as a *nobody*. This is the silent revolution—the allowing of life to create through you.

## Allowing life to create order

When you look at a tree you will see how its roots are in the earth and from here the trunk is formed followed by the branches, twigs and finally the leaves. The strength is at the bottom supporting the top, giving life to the fragile twigs and leaves. If we look at society we will see how it has reversed this natural process of life. The tree is in fact upside-down. Those who are weak and struggling in poverty are supporting the rest and as the weight of the tree becomes heavier, those who cannot support the distortion, who take from the system and cannot give, are ostracized. This way of living is complete disorder and outside the natural flow of life.

The whole upside-down tree is fuelled by desire and the striving to become, whether that is by fame, wealth, power, career or self-serving satisfaction. We cannot continue in this way of living for much longer, nor the abuse and separation that exists between one human and another. Each individual is required to look very closely at their own lives and see this movement taking place in their own thought world. We are not separate from the world problem—we *are* the world problem. We add to its chaos by our thoughts, words and actions.

How can we turn this tree up the right way and move as one complete humanity; one total human being? We have seen how the mind is always thinking and filling the moment with the past so there is no space for life to enter into our being. This life has an intelligence of its own and actions born from this intelligence are safety and fulfillment, yet we are afraid to embrace it and allow it in as we are in fear of it. We fear it because it is the unknown and we believe that there is no safety in this unknown so we run from it and avoid it. This is what causes the disorder; the ultimate fear of being alone, of having nothing to strive for and of being a nobody. Only when we have completely let go of desire do we enter into this void of total loneliness where we admit to ourselves that we do not actually know anything. We do not know who we are, what our life purpose is and if there is life after death.

From this point of admitting that we do not know how to live life we can begin to find out. Complete listening, seeing and being acutely aware of the moment, which is also the end of desire with its striving to obtain, is the very door to allowing this intelligence with its complete order to live through us. Nobody else can do this for us. It has to be each individual who turns within and learns the workings of themselves. There will be no outside authority to tell us what we have to do. The instruction can only come through inner listening so that the unknown communicates the action and brings order to humanity and nature.

Nobody can give us self-knowledge. We have been conditioned and this conditioning is a lie, which we have passed on through the generations for thousands of years. We are the very thing that we have been seeking, yet we believe we are separate from it and this belief has fragmented the human race. This inner revolution will appear radical to others, but there is no alternative, nor will the future bring the release from the ropes that bind us to suffering as the future is now in this moment. Self-observation, without the desire to change our self into something else, is the actual change that will come from allowing life to create order.

## Allowing truth to unfold

One of the greatest fears we have is speaking truth and living honestly. We are taught how to lie from a very young age and we continue our life in this same vein of covering the truth and the imperfections we believe we have with lies. We no longer trust each other or our self because either consciously or subconsciously we know we are lying and so we believe everyone else around us is lying too.

If you were to walk into a room full of strangers you would feel exposed and vulnerable to being judged, so we present an image to the world and project this image and people judge us according to this image. Each person in the room is doing the exact same thing and no one is being authentic as the image is a lie so truth is not expressed.

We have many images that we use and these change according to who we are with. We are not in touch with our authentic self, with truth, because we are afraid of it. If you were to ask yourself why you do not speak truthfully you may answer with the fear of being rejected as not being likeable or lovable, so we lie to get some form of affection from others, yet is this affection love or is it just a reaction of giving and receiving pleasure?

If you were to be honest about everything and everyone right across your life, including yourself, what would happen? Only by being aware of the lie you have been living can you take the necessary action to live a life of speaking truth and the first step out of the lie is the action to say what is happening in each moment. More importantly, it is being honest to yourself through the awareness of what you are feeling, seeing and thinking. Any holding back in the expression of truth also needs to be observed. Once you are honest, the lie will be seen, which comes in the form of judgments and opinions. Your conditioning reveals itself and the truth becomes clear when you are consciously aware of speaking a lie.

Most of humanity is waiting for a bright shining star to save them—to take them out of the suffering and chaos. Some are waiting for a new millennium, a planetary alignment, or the end of the world. All this is looking to the external for the solution to the chaos in order to bring about a change on this planet. Only you can take the action necessary to transform our world. You cannot rely on another, as they are also conditioned and confused. The distrust we have of our self and others and the fear of speaking truth, is a major cause of human division.

**Freedom in action**

At the beginning of this chapter we asked what we allow to flow into our life and what we allow to flow out. We have seen how most of what we do is from our conditioning. The present moment has the past flowing through it and out into the future, so our whole life is a continuation of the past. There is no space for anything new.

We cannot change the past. If there is such a thing as God even He or She cannot change it, so what are we going to do? There is only ever this moment and to allow it to unfold itself and direct you, all the past will need to be let go of. Any blaming, guilt, anger and envy will only keep you bound to living life from the past. Forgiveness occurs when the past can be looked at without any judgment, without wanting to change it or justify it. This act of complete looking will allow any feelings to emerge and once they have been felt peace can enter. We are not here to be violent; physically, mentally, or in any other form. When we look in the mirror we have so many self-judgments about what we like or dislike about our self. These are also an act of violence upon the Self because these very judgments set forth the desire to change what we do not like and then the suffering begins. The thought world is responsible for all the madness we see right across the globe.

The big question has to be, "Do you have a passion to set yourself free?" Freedom begins with listening, observing, being still, trusting and speaking truth. All of these things are allowing the real you, the sum total energy of all life, the very source of love to move through you. And when you achieve this, you will allow yourself to live in the Light. When we are stuck in the past we become a stagnant pond. When we release the past we flow with the River of Light.

---

### ☼ Light Practice ☼

Take a moment to step out into nature and look at it. Look at a tree, a flower, or a bird with choiceless observation and become aware of your thinking and feelings. See how your thoughts jump to assumptions or past knowledge followed closely by your feelings. When the mind is active in this way notice how your body becomes tense and how your energy moves up into the lungs. Breathe deeply, relax and go back to observing without getting caught up in the stream of your thoughts. Once you can see the workings of how the past moves in the moment through the senses, look at your partner, children, friends, and watch how the same thinking process occurs. Can you observe them without the past infiltrating the moment? The realizations that come from observations are a new discovery from moment to moment.

The past is another country and you do not live there anymore. The future is determined by each moment and by allowing yourself to be (which is also surrender) each moment is filled with vitality and the power of love.

---

Follow the River of Light to a treasure trove of inspirational quotes about the Light: ***www.thelightnetwork.com/thelight/lightquotes***.

# About Marci Shimoff

Marci Shimoff is a #1 *New York Times* bestselling author, a celebrated transformational leader and one of the nation's leading experts on happiness, success and unconditional love. She is the author of the runaway bestsellers *Love for No Reason* and *Happy for No Reason*, which have been translated into thirty-one languages.

Marci is also the woman's face of the biggest self-help book phenomenon in history, *Chicken Soup for the Soul*. Her six bestselling titles in the series have met with stunning success. Marci is also a featured teacher in the international hit film and book *The Secret*.

President and co-founder of the Esteem Group, she delivers keynote addresses and seminars on self-esteem, self-empowerment and peak performance to corporations, professional and non-profit organizations and women's associations. For more information about Marci, go to **www.happyfornoreason.com**.

# Happiness: Our True State of Being

☼

*By Marci Shimoff*

*Happiness for any reason is just another form of misery.*
**~ The Upanishads**

Everywhere we look the signs are clear that the world is undergoing a major shake-up. That is extremely scary for a lot of people. Yet within the dark cloud of fear that is blanketing the planet right now I believe there is a silver lining. All of us are being forced to ask ourselves: "What do I truly need to be happy?"

I have spent a lot of my life thinking about this question. As a young teen I began a personal and later professional quest for happiness that lasted over thirty-five years. During that time I took every transformational seminar under the sun. For years I studied and taught success principles. I applied them in my own life and gained a good measure of success. I had plenty of reasons to be happy: I was a #1 *New York Times* bestselling author, I had received national acclaim as an inspirational speaker and I had touched millions of people's lives. I was very familiar with what it meant to be "happy because…." The problem was it did not bring me the happiness I wanted.

Looking around I saw that the happiest people I knew were not the most successful and famous. Some were married, some were single. Some had lots of money and some did not have a dime. Some of them even had health challenges. From where I stood there seemed to be no rhyme or reason to what made people happy. The obvious question became: could a person actually be happy for no reason?

## The happiness continuum

In the course of writing my book, *Happy for No Reason*, I spent years interviewing scores of experts and happy people all over the world. This is what I discovered:

**Unhappy:** we all know what this means: anxiety, fatigue, feeling blue or low. This is not the same as clinical depression, which dramatically interferes with your ability to live a normal life and for which professional help is absolutely necessary.

**Happy for Bad Reason:** when people are unhappy they often try to make themselves feel better by indulging in addictions or behaviors that may feel good in the moment but are ultimately detrimental: drugs, alcohol, excessive sex, retail therapy, compulsive gambling, over-eating and watching too much television, to name a few. This kind of happiness is hardly happiness at all. It is only a temporary way to numb or escape our unhappiness through fleeting experiences of pleasure.

**Happy for Good Reason:** this is what people usually mean by happiness: having good relationships, success in our careers, financial security, or using our talents and strengths. It is the pleasure we derive from having the healthy things in our lives that we want.

Being Happy for Good Reason depends on the external conditions of our lives—if these conditions change or are lost, our happiness is usually lost too. That is when I realized that there is one more level on the happiness continuum—Happy for No Reason.

**Happy for No Reason:** this is true happiness—a neurophysiological state of peace and well-being that is not dependent on external circumstances.

Happy for No Reason does not mean grinning like a fool 24/7 or experiencing a superficial high. Happy for No Reason is not an emotion. In fact, when you are Happy for No Reason you can have any emotion—including sadness, fear, anger or hurt—but you still experience that underlying state of peace and well-being. Happy for No Reason is a state that has been spoken of in virtually all spiritual and religious traditions throughout history. The concept is universal. In Buddhism it is called causeless joy, in Christianity the kingdom of Heaven within and in Judaism it is called *ashrei*; an inner sense of holiness and health. In Islam it is called *falah*; happiness and well-being and in Hinduism it is called *ananda* or pure bliss.

I have noticed the widespread recognition of this concept around the world. No matter where I go, when people hear the expression Happy for No Reason, it strikes a deep chord in them. We seem to know intuitively that our innermost essence is happiness. Most of us focus on being Happy for Good Reason, stringing together as many happy experiences as we can, like beads on a necklace, to create a happy life. We have to spend a lot of time and energy trying to find just the right beads so we can have a *happy necklace*.

Being Happy for No Reason, in our necklace analogy, is like having a happy string. No matter what beads we put on our necklace—good, bad or indifferent—our inner experience, which is the string that runs through them all, is happy, creating a happy life.

### Practicing the happiness habits

So why aren't we experiencing more happiness in life? The answer is surprisingly simple. Psychologists say that at least ninety percent of all behavior is habitual. Happy people do not have special powers, an extra heart or x-ray vision—they just have different habits. So, to become happier, you need to look at your habits. Some books and programs will tell you that you can simply decide to be happy. They say just make up your mind to be happy and you will be. I do not agree. You cannot just decide to be happy any more than you can decide to be fit or to be a great piano virtuoso and expect instant mastery. You can, however, decide to take the necessary steps, such as exercising or taking piano lessons— and by practicing those skills you can get in shape or give recitals. In the same way, you can become Happy for No Reason through practicing the habits of happy people.

All of your habitual thoughts and behaviors in the past have created specific neural pathways in the wiring of your brain, like grooves in a record. When we think or behave a certain way over and over, the neural pathway is strengthened and the groove becomes deeper—the way a well-traveled route through a field eventually becomes a clear-cut path. Unhappy people tend to have more negative neural pathways. This is why you cannot just ignore the realities of your brain's wiring and decide to be happy! To raise your level of happiness, you have to create new grooves.

Scientists used to think that once a person reached adulthood, the brain was fairly well set in stone and there was not much you could do to change it. But new research is revealing exciting information about the brain's neuroplasticity: when you think, feel and act in different ways, the brain changes and actually rewires itself. You are not doomed to the same negative neural pathways for your whole life. Leading brain researcher Dr. Richard Davidson of the University of Wisconsin says, "Based on what we know of the plasticity of the brain we can think of things like happiness and compassion as skills that are no different from learning to play a musical instrument or tennis…it is possible to train our brains to be happy." Put another way, we each have a happiness set-point that determines our level of happiness. No matter what happens, whether it is something as exhilarating as winning the lottery or as challenging as a horrible accident, most people eventually return to their original happiness level. Like your weight set-point, which keeps the scale hovering around the same number, your happiness set-point will remain the same unless you make a concerted effort to change it.

The great news is that you can raise your happiness set-point. In the same way you would crank up the thermostat to get comfortable on a chilly day, you have the power to reprogram your happiness set-point to a higher level of peace and well-being.

The secret lies in practicing the habits of happiness. Here are ten powerful happiness habits you can adopt into your life:

**1. Incline Your Mind Toward Joy.** Have you noticed that your mind tends to register the negative events in your life more than the positive? Reverse this by consciously savoring the positive experiences as they happen: the sun on your skin, the taste of a favorite food, a smile or kind word from a co-worker or friend. Let the good feelings sink in!

**2. Lighten Your Load.** To make a habit of letting go of worries and negative thoughts, start by letting go on the physical level. Cultural anthropologist Angeles Arrien recommends giving or throwing away twenty-seven items a day for nine days. This deceptively simple practice will help you break attachments that no longer serve you.

**3. Get Your Happiness Rest.** One sure-fire way to boost your happiness level is to go to bed by 10pm for three consecutive nights. You will find that the world is a different place when you are rested and fresh.

**4. Become an Inverse Paranoid.** Choose to believe that this is a friendly universe—one that is out to support you, rather than out to get you. When you find yourself facing a challenging situation ask yourself, "If this were happening for a higher purpose, what would it be?"

**5. Hang with the Happy.** Study after study indicates that happiness is contagious! Spend as much time as possible with people who are supportive and upbeat to amplify those qualities in your own life.

**6. Do Not Believe Everything You Think.** Interrupt the downward spiral of worry and anxiety by questioning your negative thoughts. Just because you think something does not make it true.

**7. Seek Out Silence.** Prayer, meditation and being in nature have long been recognized as ways to access a deep place of peace and strength inside.

**8. Move Your Body.** All the experts agree that some form of exercise is essential for maintaining optimal well-being. The next time you start to feel glum, get your blood moving faster—even if it is just by standing up and moving around while you talk on the phone or parking farther away from your destination and going the distance.

**9. Ground Yourself in Gratitude.** Research shows that thinking of the things that you are grateful for in life definitely raises your happiness level. Writing them down is even more powerful. So start a Gratitude Journal today.

**10. Wish Others Well.** Try beaming love to people—your friends and family, as well as strangers you pass on the street. It fills your own heart in the process.

---

### ☼ Light Practice ☼

1. From today, begin registering your happy experiences more deeply by consciously looking for them. Make it a game you play with yourself. Have the intention to notice everything good that happens to you: anything you see, feel, taste, hear or smell that brings you joy: a win you experience, a breakthrough, or an expression of your creativity—the list goes on.

This intention triggers the reticular activating system (RAS), a group of cells at the base of your brain stem responsible for sorting through the massive amounts of incoming information and bringing anything important to your attention. Have you ever bought a car and then suddenly started noticing the same make of car everywhere? It is the RAS at work. Now you can use it to be happier. When you

---

decide to look for the positive, your RAS makes sure that is what you see.

2. One of the most prevalent habits that happy people share is believing the universe supports them—that this is a friendly universe. When things do not seem to be going their way, they look for the lesson and the gift in the situation. In other words, they believe there is a higher purpose that is supporting their ultimate good.

Practicing this one habit has made a huge difference in my own life. Try it yourself: the next time you face a challenge, take a moment to reflect silently, asking yourself, "If this were happening for a higher purpose, what would it be?" I am certain that whatever answer you discover will be illuminating, but more importantly you will begin tapping into that state of inner peace and well-being on a regular basis.

## The benefits of happiness

While success is not the key to happiness, happiness is the key to success. Happy people naturally have greater opportunities, better health, deeper friendships and more customers.

But these benefits are just the icing on the cake because being happy is its own reward. When you are Happy for No Reason it is not that your life always looks perfect—it is just that however it looks you will still be happy. Being happy creates a wonderful sense of lightheartedness within, which relieves tension and allows us to shine to our full potential.

We know something that will make you happy right now! Go to **www.thelightnetwork.com/thelight/cartoons** and you will smile and glow all day long!

# About Terry Tillman

Terry Tillman has hosted engaging, inspiring, life-changing personal development and leadership seminars since 1977. He has worked in ninety-four countries to help people find their life purpose and connect with their true Self.

Terry often calls himself a *recovered businessman*. Once a Type A workaholic, he turned his life around after being introduced to the world of transformational education. More dramatic change occurred after an accident in which doctors told him he would never walk again. Nine months later Terry proved them wrong and today he is as fit and healthy as ever.

Nowadays Terry works with a select number of companies and individuals who seek excellent results and he teaches self-development in the wildernesses of Idaho and Patagonia. His book about peace, *The Writings on the Wall*, was an international bestseller. His next book, *The Call*™ is coming soon.

For more details about Terry, log on to ***www.227company.com.***

# Getting in Touch with Your True Self

*By Terry Tillman*

*This above all: to thine own Self be true and it must follow, as the night the day, thou canst not then be false to any man.*

~ **Shakespeare**

I am often asked how I can walk on stage in front of audiences of up to fifteen thousand people without knowing what I am going to say. This approach only works when I am in touch with my true Self. My brain—the part of me that wants to control and organize and be certain not to make a mistake—used to go nuts with that concept. But connecting to the true Self gives me access to information and knowledge way beyond anything I have ever learned in a book or the limited amount stored in my memory.

I am in a big room right now with a lot of volume and real high ceilings. I am putting my hands together as if I am holding a baseball. The amount of air right here in my hands is the same as the air in all of this room, but it is not all of the air in the room; it is part of it, connected to it and of the same essence. It is holographic, which means the whole is in every part. I think of my true Self in the same way, so I know if I can tap into it I will have access to all the information I need.

**Who am I really?**

Most people at some introspective point in their lives ask

the existential question, "Who am I and why am I here?" They suddenly wake up to the fact that there must be more to life than working every day, paying the bills and an annual two-week vacation. While living their day-to-day lives most people identify with the body, the mind and the emotions, however that is not who they really are. I call myself a recovered workaholic because at one point I owned and ran six businesses and while I did well externally, I felt unhappy, off-course and bankrupt inside. I was not operating from my true Self.

The true Self is in the invisible world—in the ninety percent we cannot see. Most people see something solid and think it is real, whereas it is only a small fraction of the true reality. The choices available to us in the ten percent we can see are extremely limited compared to the infinite choices available from the ninety percent. With this in mind, I do my best to let the true Self lead me and when I do this life works fantastically. It is magical, marvelous, amazing, easy and it flows. It is full of loving and kindness and joy and laughter and compassion. Nevertheless, when I do not live from my true Self, I come up against all the fetters, dross and tediousness of the world.

Many people have tapped into their true Self on occasion, but they do not believe they had anything to do with it. I do not know anyone who lives from their true Self one hundred percent of the time, but I do know that if we set that as the direction and intention, we can live there more frequently and for longer periods. And when we do, our experience and the environment around us grows better and better. One way to do this it to be willing to look at things differently.

---

### ☼ **Light Practice** ☼

Place your index finger above your head pointing upwards and turn it in a clockwise direction looking up at it. Keep turning it in the same direction and bring it down to eye level. Now move it below eye level so you are looking at it from above. What direction is it turning—clockwise or counter-clockwise? Which is the right direction? It is both. The correct answer all depends on your viewing point or point of view.

Every disagreement between two people occurs because of differing points of view, often called opinions and who is right? Well, all right means is consistent with my belief or consistent with my point of view. Beliefs are not necessarily true and there are many points of view. Therefore, if you expand the context so it includes clockwise and counter-clockwise, you will have more options, which can lead to more effective choices. You will become more compassionate, more understanding, wiser and life will improve many-fold. The false self only sees clockwise or only sees counter-clockwise, whereas the true Self is able to see infinite ways.

**Positive and negative**

The true Self is also known as the heart, the essence, or the Soul; the part of us that just knows. Then there is the mind, emotions, body and unconsciousness, which is where most people live their daily life from because they see it as reality. I call that the negative or lower level, but that does not mean it is bad. It is like the poles on a battery; positive and negative are both necessary in order for it to function.

Perhaps you have heard the question, "Are you a body with a soul or a soul with a body?" The answer to that question is, "I am a soul with a body" or a spirit having a human experience. The soul, unlike the body, does not disappear, decay or corrupt, unlike everything material. The invisible, the Soul, is enduring and immortal.

The first time I was with someone when he or she died I said, "Wow! he was there and then he wasn't." So who or what is the "he or she?" For me it was undeniable and palpable. The he or she that exited was an energy and all that remained was the physical body with no sense of life or vitality. We say the body is dead then it decays and returns to the nothingness from which it came. That is part of the false self. The true Self is with us forever as it is of a higher matter and connected to the all knowing.

**Like attracts like**

One way I stay in touch with my true Self is to meditate every morning. Meditation literally changes our vibration and as like attracts like it is also a great way to manifest a new reality.

I first saw the evidence of energy resonance at the age of twenty when I was in a band. One day I went to tune the instruments. I sat next to a piano and hit one of the keys to tune the banjo. I tuned all the strings of the banjo then I picked up the guitar to go through the same process. The third string was the note G, so I hit G on the piano and my banjo sounded, even though it was sitting about five feet away from me. I thought, "Boy that's weird," so I moved the banjo ten feet away, hit G on the piano again and the G on the banjo, untouched, sounded again. I later discovered that I had witnessed *sympathetic vibration*; anything with "G" vibrates in sympathy or responds. And that is very much like us. If we meditate every day with an intention and focus on being loving, kind and giving we tune our human instrument into that vibration and we radiate that frequency. Then people and things in the world tuned into that frequency will resonate and show up in our environment. But if we choose to focus on negativity, such as anger, resentment, hatred and vindictiveness on the inside, on the outside we will see a lot of fighting, separation, difficulty and war.

**Where you look is where you will go**

One of my major teachings is, "Where you look is where

you go." Other ways this is said are, "As you sow so you will reap," "As you give you're given unto" or "What goes around comes around." Basically, it means that whatever you give out, you will get back. But you cannot give with the sole purpose of getting something back. You cannot say, "Right I've given it so now can I have it?" That is a completely different energy. The giving needs to be unconditional with no expectation of return. The natural result of this cycle of giving and receiving, when it flows freely without blocks, strings or conditions is known as the *Universal Law of Abundance*.

Planet earth is like a big classroom and every action has a consequence. The law says all actions are balanced, so if we do actions which are harmful, the harm will come back to us. The painful or difficult results come from the false Self. Most people say, "I don't want pain, suffering, difficulty, doubt, despair, hurt, or discouragement in my life so how come I have it?" Well, you have it because of the choices you have made, if not in this life then in a past life. Take a look at what you are holding inside energetically. We are responsible for everything in our life, so we create our reality. Your vibration (whether conscious or unconscious) attracts its like kind and that is what you notice in your environment, situations and circumstances. If you want a different reality simply change your focus toward what you want more of. That last sentence is an important one. You may want to re-read it for it contains the solution many are looking for.

**So how do you connect with the true Self?**

### 1. Notice – Observe – Meditate

Well, as I mentioned earlier, meditating regularly and consistently is one way. To meditate simply get comfortable, relax and observe your body, breathing, feelings and thoughts. You do not have to understand them, figure them out, correct them, or argue with them—just notice. I am not responsible for what comes into my mind, only what I hold there. So observation is a key.

Then ask yourself, "Who is doing the noticing?" Is it the mind noticing or is something else noticing the mind, body and emotions? Who is that?" That is the true Self.

I constantly work on my impatience. When I am driving on the Los Angeles freeways and someone is going slowly in the fast lane I often grow impatient and irritated. But that is not what I want my daily experience to be. I become aware by noticing how my stomach tightened, how I clinched my jaw, or the negative thoughts and judgments in my head. I then connect back to my true Self, which is the one noticing and through observation my tension begins to disappear. Simple awareness is often curative. Anger, impatience and irritability do not exist in my true Self.

## 2. Build your support team

I used to hear myself say judgmentally, "If I want something done right I need to do it myself." The result was that I did a lot of my work alone. This was hard. And stupid. I found that it is much easier, more fun and more effective to work cooperatively with others. The group solution is always superior to any one individual's solution and none of us knows as much as all of us, so it is a good idea to build your own support team. I have an inner and an outer support team. I speak to a friend once a week and I also belong to the Transformational Leadership Council (TLC) founded by Jack Canfield and made up of members who are living lives of purpose and service.

I also have an inner support team, which consists of three of my best friends who live in different cities. Often I simply go inside and converse with them. They each have different personality traits which compliment my own. You may wish to form an inner support group with people you admire who have passed away, such as Jesus, Buddha or Mother Teresa. Your team can be as large as you want, but it is real. Meet them and talk to them whenever you fancy and you will be amazed at the support and wisdom available.

**3. Get clear on what you want**

To discover what you really want from life ask and answer some structured questions, such as the examples below:

*Q: What do you want?*

*A: I want a new car.*

*Q: What experience are you looking for?*

*A: I'm looking for an experience of abundance.*

*Q: How can you get it?*

*A: I could go down to the showroom and start looking.*

Then return to the first question, "What do you want?" Now take the answer to the last "What experience are you looking for?" question and plug it into the beginning:

*Q: What do you want?*

*A: Abundance*

*Q: What experience are you looking for?*

*A: Sufficiency, knowing that my needs are met.*

*Q: How can you get it?*

*A: By trusting and noticing that they always have been.*

*Q: What do you want?*

*A: Sufficiency—trusting that I'm connected with, loved by and taken care of by the Source. (Once again the last answer becomes the first answer as I cycle back through.)*

*Q: How could you get that?*

*A: By going inside more often.*

Keep cycling through the questions until you reach an inner truth. Clue: it will be associated with your *beingness* rather than your *doingness* or *havingness*. Finish with "How could you get that?" so you have a specific next action step.

---

### ☼ **Light Practice** ☼

Here are a couple of other methods to help you to get in touch with your true Self:

1. Write down all the things you can think of that you would describe as peak experiences in your life, especially

activities you loved doing, including moments of joy, loving and bliss. Include both qualities and experiences, as well as the way you expressed the qualities. Start at the youngest memory and work through the timeline. You could also do it geographically via the places you have been. Do not analyze or think about it, just write everything down as fast as you can.

2. Go back to when you were a child, under the age of twelve or seven and think about what you loved to do. Make another list.

You should see a common line running through those lists—learning, teaching, exploring, creating, guiding, scouting, serving, dancing, moving, risking, adventuring, playing, writing, reading, researching and that is your purpose in life, which comes from the true Self.

## The comfort zone and resistance

We generally meet resistance—usually in the form of stress or tension—when we begin to step outside our comfort zone; that place which we already know and feel comfortable with.

Look at this figure. The heart in the center represents the true Self—you. The line of the circle represents the limit of your current experience. Everything inside the circle you already know or you have already experienced—commonly known as the comfort zone—and everything outside the circle is unknown and unfamiliar. So if you want to learn and grow or if you want more of something in your life—perhaps something tangible like money, a new car, a bigger house; or something experiential such as happiness, joy,

love, or peace, do you look around inside the circle, where you have already been or do you look outside of the circle where you have not been? You will start by saying you want something, you will take a step and at some point you will get to the place beyond which you have not been (the line of the circle, the edge of your comfort zone). That place is very interesting because it is where resistance shows up and if you can break through it your circle will expand and you will become bigger in some way. In order to get outside of the circle you really need to go inside the circle into the heart. As Edmund Hillary, the first guy who climbed Mount Everest said, "What we really conquer is not the mountain but ourselves."

The resistance may show up physically (headache, tiredness, hunger) mentally (explaining, reasoning, using logic), or emotionally (fears and tears). When most people experience the resistance they stop moving forward and return to old habits, defend an opinion, justify their choice, take a pill, have an alcoholic drink, argue, defend, explain, fall asleep, open the refrigerator door…something to avoid the discomfort. They stop, turn around and go back to where it is more familiar and comfortable. They return to their comfort zone.

The way to get where you want to go is through what is in the way. The way to is through! Once we move beyond the fabricated boundary and get what we say we wanted, that now becomes part of our experience. It is now in

our zone of familiarity, in our comfort zone. We have grown and we have expanded our comfort zone. We now have more choices available and so we experience more freedom.

Remember, "If you always do what you have always done then you will always get what you have always got." So in other words you have got to be willing to look at counter-clockwise. If you are not prepared to do this, if you defend your current point of view, belief or opinion you will stay right where you are and nothing will change. If you want to see more in your life, you must learn how to expand your comfort zone by moving into what is unfamiliar and unknown. If you do not your life will be pretty mundane and fruitless. It is your choice.

### Identifying your limiting beliefs

If I want what I say I want it is important to let go of the reason why I do not have it; the justification, the explanation, the logic. Results and reasons are mutually exclusive. If I am giving reasons I will not get results and if I want results I need to let go of reasons. If I say, "I want more money but I am not educated enough yet" that is a limiting belief. Whenever I hear myself explaining or justifying that is most likely a red flag. If I catch myself doing this I stop and say, "Wait a minute, is that true?" The boundary in your circle is defined by your belief system and your beliefs are not necessarily true.

Most of our beliefs are in the form of I should, I shouldn't, good, bad, right, wrong, always, never and so on. It is a good idea to examine your beliefs. If they do not work throw them away and if they do work, keep them.

If your parents told you something when you were seven and now you are forty, why should you allow the choices of a seven-year-old determine your present actions? Create a new belief and validate it through experience, observation, or via techniques such as Neuro Linguistic Programming (NLP), tapping, the Lefkoe Method, affirmations, visualizations, experiential seminars or other ways you have learned from this book.

### The importance of focus

Energy follows thought and manifestation follows energy. Something becomes manifest (material) as a result of energy moving towards it. We direct that energy by what we focus on. Most people believe the focus is what they think about, but it is more than that; it is also what we see, say, imagine, hear and sense. We direct the energy with our focus, so the key is to focus on what we want more of from the true Self.

Remember: "Where you look is where you go." I constantly focus on the things I want more of, which are typically positive and uplifting. For example, I stuck a page of a magazine on my wall that says *easy*. I was tired of hard work. I wanted to earn more doing less and I wanted to experience it with ease. I subscribed to magazines on subjects I am interested in. The screen saver on my computer comprises a collection of photos depicting things I want more of. The key is to follow the joy, follow the bliss and follow your heart.

Whatever you want, you must be prepared to get whatever comes with it as well. For example, I always thought I wanted a lot of money. Well I achieved my goal, but I also had to deal with the unexpected misery and unforeseen responsibilities that came with it. It turns out it was not the money I really wanted. I actually sought the experience of greater freedom and peace of mind, however instead I just grew more and more stressed. I thought if I had more money and a bigger house, I would feel free, happy and at peace, but that is backwards. Instead of have > do > be what works is be > do > have. I found that what works is to first put my energy into *who am I* and express that. Start with the intention then take a step—even if it is a miniscule step—in that direction.

Here is a subtle distinction that many people do not understand. When I say I want something I am coming from a place of not having—lack. And because like attracts like (remember sympathetic vibration) that lack tends to attract more lack, more of less. So how do we get around this? First let your wants come from the true Self because there is no lack there. And then learn detachment. Recognize that you can never have something until you let it go by connecting with the place inside that is absolutely *ok* with not having whatever you say you want. That place is the true Self. For me that works by reducing the desire to a preference—I prefer to have more money, a new car, more joy, greater freedom. I acknowledge that I will start with choice A and if that does not show up I will take choice B and if that does not show up I will take choice C. This is much easier when I have an attitude of gratitude; feeling grateful for what I do have.

Most people try to solve a problem, yet if you focus on solving a problem you energize problem and thus continue to have a problem, often a growing and bigger one. Remember, where you look is where you go and energy follows thought, manifestation follows energy. Every parent has said to their child, "Don't spill the milk." Then what happens? The milk spills. It is not because the child is clumsy, disobedient, rebellious or stupid. It is because the parent does not know how to give a good instruction. They have created an image of spilled milk, so that is what the child manifests. It would be much more effective for the parent to create an image of what they want. For example, "Drink the milk," "Hold on tight to the glass" or "Put the glass down on the table"—focus on the solution, what you want more of.

## Challenges along the way

When you decide to live your life from your true Self it is inevitable that you will face a number of challenges. For example, you may need to walk away from your old friends or even family members. I hardly spoke to my own mother and father for many years. I discovered I had been living my life according to what I thought others expected of me, which was inconsistent with my true Self. It was not only my mother and father I attempted to please, but also teachers, peers and business associates. When I realized this, I knew that I was not really living my life but someone else's. I was not being true to my Self. No wonder I did not feel happy. I was living my life by someone else's beliefs and expectations. As a result of my behavior I had trained my mother to know she could manipulate me into doing what she wanted. She often said, "Well, I am your mother," as if that gave her the special privilege to control my behavior and live through me. When I realized this and made choices consistent with my true Self, I began to choose what felt right for me rather than anyone else. I did not do this as an action against my mother, but rather as an action for me. I did not see her or talk with her for a while until she accepted that I was living my life to my liking, whether she agreed or not. We now relate just fine.

The true Self leads us and always supports our higher intentions. We do not always know what those are initially. Understanding follows experience and the clarity shows up along the way, never ahead of time. If you wait until you are completely clear and certain you might never take the necessary steps.

It is a challenge, it is simple, but it is not necessarily easy. It is a learning process and it involves practice and a lot of trial and error along the way.

## To conclude

In a nutshell, when you follow your true Self the experience of life is good—joyful, easy, flowing, relaxed, abundant, peaceful, confident and loving. You will be living a life of purpose, meaning and contribution. When this happens we become like a magnet and others are attracted to us. It might look like people are following you, but really you are just leading yourself at a high level of integrity. You are being true to your *Self*. This is how we connect with and radiate the Light on this physical level.

**Next, Janet Attwood shares real life examples of how she lets her true Self lead her and regularly follows her heart.**

Take a step outside your comfort zone by donating money to our *Spread the Light Campaign* today. Even a donation of $1 counts towards our one million dollar goal! Go to **www.spreadthelightcampaign.com/donate.**

# About Janet Attwood

From her own remarkable experiences Janet created The Passion Test. This simple yet effective process has transformed thousands of lives all over the world and it is the basis of the *New York Times* bestseller *The Passion Test: The Effortless Path to Discovering Your Life Purpose*, co-authored with Chris Attwood.

Janet has been a professional speaker, trainer, entrepreneur and coach for more than thirty years. She has shared the stage with leaders such as His Holiness the Dalai Lama, Sir Richard Branson, Nobel Prize winner, F.W. deKlerk, Stephen Covey and Jack Canfield.

Janet is a founding member of The Transformational Leadership Council whose one hundred plus members serve over ten million people in the self-development world. To find out more about Janet, go to ***www.thepassiontest.com.***

# An Experience of Following Your Heart

*By Janet Attwood*

*Your time is limited, so don't waste it living someone else's life. Don't be trapped by dogma, which is living with the results of other people's thinking. Don't let the noise of others' opinions drown out your own inner voice. And most important, have the courage to follow your heart and intuition.*

~ Steve Jobs

This is the story of how following the call of my heart and getting in touch with my true Self transformed an abused and drug-addicted adolescent into a passionate woman living her dream. It is the story of how I discovered that what we love and God's will for us is one and the same and ultimately how all heartfelt passions and desires lead to a life of service.

## My childhood

As a young child I had the most beautiful relationship with my mom. We spent hours playing and hanging out together. Then when I started school my mom missed me so much that sometimes she would tell the principal I had to go to the doctor just so she and I could play together. We would sing in the garden, watch our favorite movies in bed and eat *fishes in the dishes*—sardines and crackers. Our connection was clearly magical. However, when I was seven, my mom's demons came back to haunt her and she became a raging alcoholic. My world cracked open. As a child my first thought was, "Did I do this?" From then on I transformed into the black sheep in school and my world became a nightmare.

My mom and dad eventually divorced and my life spiraled out of control. At the age of seventeen I was physically molested by my brother's two best friends. Then I got into drugs. At eighteen I was strung out on LSD. At nineteen I lived with the president of the Oakland Hells Angels. And at twenty I lived in no less than twenty-one different places in one year. I was on a roll of the lost kid. One day I had the realization, "If I don't stop this then I will end up like my mom or worse."

I had a boyfriend who was not into drugs and one day when we were talking I said, "Do you know what I think?" He said, "You don't think. You don't even have a brain." It felt like someone had taken a sledgehammer and hit me hard. I was mortified that someone I loved had said something so awful to me. In tears, I called my brother who lived eight hours away. In his sweetest voice he said, "It's ok little sister, you'll be alright. I've just discovered something wonderful, it's called transcendental meditation. Don't worry, everything's going to be ok." Four days later he turned up at my door, walked into the house, packed my bags and together we moved to Santa Barbara, California, where he lived with me until I got off the drugs and learned how to meditate. That marked the beginning of my life turning around for the better and it was a big sign from Spirit. I believe that learning how to meditate saved my life.

**Beginning to follow my heart**

A miraculous series of events followed, which led me to go from a completely broke meditation teacher to following my dream of becoming a transformational speaker and seminar leader.

Then one day I opened an email from someone I did not know, which is unusual for me. It said: "Dear Janet Bray Attwood, we are group of women in Miami. We are putting on a day where we are going to bus in two hundred homeless women in transition to a five star hotel. We are going to feed them on china, give them presents and we would love you to come along and be the keynote speaker. And by the way, we can't pay you."

This deep inner knowing that I had to accept their invitation came over me. A light went on inside and as I sat there reading the email, I felt like crying. I knew I had to say yes. I received another message from Spirit while I was on the plane: "Do not give these women your usual opening speech." When I arrived I took one of the organizers out for dinner and asked her what the women from the shelters were like. She said, "Well, they have a five to ten minute attention span, many of them are coming off drugs, they'll be running back and forth to the bathroom to smoke and they'll probably be the worst audience you've ever had." At that point I felt very depressed. I did not want to disappoint these women and I did not have a clue how to capture their hearts.

That night before bed, I said a prayer, "Please let me know what to say to these women tomorrow." When I woke up I went straight to my computer and started writing. When I walked on stage, I took out my piece of paper and read it to them. It went like this: "There once was a little girl and she had a magical relationship." And I went on to tell the story about this little girl getting physically molested, taking drugs, riding with the president of the Hell's Angels and then realizing she would have to change her life or else she would end up just like her mother. At that point I got real quiet, looked out at the audience, took a breath and said, "And that little girl was me." The women got up out of their chairs and gave me a standing ovation. There was not a dry eye in the house. It suddenly became clear why spirit had led me here. As I looked out at each and every one of these precious women, I saw my mother. In that moment a healing took place in my heart and it was so huge that I would never be the same again. I knew without a doubt that everything I needed to heal with my mother was healed in that moment.

## Following the direction of Spirit

I have noticed that the best moments of my life have been when I can not make sense of why I am there. I have also come to understand that all of us are here to give and it is the giving that creates happiness. When I follow the direction of Spirit—follow the Light—in the highest sense I am looking out for number one and that is where I find the biggest gifts.

There are a number of things that I have found get in the way of being able to listen to Spirit. Some of those are false beliefs and caring what other people will think. By having the courage to listen to and trust my intuition, I create the courage to listen to it again and again. Every time I listen and trust, I realize even more that it is the only voice which will guide me safely to my destiny. There are no mistakes in the universe. Every single step you take leads you right to where you are supposed to be. My desire is that everyone has the courage to listen to their true Self and follow their heart. It is always the path of least resistance.

## My trip to India

Some years ago I was on my way back from India and making some jewelry on the plane to pass the time. This Indian woman passed my seat, looked down at me and having noticed the pearl necklace I was making, she said,

"Nice." We got talking and I learned that she was on her way to give a talk to the United Nations on the Repression of Women. She said her name was Ruth and she told me that she ran an organization in Bangalore for twenty-six thousand repressed women. By the time we arrived in Amsterdam Ruth and I had become fast friends. When we were saying our goodbyes Ruth turned to me and asked, "Janet, do you think you could come back to India sometime and teach poor women how to make jewelry?" I said, "Sure." We hugged goodbye, exchanged email addresses and promised we would stay in contact. When I got home I could not stop thinking about Ruth and her invitation. On the sixth day the desire to return to India was so strong that I bought myself a ticket, packed my entire jewelry-making kit and drove to the airport. I had not even managed to contact Ruth to tell her I was on my way. All of a sudden, while I was on the plane it felt like I had just woken up from a dream and I thought, "What the hell am I doing? I must be totally crazy. I don't even know if Ruth is in India right now."

En-route to India the plane stopped at Amsterdam and I ran straight to the computer lounge to see if Ruth had emailed back. I breathed a sigh of relief as I opened my emails and saw one from Ruth saying she would be in Bangalore on my arrival and that there would be twenty women for my first jewelry course. When I arrived at Ruth's door, she immediately fed me and whisked me into a filthy, windowless room where all these girls were waiting.

Ruth told me that these girls were so poor they lived in cardboard houses and that some of did not even sleep in their boxes because when it got really warm the rats would come out and chew on their feet while they slept. So instead they would sleep really close to the highway so the noise from the cars would keep the rats away. My heart went out to them.

For a whole week I sat on the floor and taught these girls

how to make jewelry. I decided to start a club and call it the Janima Jewelry Club. At the end of the week each one of the girls were graduates of the club and I told them I would take their jewelry to the US and sell it so they could start making some money. As I was leaving each of the girls walked up to me and said, "Thank you Janima. We love you."

That trip to India, listening to my heart rather than my head, which told me all along that I was insane to travel back to India after only being back for six days prior, was probably one of my most life-changing experiences ever. It was scary, insane and unreasonable. I had never been to India alone, I did not know Ruth very well and I was only an amateur jewelry maker. And yet, I am the kind of person who jumps when my heart is calling and afterwards I look to see how far down I might fall. I have come to trust my intuition, regardless of whether or not I can see the end result. Sometimes there might be a dead end here and there, sometimes I might fall on my face, but most of the time it is the richest part of my life and for that I am so thankful.

## Being in the Light

Each one of us is a conscious creator; we are all conscious of those subtle thoughts and stirrings in our heart, if we will only notice and then trust enough to act. I have learned that every single moment is a gift and every one of us is here to share our gifts with the world. And when we get a little off-course, the wonderful gift is that we can then re-align to our true purpose.

Following our heart is absolutely the most effortless path. It involves each of us having the courage to listen for direction. By doing this we will be guided to things which hold the most importance for us. This is the path that each and every one of us is destined to travel so that we can be in the Light and reclaim our power.

This story has been edited and modified from a chapter in Terry Tillman's book, *The Call*, which includes inspiring, transformational stories from luminaries who have followed their heart. For a deeper look at the code revealed in *The Call* log on to *www.227company.com*.

If you have an experience of the Light for potential publication in a future *Light* book, or for our website, please go to *www.thelightnetwork.com/storysubmission* and fill in your details.

# About Lauren Sebastian

Lauren Sebastian has worked in Community Arts and the Public, Education and Creative and Cultural Sectors. This winding path of exploring learning, creativity and well-being inspired her deep interest in what it means to follow our bliss. She is currently writing a practical book about this, which will also unpick the dynamics of a consciously aware creative process and the shadow blocks that can prevent us from accessing our innate creativity.

In summer 2009 Lauren fully pursued her creative dreams by moving to Spain to become a freelance illustrator. For more information, log on to ***www.laurensebastian.com***.

# The Divine Artist

☼

*By Lauren Sebastian*

*Every creative genius has been a channel. Every master work has been created through the channeling process.*
~ **Shakti Gawain**

All beings are innately creative. If we open to the possibility that we are born with inherent creativity, we come to realize it is the Essence of our true nature and that creating is essential! We have an endless spring of creative potential to draw upon and either knowingly or unknowingly every single one of us is a channel for this creativity. I define creativity as "the perpetual unfolding of the unified fabric of life." We are each a unique expression and as such a work of art.

I have encountered many people from all walks of life and it has become apparent that people's capacity for creativity is influenced by their perceptions, which are rooted in deeply-held beliefs that often vary radically. From health and well-being to religious persuasion these perceptions can become misconceptions about creativity and later develop into blocks to freely accessing our creative potential within.

## Misconceptions about creativity and creative potential

What if it were possible to move out of a subconscious creative process into a consciously aware creative process? What if all we need do is redefine some misconceptions we hold about creativity and our own potential, recognize that between each moment of unfolding life there is an ocean of creative life force animating each of us and removing any *blocks* that may be obstructing the authentic expression and flow of our creativity? As I grow both spiritually and creatively I have discovered some key affirmations related to accessing our innate creativity:

☼ All beings are innately creative and creativity is not restricted to the domain of the Arts alone. Creativity permeates *All That Is.*

☼ We are all connected beings; separation is an illusion.

☼ Success and failure are subjective judgements; we have value from the moment we are born and continue to grow and learn through the creative process of life itself.

☼ Lack is only a perception, therefore abundance is unlimited.

☼ There is not a right or a wrong way, there are only different ways to do something.

☼ Criticism can be constructive.

☼ Creative expression can be effortless and is our natural state; the process can enhance our experience of living and it can also be healing.

☼ When we bring our awareness to the present moment and trust in the unfolding of life, we express our creativity through actions that can be described as blissful.

☼ We are all part of the creative flow of life; struggling against this flow requires effort and can cause a stagnation of our energy, which blocks all creativity.

## How do we find our Source of creativity?

First we must intentionally become aware of when bliss feelings arise within us. A bliss feeling is an inner feeling of unbounded, joyful awe or deep, abiding peace or happiness, which can permeate our entire being. Our bliss is a built-in guidance system from Source, which indicates when we are truly living in the moment and creatively being who we were born to be. When we are not lost in the past or planning the future but simply awake to the present moment, we are in alignment with *All That Is*. Then we are being true to ourselves and we are purposefully participating in the creative flow of life. A blissful thought, prospect or action will make our hearts rise and sing, whether quietly sitting watching the waves of the ocean, breast-feeding our new born baby or eagerly composing a symphony.

How do we tell the difference between blissful guidance and an ego-fuelled desire? Egoic desire results in a temporary pleasure or a short-lived cessation of feelings of lack. However, blissful guidance generally feels expansive and connects us to our entirety. We will experience our connectedness to all beings, joy, serenity, peace will flow and the chattering ego-mind will become still.

When we become consciously aware, we start to silence the distracting noise of the mind and acknowledge the *magnetic* pull of our infinite creative potential, calling to be made manifest. By listening and responding to this natural, compelling, inner urge and allowing our creativity to flow, we become a true expression of the Source. In other words, we do the thing we love to do, for example, paint a picture, conceive of a new scientific paradigm, sing to a live audience, raise and nurture a child, plant seeds on an allotment or tend to a garden. The universal life force is like oxygenated air and part of the creative process is the act of breathing this universal force in and out of ourselves. The exquisite moment of stillness that exists between the breaths is where we find the Source, the Light, the abode of the Divine Artist.

**What is inspiration?**

Many classic symbols depicting inspiration often include light in some form, be it a candle flame, the rising sun, a glowing ember, a halo or a switched on light bulb. I see inspiration as a spark of insight pulsing from the eternal Light of pure awareness, which permeates all our cells. Inspiration is the breath of life that animates us and initiates movement as an energetic vibration maintaining our vitality. The verb *to inspire* also means *to inhale*. So we could say it is an acknowledged idea that breathes life into any creative venture, motivating us to take action.

There are several key stages in a consciously aware creative process and each stage could be described as an island in an ocean of creative possibility. Within the process, creative blocks or inhibitors may be encountered. The first stage then is *to be inspired*, to breathe life into an idea. If we have a creative impulse but we cannot seem to follow it through or to make it manifest, we have most probably encountered the first block, which I call the *Shadow Layer of Suffocation*. If you currently feel lost when it comes to your creativity, this understanding may return you to the true path of your creative journey. Equally, if you are someone who is already familiar with regularly expressing your creativity, this insight may enhance your flow.

**How does this *inspiration* translate into our daily life experience?**

Having an inspired idea or flash of insight can often seem like an event with a Divine quality to it. When inspiration pulses into our fertile consciousness, like a seed of Light being planted, it can feel as if we have been spontaneously gifted. Simply put, we have been receptive and open to infinite possibility.

Effortless inspiration can be induced by dynamically opening to the Divine within us. It can be as simple as placing awareness on one's breathing. Allowing for the existence of limitless potential is a profound act because it removes all boundaries and liberates possibility.

> *Everybody has the capacity to be inspired because everybody has the capacity to breathe. When we are receptive in any given moment we can tap into the Divine Artist.*

Inspired thoughts are not butterflies of Light that we must frantically grasp at outside of ourselves. Instead, we need only surrender and allow for inspiration to be revealed naturally within us. Of course, in words, this may sound easy. But in action, we often find lurking inner shadows cast by *obstacles* that prevent us from shining at our brightest and thus blocking our inner visions from view and stemming the flow of creativity.

## The shadows

The importance of lurking inner shadows is that they indicate the shape of the obstacles we wish to clear and they give us insight into what needs to be released or transformed. We unknowingly create these obstacles, through harbouring negative thoughts or repressing emotions, so they quietly grow as we stubbornly refuse to acknowledge them. They then fester within us and go on to create the shadows that attract more of the same negativity into our lives. When we only see the shadows we invariably fear them and they become our *shadow self*.

The interesting aspect about shadows is that they can only exist in the presence of light. They are dependent on the position of an object in relation to a light source. A huge shadow can give the illusion that the creating obstacle is also huge when in reality the obstacle might be very small. Until we dare to look beyond our *shadow self* at the obstacles creating it, we will have difficulty moving through our inner blocks or to connect with our creative flow. The closer we are to the Light, the smaller the shadows are and the more we can see with clarity. If we allow the Light within us to shine from the core of our being, then shadows might cease to exist altogether.

Many artists throughout recorded human history have used shadow and light (*chiaroscuro*—an Italian term literally meaning *light-dark*) in their art work to clearly define tonal contrast, which also represents the inherent duality or conflict between light and dark. However, the conflict only arises if we resist bringing the Light of our pure awareness to whatever is going on inside us. Shadows provide definition and information. They give us insight and provide depth and wholeness to our life experience. Without shadow as a contrast to light and to define form, a painting or drawing can appear visibly flat. It is this use of contrast that gives the illusion of three dimensions on a two-dimensional surface. Perhaps now is the time to embrace our *shadow self*, not fear it nor assume it is ugly. In reality, it is merely a trick of the light, with layers of information vital to our well-being.

## Recognizing the shadow layer of suffocation

As we move through life, it can often seem that we are faced with a relentless line of challenges. This is what I call the *Layer of Suffocation*. This shadow takes our breath away. It removes our ability to breathe deeply. It is the rapid, shallow intake of breath associated with anxiety, panic attacks, insomnia and insidious worry. This *Layer of Suffocation* is created by the clatter of the ego-mind with its endless mental faculty analyzing, comparing and judging. It can remain in overdrive even though it impairs every aspect of life. It is clear that a life of gasping suffocation will take its toll on our health and well-being. The *Shadow of Suffocation* wants to inhibit access to our inspiration. It holds us back from insights because this aspect of our ego feels strangely safe in the suffering it knows, believing life would be worse if we were to make changes. It feels that at least in habitual routine we know what the threats are and how to complain, worry or fret about them. Thankfully, there is another way; it does not occur to the ego that life can be lived truer to the Source, with more freedom, creativity, fulfillment and happiness. When we bring Light to this particular shadow layer and expose the ego-mind obstacle creating it we are guided to accessing our inspired-mind. We support this process by being dynamically open and receptive to the ocean of possibility.

**What are some ways in which we can start to become more creative?**

Many people have told me they desperately want to express their creativity, but they cannot think how or what will make them feel creatively fulfilled. In the process of embodying your Divine Artist, it is preferable not to think and particularly not to desperately think. In fact, there is no need for us to think anything. When accessing innate creativity, we need only open our hearts and allow the Divine within to guide us through those blissful feelings. Trying and thinking require effort, plus judgment and analysis. The ego-mind loves trying hard, assessing and analyzing but it is important that the ego-mind takes a back seat. Compassionate, constructive criticism and interpretation can come later when we reflect on our creations.

I invite you to relax, be still and be effortlessly receptive as you try this Light Practice. By doing this I believe the creative process will unfold before your very eyes.

## ☼ Light Practice ☼
### inspiration meditation for
### dynamic opening and receptivity

Aim to engage in this Inspiration Meditation every day for twenty-one days, at the same time each day. It is a good idea to do this in the same space and at least an hour after eating. The exercise will take approximately twenty minutes and you will need a notebook and pencil. Please read through the entire exercise before you begin.

1. Close your eyes and take a few moments to settle, whilst breathing normally. Inhale deeply through your nose. Gently allow your abdomen to expand and protrude as your lower lungs, followed by your upper chest, fill with air. Stop inhaling just at the point before it might begin to feel uncomfortable, because this is not intended to be a strained exercise.

2. Pause for a few moments before gently exhaling. Feel your lungs slowly emptying and, the emptier they become, notice your abdomen drawing in to expel the very last bit of breath.

3. Repeat this cycle three times and then allow your breathing to normalize.

4. Begin to focus your attention on the inhale only and repeat for approximately ten minutes.

5. Next, follow every breath as it enters into your heart space and consciously imagine your heart opening and expanding. Keep your focus on the expansion and opening of your heart as the exhale takes place. If it helps, you can visualize a glowing, soft pink/golden/white spherical point

of light that gradually expands and glows brighter with every inhale.

6. You may also choose to silently affirm, "I give and receive love easily, for I am LOVE." Repeat this for as long as you feel you want to. If you suddenly realize you have run away with a particular train of thought, or you become distracted by any other sensation in your body or a sound in your environment, simply return your awareness to following the inhale into your heart space and opening your heart.

7. Finally, shift your attention back to the process of normal breathing and come fully present again.

8. Take your notebook and write, draw or doodle anything that pops into your mind. Do this for five minutes. Do not worry if your musings seem bizarre or tedious; simply allow them to flow. If you feel stuck at this point, place your pencil on the page and begin to draw a line and just let the line crawl over the page wherever it wants to go.

9. Lastly, put your pencil down, look at or read what you have jotted down and ask yourself, "Beloved one, what next?" Then, on a different piece of paper, write down your immediate response to this from the heart.

10. Over the period of twenty-one days keep all your responses to that final question. You may see a pattern emerging. You may get goose-bumps as your inner creativity is allowed to be expressed. You may have an idea or several ideas. These things will undoubtedly open you up to your next step and reveal how you can allow this flow of creative Light to continue to illumine your life as the Divine Artist.

**Why bother to create?**

I believe that it is vital to our well-being and happiness to create. I speak from my perspective as an artist / illustrator because that is how I choose to express my innate creativity. Yet, regardless of how we each choose to express ourselves, the important thing to recognize is that we have the *ability* to consciously create. Conscious creation is one of the greatest gifts we can offer humankind. The only thing that stands in our way is to become afraid of our own shadow. We are timeless, ageless creative souls—Divine Artists— some of whom have forgotten our greatest potential, instead choosing to be spooked by our own lurking shadows.

Bring the Light of your pure awareness to this moment, take a chance on your creativity. You need not hide in the shadows. You have an amazing opportunity to shine and express your Inner Truth right now.

**What makes art original?**

When we create—produce a work of art, write lyrics to a song or decorate our homes—we usually want to end up with something original. So what makes a creation original? I feel, in order to be original as Divine Artists, we simply allow ourselves to return to our origin by being open and receptive to Source. Therefore, to be original means we need only express ourselves with truth and authenticity from a place of connectedness. When someone creates from the place of Light and Love the subsequent viewer is also transported into the experience. In reality, the viewer is just as much a co-creator through the conscious observation of the creation. The artist is not separate from the viewer because we are all connected beings.

**What happens when humanity loses creativity?**

It is not possible for humanity to lose creativity

because we are the creative expression of life force flowing from Source. However, it is possible for the quality and authenticity of our expression to be diminished if we default to an automatic creative process informed by subconscious beliefs born out of distorted perceptions of reality. In that case what humanity can lose is the uninhibited freedom, well-being and blissful peace of mind, which emerges from expressing creativity through a consciously aware process. Therefore, identifying with the Light of our pure awareness is essential to the quality and conscious experience of our creative expression.

No one owns creativity because we are all Divine Artists actively participating in the creative process, either knowingly or unknowingly. At any one time we are either unconsciously or consciously connected to the flow of life. Inspiration exists within each of us, like a seed waiting for the Light of our pure awareness to illuminate it.

Everything is continuously unfolding, yet all exists at the same time, because Source is not defined by time. It is an illusion to imagine an individual accessing inspiration before another individual because we are all playing the same game. We are all on the same team. We are all tapping into the same ocean of creative possibility. It is only the ego-mind that gets competitive about being the first to have a particular idea. Life unfolds exactly as it is meant to in the same way as the exhalation of an infinite breath expanding out into the universe. Maybe one day we will contract as that infinite breath is inhaled once more on the grandest of scales.

**What is the goal of art—what can we receive by looking at it?**

It is very beneficial to nourish your Divine Artist by enjoying other creative and beautiful works of art, music, books, spending time in places where you feel at peace, or collaborating with other Divine Artists. You could begin by having an inspired idea followed by a nourishing period of further investigation around that idea. Alternatively, the way in which you nourish your Divine Artist can inspire you to have an insight or *inner sight*.

## Conclusion

I believe we are all Divine Artists. This does not mean we are all meant to hold a paintbrush, sculpt stone or play the piano. Instead, it means we all have the capacity to consciously create in whatever ways come naturally to us. Have you ever noticed that creativity is a hybrid of two other words: *creative* and *activity*? We each have talent, skill, genius, purpose and devotion aligned with the compelling urge to express our Inner Truth. However, many of us have allowed our confidence, self-esteem and well-being to diminish to such a degree that we feel stuck in a rut. Sometimes we quash this inner calling with distraction tactics, such as too much alcohol or too much television. Yet, we each continue to create our reality in every new moment of every second of every minute of every hour of every day. We can choose to center ourselves, breathe deeply and open to Source and then imbue our unfolding experience with love, forgiveness, gratitude, compassion and conscious creative activity. When we do this we fully integrate and become the Divine Artists of the masterpiece that is Life itself.

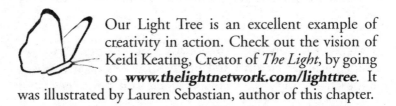 Our Light Tree is an excellent example of creativity in action. Check out the vision of Keidi Keating, Creator of *The Light*, by going to **www.thelightnetwork.com/lighttree**. It was illustrated by Lauren Sebastian, author of this chapter.

# About Barbara Marx Hubbard

Barbara Marx Hubbard has been called "the voice for conscious evolution of our time" by Deepak Chopra and she is the subject of Neale Donald Walsch's book, *The Mother of Invention*. A prolific author, visionary, social innovator, evolutionary thinker and educator, she is co-founder and chairperson of the Foundation for Conscious Evolution. She is also the producer and narrator of the award-winning documentary series *Humanity Ascending: A New Way Through Together*. She is a partner of The Shift Network as a global ambassador for the conscious evolution movement; a shift from evolution by chance towards evolution by choice.

In 1984 her name was placed in nomination for the Vice Presidency of the United States on the Democratic ticket, calling for a *Peace Room* to scan for, map, connect and communicate what is working in America and the world.

For more information about Barbara Marx Hubbard, go to ***www.evolve.org***.

# Peace Through Co-Creation

☼

*By Barbara Marx Hubbard*

*Behold, I show you a mystery. We shall not all sleep.*
*We shall all be changed, in the twinkling of an eye.*
*~ 1 Corinthians 15:51*

What is peace? What has it to do with you? When I talk about peace I am thinking about it particularly in an evolutionary context. So how would I define it?

**Peace is a signal that we are in an environment in which each person is free to express their potential for the greater good.**

In other words, peace is a result of a certain state of being and also creating. A person can be peaceful, but if they are not expressing their creativity and impulse to be who they truly are, they will become depressed or addicted or violent or bored. So peace through co-creation is the expression of the inner well-being that comes from tapping into the Source of who you are, meeting with each other in a form of essential connection and getting over your identification with your egoic self to such an extent that you can identify with your Essential Self. Peace comes from connecting through the heart to others and to the whole of life. A new way of understanding peace is expressing your unique creativity for the good of the Self and the whole. I see peace as a fulfillment of expression, at first individually and then for groups.

Until we understand that creative inner impulse and its expression on an individual level, we cannot be of service to this world. That is why I call it *peace through co-creation,* because that peace is the Divine within. The author Abraham Maslow wrote an interesting definition, describing how the American anthropologist Ruth Benedict wanted to understand why some nations were peaceful and some were violent. She studied different nations and she put all the characteristics of the peaceful nations on one side and all the characteristics of the violent hostile nations on another side. And here was the main difference: the peaceful nations had a high synergy social structure and the hostile nations had a low synergy social structure. High synergy is one in which if someone captured the biggest prey, they would have the biggest party—it was win/win. The hostile nations, however, were the opposite, in that whoever captured the biggest prey would also take everybody's wife! So not only is peace the inner state of oneness with Source and expression of your own creativity, but it is also engendered by social synergy structures, where one person's benefit is not at the expense of somebody else. We have achieved this from time to time and in many democracies there is a sense of a rising tide for everyone. However, the minute that rising tide is controlled by a minority, where more and more wealth is going to fewer and fewer people and as jobs become scarce and inflation takes hold, one sees that even within a peaceful society there is anger, separation, hostility, sadness and criticism.

## Understanding peace

Peace through co-creation is my phrase to encompass all dimensions of peace. There are certain steps and stages towards the co-creation of peace, starting with the individual and working towards conscious evolution of the group. I also see that peace is a sign of social health. First of all there is the whole story of creation, from the origin of Creation, the Source, the Mind of God, through the billions and billions of years of transformation to higher consciousness, from single cell to animal to human and all the way on up. Now, within that context it appears that we are shifting from one phase of consciousness to the next, from the illusion that we are separate from Spirit, from each other, from Source and from nature. Millions of people are shifting their awareness to the innate awareness that we are connected through the Heart to the whole of life, awakening within as we discover our life purpose and that we are Cosmic Consciousness. We are aware we are in a Universal Intelligence of billions and billions of planets. We are alive to our part as a universal process and even a universal human and a universal humanity. We experience that we are in an evolutionary shift point, as there was from Neanderthal to *Homo Sapiens* and then to *Homo Sapiens Sapiens*. Out of *Homo Sapiens Sapiens*, a co-creative, co-evolving human is emerging. I call this human a "universal human," *Homo Universalis*: the co-creative human who feels at one with the process of creation and whose creativity is growing.

As old systems are failing, this creative urge is drawn to the development of new systems that have a higher synergy of win, win, win. Win for the planet, win for the person and win for whatever profits are needed to keep going! I believe we are in the midst of giving birth to a new culture, which we could call a planetary culture. And who is giving birth to this? It is people of this planet, the universal humans; it is people who are activated by universal principles, such as peace through co-creation.

> *As we see breakdowns in the old systems, part of peace, if you want to take it in its deepest sense, is feeling that you are drawn to co-creating a culture in which everyone is free to be and do and create in a sustainable, evolvable way. And so we become what I call a "communion of pioneering souls."*

One of the most important questions to contemplate is, "How do we create social structures to connect that which is already emerging, creating, loving and actually building a new society?" The cutting edge of social evolution is something I call *Social Synergy*, meaning the combination of our separate parts and our organizational efforts become greater than the sum of our parts. But even if individuals themselves are cooperative, when you get organizations joining and synergizing, there is often a barrier where individuals controlling companies do not want to lose their corporate identity, for example they do not want to lose their funding and they certainly do not want to be mixed up with some other organization! I am grappling with this in my own work. I have a couple of thousand students of Conscious Evolution and we want to work together in celebration of *Social Synergy* on a planetary level. I liken it to an awakening Planetary Peace Department operated by a team of colleagues, all of whom are doing great work. One of the questions we are facing is how do the people who are already emerging and creative connect in a synergistic way so that we are greater than the sum of our parts? There are now many wonderful organizations and we are capable of connecting through cell phones, internet and Skype. We are getting to know each other. We have various kinds of groups and conferences by the thousand. Everywhere I go somebody is trying to create a new internet platform. We have been calling it the *Synergy Engine*: a platform that would connect people to help them find like-minded partners, projects and team-mates. From my twenty-five synergistic conferences I did in the seventies, I think the way it works is that you see common goals, you match your needs with somebody else's resources and you start to co-create out of expanded self-development and self-interest. In other words, it is not giving up your self-interest, but fulfilling it through co-creation rather than opposition and working in harmony with each other in the deepest sense. For example, there is this book, *The Light*, which is lovingly put together. At the same time, I have a message I love to give. We make a connection, so you might say we are now working in harmony with each other, because the creators of *The Light* have a goal and I have a resource to meet that goal. I have a goal, which is to give this message and *The Light* has a resource to help me give it, so that becomes synergy! It is an expanded degree of fulfilling your own creative impulse.

> *When two or more are gathered in synergistic co-creation we are able to uplift and support each other to become something greater.*

The motivation for this is helping one another but there is also the even stronger motivation, which is is to fulfill your own Divine destiny. By combining forces in synergistic co-creation, fulfillment is possible and easier than if you worked in isolation or in opposition. In the American political system right now we have an oppositional democracy totally designed to kill each other! No matter how high up one might get, for example even a President such as Obama is going to be trapped and severely restricted in an oppositional system. However, on an individualistic level down here, nobody is stopping us from communicating and co-creating. The next stage of synergistic democracy and the basis of social synergy and planetary peace is happening right here, outside the oppositional structures, at the level of people connecting. The Occupy Movement is a good example of this. It went global in a month and it also had a certain degree of street theater! You have to be dramatic to do things; you cannot just sit quietly and tell a boring story. There is a lot to be said for the new way. When you understand your connection to Source as an individual and you make the shift to what we call a conscious evolutionary worldview, a greater impulse of life purpose is awakened. Conscious evolution is the evolution from unconscious to conscious choice, meaning that you are empowered to move from unconscious chance to one of conscious choice. And the excitement is that when you begin to have evolutionary conversations with others who share your worldview, you will cultivate the *Impulse of Evolution* by bringing forth your unique calling and creativity in the company of other pioneering souls. It marks a phase-change in evolution itself, leading to the vast empowerment of humanity in our ever-evolving universe.

## First steps towards co-creating peace

Often people ask the question, "What has peace got to do with me? I want peace in this world, but what can I do?" Well, in my experience there is a sequence to how we prepare ourselves to co-create peace. The first most simple and obvious step, we call *Heart Coherence*. As you go into your own heart and experience appreciation and love for whatever is in your domain and allow that sense of appreciation to deepen, you re-sound back and forth inside yourself with love and appreciation and this resonance actually shifts your nervous system very quickly. Your heart and brain start to synchronize and you tune into higher intelligence because you are no longer reactive. So *Heart Coherence* is the first step.

The second step is the shifting from your egoic identity of a separated Self to the identity with your own essence, which is the deeper Source of your being. And the deeper Source of everyone's being is the creator within—the Divine force of Creation—but it is localized as you and it has a unique quality. When you are in heart-connection, even if you feel discontent or self-critical, or less than someone, as long as you remain anchored in the source of what inspires you to express and to give and even if it is only a little impulse, but you say *yes* to it, that yes uplifts and releases you from negativity. You are not saying yes to depression or failure or misery, but the yes is because you are attracted here, you are going to reach out there, you are going to see who you can find and that attraction, combined with the heart connection, ignites the creative impulse, which starts to motivate you.

The third essential step is that we have to learn to recognize when and why we are not at peace with ourselves. For example, back in the fifties I met a man in a little cafe on the Left Bank in Paris and I asked him what I asked all the young men I met: "What do you think is the purpose of life and what's your purpose?" He completely surprised me by saying, "I'm an artist and my purpose is to find a new image of humanity commensurate with our power to shape the future." It flashed in my mind, "I'm going to marry you." I did and we got married on the quest for a new image of man commensurate with our powers. That was in 1951. After the romance of Paris we fell into a typically conventional marriage of that time. In fact the minute I got married I will never forget my shock at waking up as Mrs Earl Hubbard rather than Barbara Marx. I remember thinking, "Where did I go?" I shifted into the new role of housewife and later mother to five children. I was living in Lakesfield, Connecticut. I was the last generation to have babies without thinking. I loved my husband, I loved my children and I was in a peaceful environment. In fact, the whole situation was peaceful and yet I got depressed. The depression, in the *peace* of that environment was even more shocking. I asked myself, "How can I be depressed when I am in a peaceful and loving environment?"

***There I was in my early thirties with everything fine on the external level and yet I really felt like I was dying inside.***

I read Betty Friedan at that time, who wrote the book, *The Feminine Mystique* in the late fifties. She interviewed numerous women and discovered they all had this deep sense of malaise, the problem without a name! The problem without a name was that they had no sense of identity beyond wife and mother. They had no sense of unique expression. The minute I read that book I knew the problem and the reason I was not peaceful was because my identity was submerged in an exclusive role of wife and mother. I wanted to be a wife and mother, but some other part of me was questioning, so I began to say, "Ok, what is that identity?" And then I read Abraham Maslow's *Toward a Psychology of Being*. He interviewed people who were joyful, creative and productive. Even though there were not too many of them, the ones he found had all chosen a vocation or life purpose that they found intrinsically self-rewarding and of service. The self-actualizing person was described by Maslow and I realized that I was not self-actualizing because I had not found that unique expression. So whilst I loved my children, I began to search for my unique vocation. I began to discover it was around communicating evolutionary potential. I read many books, called people up and asked big questions and I took some wonderful people to lunch! And when I did that, I became peace through co-creation. The depression left me and I have never been seriously depressed since.

**My way of connecting with Source**

Throughout our lives we all lose our connection with Source but there is no need to get depressed, as we have all the tools available to enable us to reconnect. I have a powerful way to get myself back on course. Whenever I feel that I might not be doing something well, or that someone has said words that hurt me, or I am failing at something, or I am out of relationship with someone I love, or that the world itself is going to hell, I know these are times I need to reconnect! When I am disconnected I get out my journal, I sit very quietly and I get in touch with what I call the inner Impulse of Evolution, the Impulse of Creativity, the Impulse of Loving Expression; my *own* uniqueness, not everybody else's. And then I feel an inner Compass of Joy, which wants to hit the mark and guide me back on track.

*The definition of sin is when you are off the mark.*

When you get on the mark in your own life it means you are being guided by that impulse to give *your* best, *your* fullness. Almost everybody, if they are not starving or dying, wants to be able to express that potential and give it and be seen by others for who they truly are. I call this coming out of the closet as who you truly are. Do not hold back your own creativity because maybe what I am saying is an extended definition of peace. You can take it on so many levels, whether you are in a warring culture in Rwanda, or you are in ethnic cleansing, or a place where they are suppressing women—all of these things are absolutely necessary to change. When we are off the mark we often experience it as sadness, depression, a lack of internal peace, even a deep sense of guilt because our societies and political systems are telling us how we have it so good. From here the spiral of life can take a downward turn into addictions and self-abuse. How do we rise out of this malaise? It is our birthright to find our unique expression and to shine.

## How can we be at peace with ourselves?

When we are not at peace, when we are feeling depressed, empty, sad, unfulfilled, lonely and lost, it is absolutely the time to start questioning. Not the "why me?" of a victim's stance, but the warrior's stance of, "How can I express my uniqueness? How can I discover and give my best to others? Where am I being guided? What is it that I am not doing?" I absolutely know that crisis precedes transformation, problems are evolutionary drivers—that is true in all of evolution. In our personal lives, if we have a very challenging situation and we can understand that it is an evolutionary driver designed to release more of our creativity, in the design of things we might say these events were needed because we can see with hindsight we were in danger of staying comfortable, but not being creative. Like me being a housewife in Connecticut. If I had not felt depressed, I would not have asked the bigger questions. I would not have found my potential for creative expression.

*A lot of women that were around me at that time accepted depression as inevitable and I was saying, "It is not inevitable, I am going to discover what wants to be born in me."*

☼ 153 ☼

Often people of that time were distressed by me. I made them uncomfortable because around me they could not say, "Well there's no way around this depression." I was saying, "I am going to find out about it," and I did! So then I went back to the people who had not found out about it and I had to be careful that they did not end up feeling humiliated. It is a subtle thing, but less so now than when I got started because there are so many movements of personal and social evolution and spiritual growth. We are going beyond the boundaries of dogmatic religion. Very many of us are going into a more innate spirituality that comes out as each person's unique expression of the Divine. That is a big step forward for humanity. It is very important right now, at this crucial time of change on earth, for us to be at peace. The rotten structures have to fall. It is so important that we associate the word peace with these changes and that each individual knows right now that peace comes through giving that greater gift to each other. This is where joy and happiness comes from. In the USA we have Life, Liberty and the Pursuit of Happiness and I have asked myself, "Who is happy?" Well, in my experience, the happy ones are actualizing their creative gift for service to others. And when we are able to share our creative gift in a synergistic way, we are always rewarded.

**Peace in times of turmoil**

In these times of great change, many ask, "How do I share my sense of peace and find like-minded individuals?" It is a beautiful question to be asking and it is exactly at this threshold that we find the humans who already have freedom and a certain degree of well-being. Profound change is something the whole human race is facing. We are experiencing lack, deficiency, struggle and war. However, when we are relatively comfortable and successful and something is still driving us on to express ourselves fully, that is the growing edge of humanity. When people who have that opportunity to begin to discover and know their inner Light, it is a revelation.

*It is the Oneness within, the love, the heart, the unconditional connection with spirit, with nature, with each other and the expression of unique creativity, which is uniting us. Like points of light emerging from the darkness, we will find each other.*

If you have everything that modern civilization has to offer and you are anywhere where *that* capacity for individual expression exists in its fullest sense, *but* you do not *also* have that deeper yearning to express uniqueness for the good of the Self *and* others, then there will be a natural depression and a sense of malaise. And that malaise is a signal that something more wants to be expressed. Now I realize there are deep psychological maladies and I am not speaking of them, but the type of depression I felt back in the fifties when I had the sense I was dying on the inside. It was not a psychological abhoration, nor was it death; it was actually an impulse of life! And I learnt from that *Impulse of Life* to be more, to do more. When I read Maslow, his research confirmed this, unlike the Freudian analysis, which was described as neurosis.

*I used to think of myself as a neurotic housewife, when actually I was a potential evolutionary!*

I also believe that we model this peaceful fully co-creative way for each other. Many of the contributors in this book have stepped beyond and through difficult life experiences and yet by sharing their experiences, those who read and learn of these situations will say, "If these contributors have done this then I can discover what I can contribute to the world, not in the same way but in my own unique way." And we will know that peace comes from connecting through the heart to others and to the whole of life. We will then be expressing our unique creativity for the good of the Self and the whole and we will become beacons of Light in these times of great change. We will know that we all are connected to one another and to God. It will become a shared experience on a planetary scale. I have always held a passionate intuition of something great coming from all the power. Many people are afraid of technological power because of its obvious destructiveness. But I have always thought we would not have had all this power if there was not a purpose. It is somewhat arrogant to sit here and say all these hundreds of years of effort have been a mistake and that we should go back. We cannot anyway. What is biotechnology, nanotechnology, artificial intelligence, artificial life? Does this have a meaning? On one level I believe it is to knit the planet together into a conscious organism. Each person has the potential to self-actualize within that organism and to actually feel themselves as linked to the whole. I have contemplated what could be the connection with this and Saint Paul's words, "Behold, I show you a mystery. We shall not all sleep. We shall all be changed, in the twinkling of an eye."

Peter Russell, in his book *The White Hole in Time*, has spoken of the acceleration of consciousness and he describes it as a black hole, which suddenly becomes so dense that all light is absorbed in it and never escapes. Peter says there is a time on the planet where all light connects and you have an explosion of consciousness, of white Light, which radically transforms our consciousness collectively. And the vision here is that we would have the awakening of a co-creative humanity—a totally Divine Creativity in our species.

I call this new phase of evolution the *birth* of a universal humanity. We realize that we are one, we are good, we are born into a universe of immeasurable dimensions and trillions of other planets, some of which may have life comparable with our own. This convergence of what is emerging will contribute to making the shift toward the next era in evolution.

*The Light* is an example of achieving peace through co-creation. An amazing twenty-two luminaries have come together to shine their Light and spread an important message to the world at the same time as helping to raise money for seven charities. To see the whole list of contributors and read more about them go to **www.thelightnetwork.com/thelight/about/the-contributors.**

# About John Perkins

As Chief Economist at a major international consulting firm, John Perkins advised the World Bank, United Nations, IMF, U.S. Treasury Department, Fortune 500 corporations, and countries in Africa, Asia, Latin America and the Middle East.

His books on economics and geo-politics have spent more than seventy weeks on the *New York Times* bestseller lists and are published in over thirty languages. He is a founder and board member of Dream Change and The Pachamama Alliance, non-profit organizations devoted to establishing a sustainable, just, and peaceful world. He has been featured on a number of television programs and in publications including *The New York Times, The Washington Post* and *Cosmopolitan*. He was recently awarded the Lennon Ono Grant for Peace 2012.

His books include *Hoodwinked, Confessions of an Economic Hit Man, The Secret History of the American Empire, Shapeshifting, The World Is As You Dream It, Psychonavigation, Spirit of the Shuar* and *The Stress-Free Habit*.

For more information log onto **www.johnperkins.org**.

# An Enlightened Economy

*By John Perkins*

*It is important to pray for peace. But you must also
take actions to make that happen. Every single day.*
~ **The Dalai Lama**

The world economy today is a total failure. Less than
five percent of the world's population lives in the
United States and we consume nearly thirty percent of the
world's resources, while roughly half of the world is close to
starvation or actually starving. That is an abject failure. It
cannot be repeated in any other country because, apart from
anything else, this disproportionate distribution of resources
is unsustainable. We have created an economy that is based
on death and ruthless destruction. It is highly militarized and
it is dependent on destroying nature. I call it a *death economy*.
What we need to create now is an economy that is based on
improving and honoring life of all types; plant life, animal
life and human life, in other words a *life economy*.

Before the big turning point in my life, I was known
as an *economic hit man*. I played a part in creating the first
truly global empire, which is run by the biggest corporations
around the world. There are many methods that economic
hit men employ to accomplish this but the most common
is identifying a third world country (one that has valuable
resources, such as oil) and then arranging a huge loan to
that country, through one of the large financial institutions.
Yet the money does not go to the country. Instead it goes
to our own multi-national corporations in order to build
big infrastructure projects in that country, such as electrical

power systems, highways, ports, airports—systems that only benefit a few wealthy families, as well as the corporations. The majority of the people do not benefit from these investments because they cannot afford to buy electricity, they do not have cars to drive on the new highways and they do not use ports or airports; yet they are left holding a huge debt.

At some point the economic hit men go back to these countries and say, "Hey, you can't repay these debts so you must sell your oil real cheap to the international oil companies (or whatever the resource is), without any environmental restrictions or social regulations." Or "Allow us to build a military base on your soil." Or "Vote with us at the next critical United Nations vote." In the few cases where economic hit men fail, where the leaders of these countries do not agree to the onerous terms, people we refer to as *jackals* are called in to either overthrow the governments or assassinate the leaders.

I worked for a private corporation (Chas. T, Main Inc, which has since been sold and the name changed). My official title was Chief Economist. My corporation would sign contracts with the World Bank, the Inter-American Development Bank, the US Treasury, the State Department or one of the other international development organizations to do a particular job.

One of my assignments was in Ecuador where the then president Jaime Roldos was the first democratically elected president after several years of military dictators. The military dictators had given in to the economic hit men and they had put their country into massive debt. They had hired outside firms to come in to build infrastructure projects and allowed oil companies to do pretty much whatever they wanted. Jaime Roldos ran a campaign that said he would rein in the oil companies and stop Ecuador from being a servant to the big corporations. He won the election and then economic hit men, myself included, tried to convince him not to keep his promises. But Roldos would not give in. He had tremendous integrity. He kept his word to the people. So the jackals assassinated him. Officially he died in a private plane crash, but there is no question that he was assassinated.

## The Mayan Prophecy

The fall of the material world is the first step in making us realize that we have to transform. The Mayan Prophecy relating to 2012, taken directly from their sacred text the *Popul Vuh*, is very optimistic, unlike the Hollywood version. It says that there was a time in history that was ruled by a king named *Seven Macaw*, who was brutal, exploitative, selfish and highly materialistic. His head was cut off by the *Hero Twins* and he was replaced by a new ruler named *Hunah Poh*, who is characterized by compassion, cooperation and spirituality. The Mayan elders say that *Seven Macaw* represents the old paradigm, the system that we have been living in for several thousand years and that now the *Hero Twins*, we the people, have to come along and sever the head of that old paradigm and replace it with a new form of leadership, which offers compassion, cooperation and spirituality. It is very clear that our current leaders will not make this happen. Just as *Seven Macaw* was not going to replace himself, the corporate systems of today will not replace themselves. We the people have to do it. We—you and I—must join together to turn corporations and governments around and help them understand that we will only buy from and vote for them if they are committed to creating a sustainable, just world where all of us can thrive. I have worked with indigenous people on every continent and they all have prophecies telling us that we have entered a time with tremendous potential for transformation.

*We are moving out of an old system that is insane, not working and self-destructive—a death economy— and into a new system, which we can call a life economy that is based on spirituality, cooperation and compassion.*

**My journey**

After I left business school, from the years of 1968-1971 I was in the Peace Corps in the Amazon Rainforest and the Andes. At one point I became very sick and was cured by a shaman. In return, he requested that I become his apprentice. As a business graduate, I had no interest in shamanism at that time. But I had no choice; he had saved my life. So I learned the art of shamanism. The best short definition for a shaman is "a person who journeys to other worlds (the subconscious or collective conscious) and uses what he or she learns there to effect change in this world." This change may take the form of healing people or of helping individuals or communities explore new ways of relating to others and the environment.

After three years in the Peace Corps, I was recruited into the ranks of the economic hit men. To begin with I thought I was doing good work because the system of investing money into infrastructure projects in poor countries was taught in business schools as the best way to help those countries grow wealthier. What the statistics do not show is that almost all the economic growth occurs among only the wealthiest people and the poor people do not benefit much at all; usually they get poorer and poorer relative to the wealthy people. Over time I began to see that this way of business was fatally flawed. After ten years of being an economic hit man I quit. I returned to the Amazon and the Andes where I offered to help the people and cultures I had lived with and to learn more about their ways. I also began to write books on shamanism. Today I can see that the whole idea of shamanism, which is about transformation and changing the way we think and feel, is an important part of the process we must go through in order to pull ourselves back from the economic and political precipice.

**The meaning of success**

For me success means doing what brings us the greatest joy

and pleasure; the most meaningful thing in our lives. I have known a lot of very wealthy people and I do not think many of them are happy. It is the same for countries. The United States is one of the most prosperous countries in history and yet statistics show that we are not very happy. We have high rates of suicide, drug abuse, divorce, child molestation and homicide. We only have to look at individuals and cultures to see that the wealthiest ones are not necessarily the happiest. I can see this when I look at my friends, the *Achuar* and the *Shuar* in the Amazon, with whom I work extensively. According to the World Bank and United Nations these people are extremely impoverished and yet if they live their traditional lives, even though they have little or no money, they are very happy. They have plenty of good food, the kind of shelter they need, all their basic needs met and they have a lot of time to spend with their families. So success should be measured by how happy and fulfilled we are, not by how many material possessions we have accumulated.

**How you can help?**

Today corporations, not governments, control global economics. And yet, we all have to take responsibility for the mess we are in. We are the corporations. Many of us work for them and almost all of us buy from them. Up until now we have sent a strong message that we want high quality but inexpensive shirts and jeans and that if they are made in sweat shops in Asia or Latin America, we will turn a blind eye and look the other way. We send the message that we want cheaper petroleum for our cars and if that means destroying the Amazon rainforest, then we will simply turn a blind eye and look the other way. This has to change. We have to take responsibility as consumers. It is up to us to turn things around.

One of the primary factors behind where we are today is that in the 1970's a new goal for corporations and businesses was defined, perhaps best expressed by Milton Friedman in the Chicago School of Economics. He stated that, "The only responsibility of business is to maximize profits," regardless of the social and environmental cost. When I went to business school in the late sixties I was taught that businesses should make a decent rate of return for their investors but that a good CEO should also take really good care of his employees, give them health care and retirement benefits and take a cut in his own salary before laying people off. He should be responsible to his customers and suppliers and be a good community citizen, pay taxes and even go beyond that and donate money towards schools and recreational centers. That all changed in the seventies when Milton Friedman defined this new goal and every major world leader since has bought into it. It is a terrible goal. Businesses need to be public servants and take responsibility for creating a better world for ourselves, our children and our grandchildren. The new goal should be: businesses can make a decent return for their investors but only while being socially and environmentally responsible. The key to creating a new economy, a *life economy*, is for businesses to redefine their goals and say: "Our purpose and intention is to make a decent rate of return on investment while at the same time creating a just, sustainable, peaceful world for all beings."

We must recognize that we live on a very tiny and fragile space station. Unlike the one our astronauts built, this one does not have any shuttles, so we cannot get off. For the first time in history we have to see that it is not enough to take care of any particular country. In order for my five-year-old grandson to grow up in a sustainable, just and peaceful world every child on the planet has to grow up in a sustainable, just and peaceful world. And that does not only apply to human children but to the children of all animals and plants; the whole system. Our entire space station has to function properly or else none of it will function.

We the consumers, the people, have a great deal of power and responsibility. The marketplace is essentially a democracy if we choose to make it that. So every time we buy something, or elect not to, we are casting a vote. I think this is an even more important vote than the one we cast in the voting polls for politicians because this vote is cast every time we shop. It is imperative that we only purchase goods from corporations and businesses committed to creating a sustainable, just and peaceful world.

For example, many clothing companies employ cheap labor in sweat shops in Asia and Latin America. It is important for these people to have the jobs but it is also essential that they earn a good wage and get health care and retirement benefits so they can live good lives. We should decide *not* to spend money with any company not committed to making that happen. We need to send a message to those companies that are not acting from a place of integrity that we will not buy from them. In the same way we need to let those companies that are doing a good job, know we appreciate it and that we will continue to buy from them. This has worked in the past. When I was in college there were rivers in Ohio that were on fire with pollution. We boycotted the corporations that were polluting the rivers and they cleaned them up. We also got corporations to open their doors wider to women and minorities and to hire more people from diverse backgrounds. We can be pretty successful when we put pressure on these corporations. Now we need to take it up a notch and not just go after individual causes; we must make it clear that we will not buy from corporations whose goal is to only maximize profits. We will only support businesses that are dedicated to creating a world our children and grandchildren will want to inherit.

## An enlightened—*life*—economy

I think lots of countries are now moving toward an enlightened economy. I like the term *life economy* as opposed to *death economy*." I first heard *life economy* used by the co-host of 21st Century Radio, Dr. Zohara Hieronimus. Some of the countries in Latin America are taking pretty aggressive stances in that direction. Ecuador is attempting to create a new currency that is not based on a central banking system of interest rates and debt. We are also seeing countries like Ecuador and Bolivia adopt new constitutions that give nature rights. Bhutan has a happiness index, which is much more important than the traditional economic indices. There are a number of communities throughout Europe and the United States that are developing their own currencies locally and emphasizing the importance of supporting local banks and local businesses.

Today most of the leadership is coming from individuals: writers, philosophers, teachers, show-makers, activists and movements like The Occupy Movement. As the prophecies tell us, the leaders are not likely to make this happen because they are in too cozy a position right now. Nobody gets elected to a higher position in any of the so-called democracies without support from corporations. Once the corporations give campaign money to any politician or political party, then whoever gets elected is controlled by the big corporations. These global companies also control the mainstream press either through outright ownership or the investment of huge advertising budgets. The corporations are very much in control of our current leaders. Consequently, to create enlightened economies we need to look elsewhere, to people who are not necessarily mainstream or known leaders.

**Money and the world**

Human beings do not need money to exist. We have lived for hundreds of thousands of years without it. There are people living in the Amazon and other places who do not have any form of what we call *currency*. Nevertheless, I cannot imagine most of the world today without some form of currency, because it makes exchange far easier. I think the real questions revolve around the types of currency and the institutions that back them up. The central banking systems in place in much of the world today are corrupt and inefficient; they serve the interests of the very wealthy and not the majority of the people. This private money system based on debt and interest rates is exploitative; it leads to corruption and inequality. Therefore, we must replace it with a different type of currency, a different system.

The point of money as energy is important for us to understand. For example, if I go out and dig ditches and get paid for it, then I am being paid for the energy I have put into digging the ditch. Then I might use that money to buy a loaf of bread or get a new pair of pants, so again the money represents the energy that went into baking the bread or making the pants. When we understand that, we also see that money is really just a form of making the barter system a lot easier. But that does not require a central banking system, which is usually privately owned by somebody or by a group of people who benefit greatly by the fact that the government borrows money and pays high interest rates—in essence a form of taxation for the rest of us. The current systems only work to the advantage of the very wealthy. Today, thanks to technology, it is fairly easy to implement a digitalized form of exchange where we do not need printed money. Several countries in Latin America have joined together to consider introducing this type of exchange. They are calling it the *sucre* named after a famous general in the war for independence from Spain. It is basically a computerized form of money, a bit like having a credit card but with no need to pay interest.

**From lack to abundance**

We have grown up with a world-view that says we are lacking and that there is a limitation to everything. For example, the belief that there is a shortage of oil and that someday we will run out. The real issue is not whether we have a lack of oil; rather it is the fact that we really have an atmosphere that cannot handle the carbon dioxide produced by all the oil currently available under the ground. But there is no lack of energy. The sun is an extremely powerful source of energy: hence, we could satisfy most all of our energy needs from solar if we set our hearts and minds to it. The same is true of other resources. There is no lack. Going back to the fact that less than five percent of the world's population live in the United States yet consumes almost thirty percent of the world's resources, it is easy to see that it is not a lack of resources that is the problem; the fault lies in the distribution of those resources. The prophecy that comes out of the Age of Aquarius, which we entered in June 2012, says it is a time to move out of old dysfunctional patterns of limitation and lack and move into a new, much more functional pattern of understanding that there is plenty. We have abundance on this amazing planet, we just need to take care of it better, distribute the abundance more efficiently and honor all life forms.

**The laws of giving and receiving**

If we are compassionate, cooperative and willing to contribute to the betterment of others, we will receive back in return. In many indigenous nations it is said that if anybody in the community is suffering and others could alleviate that suffering, but they do not, then the whole community will suffer. There may be people who are suffering and no one can do anything to help them because they have a terrible disease or they have been in an accident, but if anyone is suffering because they do not have enough to eat, they do not have good clothes, they do not have a good place to live, or because they are being treated brutally, then the whole community suffers. If someone does not get enough food from hunting then the good hunters are called upon to give a share of their food and it is recognized that their compassion will come back as a gift to them.

I am a founder and on the board of directors of a couple of non-profit organizations: Dream Change and the Pachamama Alliance. If we give time and money to organizations doing great work, we will get it back in many ways. Giving and helping people is, in its own way, a form of investment. Everything we do to make the community a better place is one of the best forms of investment for ourselves, our children, our grandchildren and for our own peace of mind. There is nothing more wonderful or satisfying than doing good work, helping other people and making the world a better place. I can speak personally. For many years I did jobs that were pretty selfish and materialistic and I was never happy. I drank a lot of alcohol, I took a lot of valium, I went through a terrible divorce and I underwent extensive psychological therapy. I was not a happy person. Now I devote myself to trying to create a better world for the generations to come. It is extremely satisfying, wonderful work.

## Philanthropy

Philanthropy is a great thing. If someone has made a lot of money then it is a good idea for them to give back. However, I advise students not to follow in the footsteps of some of the big entrepreneurs and make, for example, $80 billion then give back $30 billion. It is better to make less money and support people as we go along. Most of the famous philanthropists did a lot of bad things in terms of destroying competition, monopolizing ruthlessly the market. It is important, as a young business person starting out, to understand that better than making a lot of money and then giving some of it to philanthropy, is to do a good job as you go, encouraging competition, paying your employees really well and taking good care of the community. I am not discouraging philanthropy, as I think it is a great thing for all of us no matter how much money we have, but I also do not want to encourage the concept that people should make a lot of money, be ruthless doing it and then give some of it back for good causes.

For those who have money, my suggestion is to keep it

in local banks that invest in their community and encourage projects that stimulate the local economy. And rather than investing in large corporations, invest in people who are doing good work in the world.

## Bringing forth the Light into our financial dealings

No matter what your religion is, the greatest service you can do for yourself and for the planet is to serve others, including nature. Whatever we worship, or whatever spiritual forces we believe in, we must understand that serving future generations, serving other people, serving the earth and serving nature, is commendable and will bring us good returns, materially, emotionally, psychologically and spiritually.

## My vision for the future

My vision for the future is that we will establish a world that has a *life economy*. We will focus on cleaning up the planet's pollution. We will create societies where starving people can grow food more efficiently and store and distribute it locally. We will introduce systems that employ better forms of energy production and transportation, ones that have a much a smaller carbon footprint. There is a huge amount we can do on this planet to make it a better place. And of course, it is terribly important that we have great artists, writers, poets and musicians, since the arts inspire us and enrich our lives in so many ways. Let us focus on a *life economy*, one that encourages prosperity for everyone—rather than today's *death economy* that thrives on ripping up nature and fomenting wars.

The key to us moving into a better world is to recognize that we all have passions and talents. We can use these in different ways. We can take different paths. In my case, I focus on writing books and going on speaking tours, but we all have our own unique gifts to offer this world. If we all head toward the same goal of helping to create a sustainable, just and peaceful world—a world that the children and grandchildren of all beings will be happy to inherit—we will get there! And we must have fun on this journey, as we move along this path. Otherwise, we will burn out. It is imperative that we bring the bliss of recognizing our powers as agents of change into our every day lives.

 Practice altruism right away! For some suggested charities to donate money to log on to ***www.thelightnetwork.com/thelight/ about/the-charities.***

# Section 3

# Experience the Subtle World

*She gazed lovingly at the radiant face of the traveler.*
*"Your steadfastness will be rewarded. Your longing has attracted grace. I invite you to come with me into the Sanctum Sanctorum. It is time for the mystery to be revealed..."*

# About Julie Chimes

Julie Chimes was once a successful company director, businesswoman and part-time racing driver until her world underwent a dramatic change. Viciously stabbed and assumed dead, her subsequent survival was considered to be something of a miracle. She wrote a profound yet humorous autobiographical account of her experiences, both in and out of body, called *A Stranger in Paradise*. It created a wave of positive media attention around the world, particularly because she forgave her attacker.

Since the attack she has traveled extensively addressing and entertaining  diverse audiences around the world sharing the experiences of her many adventures and fresh insights on the mysteries of life and death. She is now dedicated to sharing the deeper meaning of life and the healing power of forgiveness. Julie has a new book coming out called *The Sutras of Suburbia* and a children's spiritual adventure story called *The Wish-Fulfilling Tree*.

For more details about Julie, log on to ***www.juliechimes.co.uk***.

# The Paradox of Forgiveness

*By Julie Chimes*

*When the violin can forgive the past it starts singing...*
*When the violin can forgive every wound caused by*
*others, the heart starts singing.*

~ **Hafiz**
**Extract from** *The Gift,*
**translated by Daniel Ladinsky**

W hy would anyone knowingly walk around with a sack of stones on their shoulders and an iron band clamped around their heart? What possible benefit is there in clinging onto pain, sadness, resentment, grudges and vengeance? And what induces us to carry this sack around with us 24/7, wearing our grim expression as a badge so others can see our suffering and martyrdom? Why would we deny ourselves the chance to live a life overflowing with joy, by doggedly hanging on to that which destroys all possibility of manifesting happiness, peace and love? Why would anyone do this? What is this load that we carry on our shoulders and what is it that slams the door of the heart firmly shut? The late Martin Luther King Jr gave us a clue when he said, "I have decided to stick with love. Hate is too great a burden to bear."

Often we do not even notice that the perceived wrongs, the rage, the tears, the hurts and even those little slights in our lives are being placed in that pesky sack, until we wonder why we are so utterly exhausted and overwhelmed, eaten away on the inside and often ill. But take heart, because there is one sure way to free ourselves from this contracted existence. It has been written about in every spiritual, philosophical and religious system and it has been practiced for centuries. What is more, anyone can do it, anywhere, at anytime; it works, it is free, it has no side effects and yet it is perhaps one of the most misunderstood teachings of all time. It is the key to finding the peace that surpasses all understanding; it is better known as *forgiveness*.

> **A modern Indian saint once said, "As long as you are unable to forgive both yourself and others, you are unable to recognize the profound love that dwells in the heart."**

I love this image of freeing up space in our beautiful hearts and allowing the sacred place to be filled with kindness, gentleness and love towards our world and ourselves.

Most dictionaries define *forgiveness* as a quality and as with any virtue it needs to be nurtured. It is a spiritual attribute, yet it is in no way limited to the confines of religious dogma; the capacity to forgive exists in every heart. We can say the words "I forgive you," but they have no meaning if we do not have the feelings of warmth, compassion, release and love that accompany the act. Forgiveness is much more than an intellectual process. It has to be drawn forth from our being, in other words through the true meaning of *to educate*, derived from *educare* which means *to bring*, and *ducere, to lead; to bring forward*. Much has been written about this subject but there are still fundamental misunderstandings about what forgiveness actually is and these misconceptions often block us from wanting to apply it or to go deeper into what I call the *Paradox*. I think clarification of what forgiveness *is not* can be helpful.

☼ It does not condone acts that are harmful to any part of creation.

☼ It does not necessitate liking the one we are forgiving.

☼ It does not mean we have to be in the physical presence of whoever we are forgiving.

☼ It does not mean we have to block our emotional responses to harmful acts against us.

☼ It does not mean we have to remain in abusive situations.

☼ It does not stop us from becoming a voice against atrocity.

☼ It is not used as a comfort blanket, negating the need for honest remorse in the perpetrators of abuse.

☼ It is never given with a set of conditions.

Forgiveness can be granted without consent or demand. In business one forgives a debt, giving up any claim. It is also defined as the giving up of all resentment, anger and desire to punish. My favorite is the beautifully simple explanation, *to forsake, to lay aside*. So how do we lay aside these burdens? Well, some people can simply just let the sack go, but for most of us it is far more complex. There is no set pattern or timescale. Just as one cannot stand before a bud and demand it to open, one cannot impose any deadline about when to forgive. That is a decision unique to each one of us and our circumstances. Take a look at the website of the charity The Forgiveness Project (*www.theforgivenessproject.com*) and read the stories from people around the world and you will see how there is no blueprint for forgiveness. This knowledge can help to alleviate the guilt we sometimes feel when we are not ready to forgive, even though we know it would be a good thing to do. Guilt, by the way, just adds another few kilos to the already hefty sack!

A spiritual master once asked his disciples to write

on potatoes the names of all those for whom they carried resentments, anger, or had unfinished business with. He then instructed each disciple to carry them in a bag 24/7 so they were aware not only of the weight, but also the eventual stinking, seeping slime. "Forgiveness," he said, "is the laying down of this festering burden." He also made the point that the only ones who suffer from the weight and stench of non-forgiveness are ourselves, never the perpetrators. As my friend Eva Kor, who survived the horrors of Auschwitz, likes to point out "forgiveness is actually an act of self love."

Beyond the personal benefits there is another very good reason to forgive. The scientists and mystics are at last coming into agreement and they know we are all inextricably linked to each other and Mother Earth. When our minds are intent on revenge or filled with sadness, we pour toxicity into Her soil and spray negativity into the lives of those around us. We forgive in order to stop ourselves becoming weapons of mass destruction. Never has there been a more urgent need to give our precious earth a break. The illumined words of the Indian saint Paramahansa Yogananda say it all: "The physical substance of our earth is held together by the mortar of forgiveness"

**My own experiences**

So who am I to discuss the *Paradox of Forgiveness*? In 1986 I agreed to let an emotionally distressed acquaintance wait in my cottage home, which was occasionally used as a waiting room for patients of my partner, the local doctor. This woman had been removed from an early morning London-bound train for behaving in a strange manner (hurling most of her clothes out of the window) and after a bizarre breakdown in communication she was eventually delivered unexpectedly early by police to the full public waiting room of my boyfriend's practice. After receiving an initial assessment she asked, as she had met me, if she could wait in the comfort of our cottage until my partner could clear his patients and give her his full attention. No one who saw her that day thought her to be dangerous and no one, including her psychiatrist, family or friends had any idea that she had recently taken herself off all the medication she took for her paranoid schizophrenia. I thought I was being kind. Within minutes of her arrival she helped herself to my largest carving knife and set about her mission of saving the world in the name of Jesus.

When the knife entered my chest something as well as shock and agony exploded in my awareness. A part of me became detached from my body and although I knew some part of me was being stabbed, it did not seem to be of any consequence. I felt incredibly alive and I became aware of a place beyond the screams; a place where calm, loving, soothing, beautiful thoughts and clear instructions on how to survive came from the authoritative voice of what felt to be a guardian angel. From this elevated perspective I was able to observe the mayhem with total understanding of her life story and why she was doing this to me—there was even a tremendous sense of humor present.

*In an upwelling of pure joy I shouted out that "I loved her," which given the circumstances was as much of a surprise to me as being stabbed.*

The physical pain was excruciating, but a phenomenal strength and focus arose within me and my friend in Spirit gave me very specific instructions, which along with the profound visions I was experiencing enabled me to eventually get out of the cottage. As I crawled to the gate, crying for help with an enormous knife in my back, I saw passers-by running away. Not that I blamed them, for in their shoes I probably would have done the same. Eventually a courageous passer-by managed to disarm my attacker as she attempted to hack off my head.

I was given up for dead by the first police officers arriving at the crime scene, but I was aware of everything, including the unhelpful onlookers who were discussing the ambulance strike; and the businessman who would not cover me with his jacket because he did not want it *ruined* by my blood. Curled in an exsanguinated foetal heap, in that cold wet driveway in the south of the United Kingdom, I was totally aware of everything going on around me. My overview came from a place beyond physical form. I still felt profound love towards my psychotic attacker and it even extended to the unhelpful accident-onlookers. "Father forgive them, for they know not what they do" was my main thought. I remember also thinking, "Look at it this way kid, from here things can only get better!" They did not, but that is another story!

## When there is understanding compassion can arise

Our healing begins with the willingness to undertake the forgiveness process and that sweetest of efforts attracts what I call *Grace*. This mysterious unfolding of the energy of intent, when unleashed, ensures that everything we need to support us arrives in our lives at exactly the right moment. The book that falls off the shelf as we walk past; the chance remark we overhear on our journey home; the old friend who turns up in our life; a random tuning into a broadcast of a story that touches our heart. When we decide we need to heal, to become whole, our efforts will be supported tenfold.

## Releasing pain

How do we safely release the contents of our sacks—all those repressed feelings—in a safe and constructive manner? Sometimes we erroneously believe that dumping our stockpiled negativity on the perpetrators head will bring about the desired sense of justice being done and an end to our suffering. But if you ask (and I have) those who have tried it, they report that the spewing of self-righteous rage and spilling of bitter tears brings neither peace nor closure. Yet we do need to express ourselves, to tell our stories and feel our feelings. It is an essential part of the process.

The simplest way is to find someone who loves you enough to listen without interruption, judgment, or a gushing need to make everything ok. Avoid the tea and sympathy brigade— their attentions only serve to keep us victims. If I see a beatific smile or hear a "you poor thing" heading towards me I swiftly change direction! If you are fortunate enough to have a true and empathetic friend, take yourselves to a favorite place and get talking. It does not matter if you make no sense. Do not think about it; just tell your story and allow all the emotions to pour forth. If you do not have a suitable friend then find a good therapist and pay them to listen instead. Whatever it takes, this backed-up energy has to be removed from the physical cells of our bodies. If not, it wreaks a silent havoc. Latest scientific research confirms that *festering* because of a lack of forgiveness leads to all manner of *dis-ease*. The perpetrators do not suffer, we do, so why give them any more of our precious lives? This research also proves beyond doubt that when we are allowed to tell our stories blood pressure lowers, stress reduces, sleep improves and our performance is enhanced. The indigenous peoples of our earth have always known this.

*They say that in our darkest times, the greatest healing of all comes when our stories are heard, when we find new ways of understanding and when we begin to call our spirit back.*

As the saying goes, "A true friend is someone who knows the song in your heart and can sing it back to you when you have forgotten the words."

Another safe way to discharge the build up of negative emotional energy is to write without censorship. Just tell your story in full detail—write until there is nothing left to say and then read it to yourself out loud. Scream, shout and cry until you are through. Get all that stale victimhood out of your system. Being a victim is not unlike illness. It is an imbalance in the system, but it is never meant to remain with us for the rest of our days. Unless, of course, we enjoy the secondary benefits of being a chronic victim—more on that later. The physical act of writing is one of the best ways I know of releasing pent-up frustration—and sometimes it even gets published! I wrote letters in my head, even during the attack and in the aftermath, to all those who had seriously upset me. When some years later I wrote a book about my experiences, the letters were still vivid in my memory and, as I began to write them down, something amazing happened. My tears of rage and frustration became tears of laughter. Something released and the ensuing hysteria shook the last vestiges of painful memory out of my system *forever*. Not only that, but readers of my story said they were amazed to find they could cry out in horror yet burst out laughing within the same paragraph. Words written from real experiences— and an open heart—have potency and the power to transmit the writer's feelings into the reader's own body and mind, whether spiritually uplifting or otherwise!

If speaking or writing has no appeal then dance your story, sing it, paint it, or sculpt it. Give it form and get it out of your system. Imagine you are performing in front of an audience who love and cherish you. And how will you know when you are done and ready for the next step in the process? Because you will probably feel exhausted and somewhat bored with the old tape that has being playing incessantly in your head. You may be laughing, but for certain a new calm, stillness will be present within and you will like the feeling.

## Understanding

As a small child I received an early training in understanding, having an older brother with a profound learning disability. Unable to speak or communicate, he would often lash out in sheer frustration and sometimes out of jealous rage he would do unspeakably horrible things to me and anything I loved. My mother would say to me, "Don't be mad—just close your eyes and imagine how he feels, trapped inside himself. Try to understand him and then you will not feel so hurt or angry." My heart would always melt when I saw the world through his eyes and we developed an extraordinary level of communication and love between each other, which continues to this day.

No matter what we think about the events of our lives, there is always a higher perspective. Closing our eyes, becoming still and entering into meditation is one of the most effective ways of getting to this enlightened overview and it is far more enjoyable than being stabbed! Meditation also releases the tension in our breathing; often we are still holding our breath in terror years after the event. In a meditative state we can contemplate three key questions, which can help our understanding evolve:

**What have I lost?**
**What have I gained?**
**What have I learnt?**

There is a place within us that is untouched, unsullied and unharmed by all of the outer experiences. If we want to experience *The State of Forgiveness*, we have to go within and find it—this is the greatest truth I know.

I was recently on a BBC radio interview with a man, who by his own definition was a serial criminal. He gave no thought whatsoever to those he robbed, cheated and battered. He considered his crime and subsequent punishment were a way of life. His victims were simply a faceless name on the police summons—*a piece of paper*. While serving yet another sentence he was asked if he would take part in a Conflict Resolution Program. He agreed and for the first time in his life he came face to face with one of his victims. When he had to listen to the consequences of his actions and the impact his brutality had on an innocent family, he felt profoundly uncomfortable. His *piece of paper* had become more than a faceless victim; it was a man, a passionate, angry man who risked his life to protect his small daughter from witnessing a brutal crime. This hardened criminal's awareness suddenly exploded beyond his own little melodrama and he experienced the power of honest remorse and as a result his life changed course dramatically. He never committed another crime and over time these two men, of very different backgrounds, learnt to understand and respect each other, resulting in a deep friendship. They also turned their experiences into something for the benefit of others, by creating a charity which encourages the Restorative Justice process and empowers victims to have a voice that is heard.

**When there is forgiveness, compassion arises**

So what is this elusive quality, compassion? And how do we get it to arise in our hearts? Its root comes from the Latin *compati*—to suffer with—and in modern language usage, *to share*. I like to think that the stem of the word, compass, points us in the right direction! If we compass the earth, we do a complete circuit; we take in all points of view. In the most ancient of languages, Sanskrit, the word for compassion is *karuna*. The beauty of this sacred language is that it provides layers of meaning, which help give definition. It defines compassion as sentiment associated with sorrow and suffering. It is a particular tone in music—there are Indian *ragas* composed especially to invoke compassion and most powerfully it is described as an action, which is holy work. It says in the ancient Indian epic book of sacred stories, *The Shrimrad Bhagavatam*:

**A truly compassionate man will consider the pain of others as if it is his own. And knowing**

*the pain of others, if he does not do anything to help them, to alleviate their pain, then there is no difference between him and a log.*

It is clear that compassion is something we feel rather than think and until we can feel it we cannot fully forgive. When we can feel the suffering of another, compassion arises. It is a soothing balm, which melts away the attachment to our own little melodramas, leaving behind a deep desire to be of service to humanity. Lack of compassion is in fact a state of selfishness. The Dalai Lama, who is the embodiment of compassion, recently said:

> *Hatred, jealousy and excessive attachment cause suffering and agitation. I feel compassion can help us overcome these disturbances and let us return to a calm state of mind. Compassion is not just being kind to your friend. That involves attachment because it is based on expectation. Compassion is when you do something good without any expectations.*

## When there is forgiveness there is peace

When compassion arises we stop blaming others and ourselves. We need tremendous courage to break the cycle of hatred, revenge and retribution in our lives, societies and the world. Forgiveness is not for cowards. As I lay in intensive care, the sound of voices around me arguing over who was to blame made me feel so ill that all the alarms monitoring my vital signs went off and the visitors who had come to make me feel better were asked to leave!

We have created societies where forgiveness is not good for business because blame and chronic victimhood can result in plenty of work for lawyers and substantial compensation for victims. Often the promise of secondary gain keeps us chained to the painful baggage.

I refused to sue anyone because I knew that no one was

to blame. I certainly suffered financially, but I have never for one moment regretted that choice. A modern sage recently said that we are all longing for peace in the world—she then added with a smile that this world does not need peace—*you* need to be at peace.

> *Forgiveness fills a soft pillow beneath our*
> *heads that ensures deep and peaceful slumber.*

Forgiveness is a paradox. It bestows remarkable healing powers upon us. It is forgiving the ignorance, but never condoning the acts that cause pain and suffering. It is having understanding and compassion, but never weakening and negating the need for others to face their demons and come to a place of true repentance. It is a state of courage, clarity and gentleness from which peaceful solutions arise. It is a state of being and the gateway to brotherhood and Universal Love. And when we attain this state, we begin to shine; we become a beacon of Light and of service to others who are suffering. Within this Light we realize the great *Paradox of Forgiveness* is that in truth, there was never anything to be forgiven.

---

☼ **Light Practice** ☼
**A forgiveness contemplation**

Choose a favorite spot where you will be comfortable and quiet, without distractions. If indoors make sure it is clean, fresh and uncluttered. Contemplation is an ancient form of spiritual practice, which is all the more potent when performed in a prepared sacred space. You may wish to light a small candle and place some flowers in front of where you will be sitting. In order to purify the space, even if outdoors, light a natural incense or burn essential oil of geranium to help release old anger and negative memories, or lavender for its healing properties, which promote a deep relaxation

---

of mind, body and spirit. It is also a good idea to play a sacred chant in the space, prior to this exercise, or allow wind chimes to resonate. If you have a treasured crystal or photograph, place it with the candle. Wear soft, comfortable clothing and preferably have bare feet to allow the energy of Mother Earth to support you. Have your favorite pen and a writing book to hand. Take a comfortable posture, either sitting cross-legged on the floor or on a chair with both feet on the ground, shoulder-width apart. Allow your spine to be gently upright, as if a silken cord is pulling at the top of your head. Inhale deeply through the nose and exhale through the mouth, checking to see that all your muscles are relaxed. Do this three times (a simple yet powerful breathing technique which can be used anywhere). You are ready. Now slowly read the following quote by Martin Luther King Jr.

> *Returning violence for violence multiplies violence, adding deeper darkness to a night already devoid of stars. Hate cannot drive out hate: only love can do that.*

Without judgment and with complete honesty, ask yourself the following questions:

☼ When in my life have I expressed violence in my thoughts or actions?

☼ How did this negativity make me feel?

☼ What effect did my action or mood have on those around me?

☼ Who or what have I not been able to forgive?

☼ Where and how do these negative feelings affect my body?

☼ Who would I be without this pain?

☼ How much more energy would I have if I was free from my past?

☼ What do I need to do to express more love in my life?

Re-read the quote out loud then choose the one question that resonates with you the most. Write the question in the center of a blank page and draw a circle around it. Repeat the question silently, breathe deeply and simply allow your feelings and thoughts to flow without any restrictions. Give time and space to this and with your eyes closed imagine you are bringing the question to your Highest Self. Pick up your pen and begin a letter to yourself, starting with the words, My Beloved......(your name). Write in a circular direction around the question and answer as fully as you can. Do not think about this, just allow a dialogue to flow until there is nothing left to write. Breathe deeply and read back your words. Ask yourself what you have lost by doing this, what you have gained and what you have learned? Ask how you will apply this new wisdom to your life. Intellectual knowledge and revelation is not enough; to truly change wisdom must be applied to our everyday lives. Write down your answers. When you have finished bring your hands together and express gratitude to your Inner Teacher.

The Forgiveness Project is one of the seven charities we are raising money for through sales of this book. You can read more about The Forgiveness Project and our other chosen charities by entering this link into your browser: **www.thelightnetwork.com/thelight/about/the-charities.**

# About John-Roger

A teacher and lecturer of international stature, John-Roger is an inspiration in the lives of many people around the world helping people to discover the Spirit within themselves and find health, peace and prosperity.

With two co-authored books on the *New York Times* Bestseller List and more than four dozen self-help books and audio albums, John-Roger offers extraordinary insights on a wide range of topics. He is the founder of many organizations including the nondenominational Church of the Movement of Spiritual Inner Awareness (MSIA), the University of Santa Monica; Peace Theological Seminary & College of Philosophy; the Institute for Individual and World Peace and The Heartfelt Foundation.

John-Roger has given over six thousand lectures and seminars worldwide, many of which are televised nationally on his cable program, *That Which Is*, through the Network of Wisdoms. He also co-wrote and co-produced the movies *Spiritual Warriors* and *The Wayshower*.

To learn more about the information presented in this chapter, please refer to John-Roger's book *Fulfilling Your Spiritual Promise*.

For further details about John-Roger, visit ***www.john-roger.org.***

# Karma and Destiny

☼

*By John-Roger*

*Every leaf that grows will tell you... What you sow will bear fruit. So if you have any sense my friend, don't plant anything but LOVE.*

**~ Rumi**

Karma is the law of cause and effect: *as you sow, so you reap.* Simply stated, what you put out, you get back. The law of karma, taken beyond the context of a single life, is the foundation for reincarnation. Often the imbalances that you have created cannot be balanced in one lifetime, so the consciousness returns to this physical level to fulfill the debts incurred and balance the action. The law of karma is a just and perfect system and ensures that those who evolve into soul consciousness, a positive and liberated state of being, have a deep and true knowledge of all levels of consciousness.

People usually use the word karma to refer to something that is difficult or upsetting, but there is also what can be called *good karma* where a positive action leads to a positive result. Here, though, I will refer to karma as an imbalance from one time that still needs to be cleared or balanced.

### The law of cause and effect

There is often a comparatively large time gap between the instigation of an action and its result. This is one reason it is sometimes difficult for people to recognize the relationship between the cause and the effect. For example, if you steal a car and go joy-riding when you are sixteen and twenty years later some kids steal your new Cadillac and wreck it, you may not see the connection. It is there, it is just your action being returned to you.

☼ 191 ☼

This also applies from one existence to another. Your soul has probably had many physical and nonphysical existences prior to this one. However, it is safe for you to consider that almost everything you have in this lifetime is connected in some way to your experiences in past existences. Sometimes the connection is big and obvious; other times, it is subtle. But it really does not matter much if something is *karmic* or not because you still need to handle the situation in this life.

Before incarnation you have free will and you exercise it; after incarnation you have free choice. Before you incarnate you freely choose the various life circumstances you will come in with, such as your parents, country, race, sex and other physical attributes, as well as many possible life scenarios. After you incarnate you choose and keep choosing which of these many possibilities you wish to follow.

Many people see themselves as the sum of the past, the result of everything they have accumulated along the way, including from past existences. I prefer to look at life another way: the person I am today is perfectly positioned for my future.

> *The way I see it, the future, not the past, has put each of us where we are in this moment, in this place, in this position in our lives, so that we can claim the potential that awaits us. In this there is great freedom, great personal responsibility and great opportunity to learn.*

## Is karma *good* or *bad?*

The earth is a classroom and everyone here is a student. The experiences that come your way and the problems that come your way are your lessons. So every person you meet is your teacher. If you can keep that in mind as you are going through your day-to-day activities you may be able to make some tremendous changes and grow very rapidly in your awareness. Problems are beautiful because every time you handle or overcome a problem your wisdom and knowledge grow. Every time you overcome something, you grow. The problems give you strength to go further and your karmic situations are your stepping stones. So love your karma. It is your opportunity to learn and to gain wisdom. By loving even your negative creations, you can shift their energy and release karma.

When you begin to understand karma, you can begin to realize that some actions that appear to be *bad* may be actions of fulfilling karma and, therefore, right and proper within that framework. For example, in a previous lifetime, a mother abandons her child and leaves it in the hands of people who do not really care for the child. Because the mother refused to accept and handle her responsibility for the child, the child grew up unloved, abused, misused and leading an unhappy, embittered life. The child then re-embodies at some point, grows up and has a child of her own, who happens to be her mother from the previous life. She may feel no love for her baby and may abandon it, giving it the opportunity to have the same experience and learn what it is like to be abandoned and unloved.

People who observe this might judge this mother for abandoning the child, when she is actually fulfilling the karma and bringing to the other consciousness the experience that is necessary to free it from the karma it had created in that other lifetime. So unless you can read the karmic records and see what is within each person's heart, it is best not to judge any action that appears to be unusual or cruel. It may be an action that is fulfilling a karmic debt.

Am I saying to dismiss people's suffering by saying, "Well, it's their karma?" Not at all. People need your love and compassion, your reaching out and your caring and it is always helpful to suspend any judgments and say, "I don't really know what's going on." When you understand how the law of karma works, you may find yourself being even more accepting, forgiving and loving. And when it is in your power to ease another's pain, do that. This would be with the people directly in your life and the people you are around. Sometimes it could involve simply being friendly and speaking kindly, offering someone a ride, listening with acceptance to someone talk and putting yourself in another's shoes. You may also, of course, feel called to assist others beyond your immediate sphere.

**How can I be in harmony with karma?**

One thing you can always do to assist is to love it all—the situation, the people involved, your own distress or upset, the whole thing. Let's say that you are upset over the violence in the world. When you are in any kind of distress over that, you are in the karma. When you can expand beyond it (that is, rise above it), you can bring in the love. Those are not just words. In your consciousness, you actually move above and expand beyond it. You turn from your thoughts about it and your emotions over it and you go into the greater part of yourself (the Soul), where there is only love for everything— the violence, the people who perpetrate it, those who are on the receiving end of it, your distress over it, your judgments that it is even allowed—everything. Only through more loving can more things be healed. And if, on some level, you feel responsible for what is happening in the world, you can let that go. Your feeling the pain of the world does not decrease the pain. But your loving in the midst of pain can only help.

The Soul looks at every situation as an opportunity to get more experience and it does not judge anything as good or bad. When we look at things from the point of view of a level other than the Soul or when we identify with something other than the Soul, we can experience suffering. When we identify with the Soul (which is who we truly are) and when we look at things from the Soul's viewing point and really know the truth of that, we can have the joy of the Spirit in the midst of suffering on another level, for example, grief and physical pain.

We do not have to suffer to get to God, yet our suffering can serve a purpose because it can make us so uncomfortable that we may say, "There must be something different," and we may turn to God. The ego and the personality are restricted consciousnesses and they cannot go into God, although God can come into them. When we begin to give up those restricted consciousnesses and their demands and desires, we may feel pain and suffering on those levels, but it is only because we are still holding on to the restriction and not moving into the freedom of Spirit.

It is important to learn to accept and work with whatever is going on in your life, without placing too many judgments or self-recriminations. When you accept, it is easy because accepting is not resisting; it is letting things pass through and saying, "Thank you, Lord, for another wonderful day." When you can do this, breaking free from karma is so much easier. So do not judge yourself or put yourself down. Just go through the experience, get out the other side as rapidly as possible and move on. Do not look back; it does not help. Do not burden yourself with guilt and remorse that you may need to handle later. Just let it go.

Even though we all have karma, we can keep our own house in order, taking care of things immediately as they appear on the scene. This life is actually very easy:

do and complete,

do and complete,

do and complete,

do and complete—no karma.

Say you are going to do and then not do—karma.

Start to do and then not finish—more karma.

Feel bad about all that—more karma. And when something happens that really disturbs you, get up instantly and release it. If it is with another person, go to that other person and clear it. If it is something within you, go to work with yourself to change it and bring it into balance so that you are happy and comfortable with yourself. The key to handling any karma, no matter the area or person, is to be loving and forgiving.

If you learn from any disturbance, you will be free of it. If you do not learn, the experience may very well come around again and again, to give you a chance to clear it and get free. You must be free to reach into the spiritual realms and into God consciousness and you will probably know if your karma in a certain situation or with certain people is complete if there is a neutrality or *clearness* about the situation or person inside you.

And you certainly can release yourself from karma through laughter. Even in your daily life, if you can laugh instead of take umbrage at some of the things that people say or do, you are already free at that moment and the situation cannot hang on you.

## Surrendering the past

When you know of the law of karma, you also know that if someone does something to you that you think is unfair, you can just let it go. You know that if it is unfair, the other person will be held accountable for that, through Spirit. You do not have to do anything. You do not have to seek revenge or try to get even. You do not even have to think about it or hang on to the experience at all. You can just learn whatever you can from it, let it go and go on to your next experience.

An attitude that will help is to realize that people, including you, are doing the very best they can all the time, considering what they are working with and where they are. When you reach into a higher consciousness, you come to the realization that we are all one Spirit in many different manifestations. So if you strike against anyone, you strike against yourself and that action returns to you. If you curse someone, that curse returns to you—maybe this lifetime, maybe a future lifetime, but it returns. So you might want to look very carefully at the actions, the words, the thoughts and the emotions that you put out to make sure that they are the kinds of things that you would want returned to you.

We are responsible for our actions all the time and at the same time there is no need to get hung up in past deeds. Awakening to Spirit involves paying attention to what you are doing in the moment, not judging your actions and doing the best you can at the time. If you have memory of negative past actions, you can forgive yourself for them and for any judgments against yourself and then be careful not to move into those areas where you know you might get into trouble again. If you do not have memory of the past—and even if you do—just love yourself in the present and be willing to move through your life in the knowledge that those things that are right and proper will occur.

Everything a person does makes both positive and negative karma, though rarely equally. Your attitude is more important than the action; in fact, probably more than any other single thing, the guilt you feel after doing something will bring karma to you. And in whatever you do, be loving and choose wisely. Disturbing action creates karma. Disturbing reaction perpetuates karma. When you change disturbing action to loving action and disturbing reaction to acceptance and understanding, you may experience love, joy, peace and fulfillment. These Divine attributes help maintain the harmony of God's creation. You can create misery, hurt, fear, revenge, or hatred, or you can create happiness, harmony, confidence, peace and joy. Each of us makes these choices many times each day.

> *When you are dealing with any karmic pattern or situation, your time and focus are much better spent on loving everything in your current life and not trying to go back and figure out anything in the past that might be connected to the karmic situation.*

Spirit is present in each step you take and each movement you make. If you bring your awareness to that each second, you are doing far more for yourself than you would do if you tried to look into the past for causes, reasons and so on. And, of course, if any memory comes up, you can do any forgiveness that is needed, bring loving to the memory and yourself and then get on with your life and with loving everything in your life.

**Grace**

The idea of needing to balance everything exactly is the idea of "an eye for an eye and a tooth for a tooth" (Exodus 21:24). The Christ action through Jesus changed that to grace. The key to grace is forgiveness—continual forgiveness—and it continues until your last breath. Being in a constant state of forgiveness is being in a state of grace.

Coming under grace would be something like, "I didn't know better, or I would have done better. They didn't know better, or they would have done better. And in that, I forgive myself and I forgive them. I love me, I love them and now we move on." The Soul energy then comes forward and suspends it. It is not just neutralized. It is suspended through grace and the loving attitude dissolves it. So you may not have to balance every little thing exactly.

God dwells within you, as you; all you need do is awaken to that presence and one way to do that is to listen within yourself to God's loving direction. Ask for God's will to be manifested through you and then listen for God's voice to speak in your spiritual heart. You do not have to be concerned about yourself. All things are already being taken care of. Your true Self is moving you forward on your Divine destiny and you do not have to look at your past actions.

*Your ultimate destiny and the ultimate destiny of each person is to be consciously aware on all levels at all times and to know your own divinity, to live and be in the presence of the living God and to know that.*

When you do this, you also know the divinity in all things and realize that it is all One. Then, what you do in your life is up to you to decide. You can do any number of things and still fulfill your destiny of knowing God.

---

### ☼ **Light Practice** ☼

How to do the next thing in front of you and then live your life as lovingly as you can:

1. Pray to be guided by God and to be aware of that guidance.

2. Ask for the Light (the positive energy of Spirit) to manifest.

3. Keep your eyes open to see what the Light shines on for your immediate level of concern.

4. Read this out loud: "I have the opportunity to change the karmic flow of my life through my ability to be loving. By loving the God in myself and others, I can move into a path of greater unfoldment. Instead of looking at the factors of my life and saying, "That's my karma, so I can't help it," say, "That's my karma and I will fulfill it so I am free. I don't have to blame the difficulties in my life on karma. Through loving, I can complete my karma."

---

Create a little good karma right now by helping us to spread the Light via our *Spread the Light Campaign*! You can either donate money or time to enable us to reach our goal of raising one million dollars for charity even faster. Go to **www.spreadthelightcampaign.com** and read about how your input will help.

# About Molly Ann Fairley

Molly Ann Fairley began studying hypnotherapy, meditation and deep relaxation in 1980. After extensive training in all three disciplines she set up a private practice in London. She went on to found the Kingston School of Psychic Studies in 1997. The psychic teachings spread to Europe and Ireland over the next five years where Molly Ann has worked extensively facilitating healing workshops.

She was not born psychic, but opened suddenly at the age of forty-five when she experienced over eighty of her past lives in one night. She attributes her psychic abilities and healing to Divine guidance and powers much greater than herself.

A number of articles have been published about Molly in the national press and health journals on the application of psychic and spiritual healing. She has also appeared on TV and radio interviews. Molly's first book *You Can Be Psychic Too* is out now.

For more information on Molly Ann Fairley, log on to **www.slimandrelax.com**.

# Connecting with Your Angels

*By Molly Ann Fairley*

*I saw the angel in the marble and carved*
*until I set him free.*

~ **Michelangelo**

Have you ever wondered what angels are, what they do and where they live? I wondered all these things until some years ago when my spirit guides informed me that angels were special spiritual beings with an important role to play. They are appointed by the Divine to protect, guide and help human beings on earth. They are God's heavenly messengers and they have never lived in a human or animal body. Angels do not know what it is like to live here on earth because their vibration is much lighter and faster than ours. They are not able to sustain life here because of its negativity and density.

Angels are genderless, which means they are perfectly balanced in their male and female proportions. They are higher up the spiritual ladder than we humans and like us they come in all different shapes, sizes and abilities because they are also evolving. Each angel is consigned to a rank and has a specific task. They evolve on one pathway—an angel pathway and we evolve on a human pathway, much like dogs and cats evolve on their own pathways and do not cross on to another's.

As a child I remember being fascinated with pictures of angels. I loved their robes, their haloes and the wonderful golden lights around them. At point I did not believe angels could have an impact on my life and this delayed my connection with them. Years later, however, my first glimpse of an angel filled me with amazement. The angel was much bigger than I had thought possible, with a huge wingspan that covered the whole right hand side of my house. He was about sixty feet high and he had come to offer advice to a group of my students about psychic protection. Only two of the students actually saw the angel in any detail, although the rest of the class sensed a Divine presence descend among us. It felt like a blanket of silence; the type of silence you experience after heavy snowfall.

I soon began to see other angels, both big and small. Once a spiritual friend told me to ask the *golden angels of the air* to clean the atmosphere in my teaching room after psychic classes. Still skeptical, but knowing he was a good channel, I did as I was told. I opened all the windows and I instantly saw a host of tiny golden cherubs fly into the room. There were hundreds of them carrying golden dustpans and brushes. They swept up everything and the scene reminded me of *Snow White and the Seven Dwarfs*. The whole room shone with the beautiful golden energy of these baby angels.

## Guardian angels

We all have a guardian angel. Your guardian angel has been appointed to oversee your spiritual progress throughout each of your lifetimes. This angel has been with you for all time and will continue to be with you for eternity. Your guardian angel was by your side when you were born and that same guardian angel will help you pass over to your loved ones when you die. Your guardian angel bestows good values upon you and quietly holds the dream for your highest spiritual growth. It gently impresses integrity, honesty, compassion and other gracious qualities upon you.

Your guardian angel cannot interfere with your decisions or your destiny. That is for you to change. It can, however, nudge you in the right direction and help you along your way. If your guardian angel sees you getting into difficulties, it cannot stop you from making mistakes, but it can help you to understand those mistakes if you are willing to listen. Under spiritual law your guardian angel is not able to help you if you do not ask for help and no request is deemed too little or too great. You can ask for anything you like, for in the angelic kingdoms there is an abundance of everything.

Angels are around you all the time, so connecting with them is fairly easy—you do not need to perform a ceremony unless you choose to do so. Nevertheless, angel innovations are very powerful. Perhaps you could begin by asking the angels for a parking space. That way you will gain proof of their ability to help you. I have friends who create parking places everywhere, even in central London in the most congested of traffic. You may also ask your guardian angel for a solution to a problem or for help with your computer. Many people have reported their computers suddenly springing back to life after such a request. You can ask for a safe journey, better health and financial help. Ask your angel to help your loved ones or another's loved ones, a sick relative or a child. Try asking your angel to surround your house or car with a ring of protective light so they remain safe while you are away. You may see these rings of protection, but angel energy is very subtle and your eyes will need to adjust for you to psychically see it. Remember it is ethereal (of the ethers) so it is not solid.

You can ask the angels for help with everything you need. If your request is not answered straight away ask your guardian angel why, then listen and sense what the angel is trying to impress upon you. You may feel emotional or suddenly realize something. We all send out vibes and if the timing is wrong, possibly because you are angry, frightened, you bear a grudge, or because you are a disbeliever, delays can occur. Having said that, miracles still take place for people who do not believe. The angels might send a human being to help you, which you may not expect.

If you have an argument with someone and feel upset ask

your angel to link hands with that person's guardian angel to bring peace to you both. If you cannot forgive, ask that your heart be softened and opened. Your guardian angel is unbelievably compassionate, full of love and never judges you. If you have been unkind to someone, it will send you love and perhaps nudge your conscience, but it cannot get in the way. Karma, or the just return of what you have sent out to others throughout all of your lifetimes, cannot be interfered with by your guardian angel. You may have something important to learn before a karmic lesson can be dissolved and without it you would not evolve. It may not seem so but karma is necessary to prevent you from getting into deeper trouble.

While talking to your guardian angel realizations may pop into your mind which may be associated with the people in your life or uncomfortable situations that have occurred. I call these spiritual insights *wake-up calls*. If you get one, ask your angel for clarification and guidance.

**Reading signs from angels**

Angels can communicate with you in many ways. You may feel prompted to watch a television show, read a book, go on a journey, or spend time with certain people. I receive messages through television, plays and films. You can also purchase special angel cards, which offer guidance, protection and answers to your questions. White feathers tend to crop up quite often around angels and people who do kind and wonderful things are often earth angels in disguise. You may get a sense of *knowing* and feel compelled to follow a message up without knowing why. You might also see energies flitting out the corners of your eyes like tiny sparks. These are spirit guides and angels. You may see a shimmering light, a bit like the heat haze which comes off roads in hot places.

Be open to receiving help from your guardian angel. Receiving can be more difficult than giving, especially if you have been conditioned to believe that receiving means you are selfish. Angels love to give, so be open and ready to receive. They have a sweet, spiritual fragrance that does not exist on our physical plane. By thinking kind and loving thoughts you will strengthen your aura and emit a sweeter fragrance, which will attract higher celestial beings. By lighting up your aura the higher beings can find you more easily. A presence may gently brush your face, which tends to grow colder as more angels build up around you. Light bulbs may flash on and off and music can grow louder and softer. You might be suddenly woken in the night and feel wide awake. If this happens to you wait for an angel message.

## Angel guidance and protection

I first noticed Jacinta seated outside the recording studio in the local radio station in Marbella, Spain. I had never heard that name before and was surprised because she was the second Jacinta I had met in less than two days. The name is Irish and it means Hyacinth. She looked glamorous and was waiting to meet me after my radio interview and introduce me to others in Spain.

One day, after we had become friends, Jacinta told me a fascinating story about her guardian angel. Some years before we met, she and her former work colleagues were driving two cars along a dangerous pass on Mont Blanc on a skiing holiday in Chamonix. Jacinta's driver was driving fast because he was nervous of the back seat passenger who kept interrupting him. As they sped around an icy corner a big lorry came hurtling straight towards them from the opposite direction. It smashed into them knocking their car hard up against a wall.

The car spun, flipped upside down and skidded across the entire road where it finally slid to a precarious position hovering on the ice. It was hanging right over the edge of a sheer drop below. Jacinta was hanging upside down in the battered car still strapped in by her seatbelt. Shocked and frightened, she suddenly felt the presence of her guardian angel and knew she would be safe. A beautiful calm came over her.

Minutes later the people in the second car ran forward and one of the men cut Jacinta's seat belt and pulled her free from the wreckage. The driver had a broken shoulder and cuts and scratches all over his body. Miraculously Jacinta had no cuts, bruises or broken limbs. Once safe all the friends gingerly peered over the cliff edge and realized how high they were and how dangerous it was. Those in the car accident were taken to hospital and treated for shock.

Jacinta realized she was being divinely protected by her angel for this had been her second car accident. In the first accident, she had walked away completely untouched whereas the driver was brain damaged for life.

## How to communicate with your angels

If you are new to working with angels or if you feel skeptical, reading books on angels and archangels will help. You will align yourself with the subtle energies of these Divine beings and connect to the author, who has a more direct link to them.

Angel rituals and invocations are very powerful and they will draw you closer to the angels, but they are not always necessary. Simpler forms of communication also work. You could talk or write to your angel. If speaking, use your own words either out loud or silently inside. For writing, you need to quietly think about the angel you are writing to. It is also possible to receive a reply from your angel. Just relax and let your hand move across the page or listen to your intuition as you await a reply. Only kindness will come back from your angel and it is a good idea to carefully lay out your question in writing so your angel can review it and bring you wise guidance. You may also write to someone else's angel.

It is useful to know your guardian angel's name. When writing or talking to your angel ask it to impress its name upon you then relax and wait for it to come through. Angels love soft music and flowers so light a candle and beautify your surroundings with flowers, crystals and pleasant fragrances. You can also ask your angel to float into your aura and lightly touch you. This will light up your energy and bring you joy. Blessing your home and your work environment also encourages angels to communicate with you. Light up your energy by walking in nature and eating healthy food to enhance the influence of the subtle energy of the angels.

Angel balls are another way of communicating. You can make a ball of color or sound by humming and then ask the angels to fill it with their light, love or compassion. These beautiful angel balls can be sent to anyone. Create an altar in your home—somewhere private that you can fill with beautiful objects and colors. This will attract the angels and help bring harmony to your ancestors.

If you manage to see an angel, please treasure the experience as angels make you glow and feel happy. They look splendid with their beautiful white gold robes and shimmering lights. If you cannot see them, use your imagination to step into their golden light and sense that golden light all around you. It helps you to realize that you are also made up of spirit and light and as such you can fly and play with them. You might see tiny, golden cherubs playing gleefully or bigger angels lovingly protecting you and enfolding you in their huge golden wings. Enjoy playing and basking in the golden light, making sure every cell in your body revitalizes.

If you wish to draw the angels to you, dive into your imagination. Breathe softly to fill yourself up with their beautiful love until you are glowing inside and out. Absorb as much of the loving golden angel energy as you can and let it penetrate your entire being until every part of you is filled with love.

To help your imagination look through books that feature pictures of angels dressed in magnificent colors and gaze deeply into their eyes. You will see an incredible depth of love, wisdom and peace staring straight back at you. As you connect with that glorious angelic energy watch for synchronicities and miracles occurring in your life.

There have been many thousands of angel sightings over the centuries. Joan of Arc had a vision and heard voices and Jesus and Mother Mary often have angels around them in pictures. Link into these higher masters to help you communicate. Angels are everywhere; they are all around you and they know everything about you. Many millions of them are flocking here right now to help mankind at this special time of spiritual ascension.

**Earth angels**

Earlier I told you that angels cannot reside in our dimension as it is too dense. So then what do I mean by earth angels? Earth angels fall into two categories. They can be humans who have agreed to incarnate to serve. These are sensitive individuals who are kind and gentle and who will do anything for you. There are also earth angels who have not incarnated, who touch down for a short time and take on human form to carry out a specific task when help is needed. I have personally experienced both types of angels. I have also come across them when spiritual intervention was needed. The ticket lady at Euston was more than likely an earth angel for she manifested out of the blue and she was very kind.

An Englishman man lost his partner in a drowning accident while on holiday abroad. He was in total shock, grief stricken and unable to speak the native language. A tall, golden-haired stranger approached and told him that he worked for the British Embassy. He told him to go to the

Embassy and fill out the appropriate forms to fly the body home for burial. The gentle stranger then hailed and paid for a taxi to the Embassy. He also wrote out the information the Embassy would require on clean sheet of white paper. At the Embassy the grieving man was instantly ushered to the front of the line and the usual complicated paperwork was completed in a matter of moments. When the man spoke about the stranger to the Embassy staff, no one had heard of him. There was no record of him. He did not exist—on earth that is.

## The different kinds of angels

There are many different kinds of angels, just like there are many different kinds of animals and humans. Some angels look after the day-to-day running of things, while others have huge universal tasks to perform with many angels under their jurisdiction. The larger angels are in charge of the mountains, deserts, forests, the sun and the stars. Others reside in the outer regions of the earth and are responsible for overseeing vast universal projects. Some reside entirely in space.

Angels can be found in three different categories; heavenly counselors, heavenly governors and heavenly messengers—spheres one, two and three.

| Sphere One | Sphere Two | Sphere Three |
|---|---|---|
| *Heavenly Counselors* | *Heavenly Governors* | *Heavenly Messengers* |
| Seraphim | Dominions | Principalities |
| Cherubim | Virtues | Archangels |
| Thrones | Powers | Angels |

The highest ranking angel is the seraphim in sphere one. A seraphim is a grand celestial heavenly counselor. These great angels surround God's throne. They have unbelievable responsibilities; in fact they administer all the universes while carrying out God's heavenly orders.

Guardian angels fall into the lowest ranking order in sphere three. They are the worker bees and they look after humans under the direction of the archangels. There are also lots of other angels that work with us. These angels heal and bring light. They are creative and they work with nature, dance and music. There are others for literature, politics, science, devotion, peace, relationships and magic.

The archangels are sometimes called *the over lighting angels* as they are responsible for large groups of people and animals. You may well know the names of the archangels, especially those who head the seven rays. These are called Michael, Jophiel, Chamuel, Gabriel, Raphael, Uriel and Zadkiel. All of these archangels have twin flames to balance their male/female aspects. There are many other archangels too, but these seven are the ones people are most familiar with.

Above the archangels are the principalities. They attend to large groups like cities, countries and multi-national companies. They have their work cut out as the world is becoming smaller, but entities like supermarkets and hospitals are becoming larger and larger. This depersonalizes things and cuts people off, as these large organizations lose their personal touch. The principalities infuse love and compassion into these establishments.

**The cosmic order of the angels**

I have very briefly touched on the different types of angels and their ranking positions to give you some idea of the gigantic scope of what takes place. The vastness of God's networking of angels throughout his mighty host of universes is quite incredible. The organization of the angels is huge and precise. It extends far beyond the boundaries of this small planet. One angel alone can hold the integrated world order of the entire planet in his heart. If you can imagine this it will begin to give you some idea of the power of these great angels. The cosmic seraphim angels administer to other planets and star systems throughout all of the universes. These powerful beings all serve God's plan.

## Where to get help

Your guardian angel will always be by your side, but you can also enlist the help of the more powerful archangels. Like all angels, each archangel has a specific task and is able to help you in a special way. It is better to ask the right angel for help. It is rather like shopping for exactly what you want. There are millions of archangels across all of the universes, but only a small number connect with humans on earth. Some of these archangels come from the mighty energy of the innermost sun; they are very powerful and accompanied by twin flames.

## Archangel Michael

Archangel Michael, the first of these, is the warrior angel who stands for courage. He is fire. He brings you courage and willpower and frees you from fear. Faith, his twin flame, encourages confidence. Archangel Michael is a leader and if you ask him he will instil the steadfast qualities of a leader within you. Michael protects and he has a host of mighty angels working with him. He wears a deep blue cloak of protection that you can ask him to wrap around you. You can also make sure others are protected by asking Archangel Michael to wrap his cloak safely around them too. An archangel's influence is very powerful indeed; it is quite possible for them to save someone's life. Protect your home, your possessions and your loved ones with the incredible might of this powerful archangel.

Ask Archangel Michael for help with:
> Courage
> Energy and vitality
> Direction
> Motivation
> Protection

## Archangel Jophiel

Archangel Jophiel is the angel of wisdom and illumination. His twin flame is Christine. Together they light up humanity. They discharge vast forces of light to dissolve negativity. These light currents flow around your brain. Whenever you get a sudden brainwave, after having tried to unravel a problem, Archangel Jophiel will bring you the solution. Archangel Jophiel is the Patron of Artists and the archangel for art and beauty.

Ask Archangel Jophiel for help with:
> Creative projects and art
> Interior design
> Kind and beautiful thoughts
> Beauty from within
> Giving talks
> Inspiration

## Archangel Chamuel

Archangel Chamuel and his twin flame Charity will encourage you to be more organized and clear-minded. Archangel Chamuel is also involved in the development of your heart. Pray or talk to Chamuel if you have lost a loved one and your heart is breaking. If you cannot forgive that person he will help you to open your heart and let go of any emotional blockages. Archangel Chamuel rules the angels of love and you can ask for these angels to help you find things you have lost. You can also ask these angels to completely engulf you in love.

## The angels of love

Bereavement or loss is part of being a human. The angels of love cannot take this away from you, but they can soothe your pain and tired emotions. They will do their utmost to heal your wounded heart. If anyone, including a child, has agreed to live certain conditions before they were born as part of their destiny, the angels cannot take this away. But praying for yourself and your friends in need will certainly open your heart and theirs, enabling the angels of love to come forward and help more easily.

## Archangel Gabriel

Archangel Gabriel and his twin flame Hope will help you to achieve your highest potential. They are able to show you what you have agreed to do on earth and they can guide you towards the right people to help you achieve your mission. If you need clarity or discipline, Gabriel will help you by aiding your ascension pathway and enabling you to absorb more light. He works with artists, musicians, architects, builders, spiritual teachers and scientists. He always attends the birth of a child to oversee the arrival of the tiny new soul.

Ask Archangel Gabriel for help with:
>Fertility and conception
>Child adoption
>Writing or journalism
>Artists and art projects
>Radio and television work

## Archangel Raphael

Raphael is a very powerful archangel, responsible for healing, abundance, creativity, truth and vision. His twin flame is Mary, mother of Jesus. Mary is the queen of the angels. These angels help doctors, nurses, healers and mothers. If you wish to open your third eye and develop your psychic vision, Archangel Raphael can help you. He is the patron saint of the blind. Raphael assists in improving your concentration and focus. He can also direct potent healing power into your heart to remove disease and bring in love.

Ask Archangel Raphael for help with:
>Addictions and cravings
>Psychic vision
>Improved eyesight
>Healers
>Healing for both humans and animals

If you have lost a pet, call upon Archangel Raphael to help you find it.

## Archangel Uriel

Archangel Uriel is the great archangel who commands the angels of peace and his twin flame is Aurora. They work on transformation and forgiveness. You can ask Archangel Uriel for guidance when you do not understand another's motives. Uriel, together with Jesus Christ, teaches selfless service and promotes closeness. This archangel is considered to be one of the wisest of the archangels.

Ask Archangel Uriel for help with:
>Alchemy and Divine magic
>Development of your solar plexus and your soul's wisdom
>Dissolution of fear in the solar plexus
>Problem solving
>Informed information
>Studying and exams

Archangel Uriel can be called upon often as he has so much wisdom about life.

## The angels of peace

Archangel Uriel governs the peace angels. They are beautiful beings of Light. If they come to you, you will feel a sense of deep peace and stillness. They may ask you to make a haven of peace in your home or town. This will be somewhere you can go to be at peace with yourself. It does not have to be very large. It may even be a special chair. Do not enter this place unless you feel entirely peaceful or else you will rock its peaceful vibrations. Think peaceful thoughts whenever you think about this place.

## Archangel Zadkiel

Archangel Zadkiel and his twin flame Amethyst bring forgiveness, compassion and mercy. He will encourage you to free yourself from negativity and any limitations. If you are willing to forgive yourself or another, Archangels Zadkiel and Amethyst will release the karma between you. They will also help you to become more diplomatic when difficulties occur. Archangel Zadkiel worked with Ascended Master, Saint Germain to bring us the Violet Flame. The Violet Flame is powerful enough to heal anything.

Ask Archangel Zadkiel for help with:
>Compassion
>Finding things
>All kinds of forgiveness
>A good memory
>Studying

## The great Lords of Karma

For a long time I thought the Lords of Karma was a stern spiritual council where everything we had done had to be brought to justice. I then realized that most of the Lords of Karma are goddesses and like all angels they are full of compassion. They reside over the *Akashic* records of all humanity (the spiritual records written in the ethers) and they keep a spiritual diary of your karma. Karma is the just return of all you have sent out. There are seven high angels on the board: the Great Divine Director, the Goddess of Liberty, Elohim Cyclopea, the lady masters Nada, Pallas Athena the Goddess of Truth, Kuan Yin the Goddess of Mercy and Lady Portia the Goddess of Justice and Opportunity. In December 1993, the Dhyvani Buddha Vairochana joined the Karmic Board. Lady Portia is the spokesperson for the Board. There are specific rituals that you can perform to approach the Lords of Karma, but I find that if I just talk out loud in my own words they hear and, if appropriate, they will carefully consider and act upon that.

**Frequently asked questions**

*What can angels do for me?*
Angels lift your energy. They can protect you and bring you love. They can guide you and heal you, your family and your friends. The angelic Lords of Karma can cancel your karma.

*How can angels help me?*
Angels can open your heart, bring love to your children, help with your marriage, partnership, finances, and rescue you. They can also cancel any vows not serving you.

*Do I have more than one angel?*
Yes, there are millions of angels overseeing our planet. You have many angels lighting up your life, but only one guardian angel.

*Should I pray to my angel?*
Prayer and worship used to be more common. Nowadays we talk more as an equal to deities of any kind. Prayer is still good though.

*Do angels get angry with me?*
No, never. Your angels love you unconditionally. They do not know how to be angry. They are too full of love.

*Why are archangels important?*
Archangels have more power than your guardian angel. They deal with specific wishes.

*Are Ascended Masters angels?*
Some of them are. Mary, Mother of Jesus is an angel and because she has lived in a physical body she is also an Ascended Master. Usually angels have never lived in a body.

*What is an Angel Invocation?*
An angel ceremony to call in angel energies to invoke positive change.

*Who are the angels of Atlantis?*
Special angels are being drafted in to lift the consciousness of our planet for the approaching golden age of Atlantis in 2032.

*What are fallen angels?*
Fallen angels once sat at God's right hand. They fell from grace and so agreed to stay behind and help humanity to resolve its karma. Lucifer is the most well-known fallen angel. It is said he works closely with God.

*Is there an angel of birth and death?*
Yes, there certainly is an appointed angel of birth and death. These powerful angels have hosts of angels working under them to ensure the safe passage of your passing in and out of the physical world. They liaise with your family in spirit at the time of your death.

***What do my angels need from me?***

They need a love vibration from you in order to come closer. This provides nourishment and food for the angels. They need you to send this love vibration to the earth and others.

***Are angels involved with crop circles?***

Yes, the turquoise angels of communication are giving us keys to unlock universal information. We understand these messages in our unconscious minds.

---

## ☼ Light Practice ☼

This short Light Practice will enable you to draw closer to your guardian angel.

☼ Find a quiet place, bless this place and make it your own.

☼ Light a white candle, be still and stare into the flame.

☼ Sense a wonderful peace within you as you close your eyes.

☼ Breathe gently into your stomach.

☼ Invite your guardian angel to come close. Feel the softness of its fluttering wings as it enfolds you.

☼ Ask your guardian angel for its name and wait. Be happy if you are given a name and patient if you are not.

☼ Wrap yourself up deeply inside its wings, in its love and

---

overwhelming compassion for you.

☼ Open your heart and breathe in all the love and security that your guardian angel brings to you. Let that love sink deep into the center of your heart.

☼ Your heart is softer, open and smiling now. Come back when you are refreshed and revitalized.

Molly's book *You Can Be Psychic Too* in the series *Light from the Elders* is published via The Light Network. If you have written a book which has a spiritual or self-empowering message, fill in your details on our web page **www.thelightnetwork.com/thelight/about/the-publisher** and if we are interested we will contact you.

# About Dr Sue Morter

Dr. Sue Morter is an internationally recognized authority on bridging science, spirit and human possibility. She is a master teacher and practitioner of the BioEnergetic Synchronization Technique (B.E.S.T.), a neuro-emotional clearing and healing process that addresses subconscious interferences within the mind, body, memory and spirit and their integrated influence on health and human performance.

Dr. Sue founded Morter Institute & HealthCenter in 1987, a multi-doctor wellness and teaching facility in Indiana that focuses on cleansing and restoring the mind, body and soul by releasing unresolved subconscious beliefs and emotions.

In addition to her private practice she has spoken at Agape International Spiritual Center, Kripalu Center for Yoga and Health, Tony Robbins Trainer Support, amongst others and she can be seen in documentary films, internet television, radio interviews and live conferences worldwide.

For further information about Dr Sue log on to
***www.suemorter.com.***

# Manifesting Miracles

*By Dr Sue Morter*

*There are only two ways to live your life. One is as though nothing is a miracle. The other is as though everything is a miracle.*

**~ Albert Einstein**

We tend to hold miracles as something spectacular, outside of our realm of probability or as separate from ourselves. But in order to allow miracles to occur more regularly in our personal reality we must change the way we see them. Most of us believe miracles supersede the realm of probabilities and by holding this belief we are unable to welcome them into our environment as readily as we could.

My invitation to the readers of this book is to see everything as sacred and possible. To do that with integrity we must first learn to hold our consciousness differently than the way we are familiar with. In order to allow something sacred or miraculous to happen more regularly in our lives, we must allow it to be a readily accepted perspective that we can anticipate and as a new way of being.

## Everything is energy

The first premise is to remember that everything in all of creation is energy and that energy is vibrating at different frequencies, ultimately determining the physical realities that we experience. If we experience something as a physical object it is energy vibrating at a particular frequency and if we experience something as an emotion, the energy is vibrating at a different frequency. Think of it as different radio stations that we dial into.

When we think thoughts we are honing energies into a particular frequency pattern. When these thoughts are recreated day after day they produce a consistent pattern of energy within which we perceive an entire world; one that either works well or seems full of despair and pain.

We have the capacity to move energy in particular patterns and pathways with our free will. We can choose the meaning something has to us and therefore have it generate a particular energy in our world. One person may be happy he has been sacked from his job, another devastated over the loss. In the highest form of truth and from the biggest perspective, this allows us to recognize our level of empowerment, enlightenment and conscious development based upon the meaning we regularly assign to circumstances.

## The template of our beliefs

The reason we experience our daily lives as we do is because we hold our filters, perspectives and perceptions in a stagnant way based upon our beliefs held both at the conscious and subconscious levels as a particular template. That template determines what gets through from the greater Reality into our personal experience and what does not. So if we want something different to manifest in our physical reality it is imperative that we change our regular pattern of thoughts and create a new and different template. To do so we must learn to blur the boundaries a bit. Things cannot continue to mean the same to us or else we have no choice but to manifest the same old non-miraculous, mundane reality.

When we understand that we have the ability to gather and generate this energy in one form or another and that we can change it at will, we wake up to the fact that there is something most sacred and miraculous about the way we can operate. So it is not about waiting for a miracle to occur, but simply waking up to the reality that we can manage and move any energy in any way we choose and thereby create a particular *reality* directly proportional to that choice. We have the capacity to shift energies from one vibrational frequency to another and change its meaning simply by changing our perception about it before *becoming* that vibration ourselves. When we become a vibrational match to the dream manifested, we invite its appearance into our lives. And amazingly it does not arrive, it simply becomes visible to us. Interestingly, this happens every time we forgive something and every time we love.

When we forgive something or someone we shift the energy around that topic from one vibration to another, say from wrong to ok. When we do this we change the energy that exists in our personal space, which in turn changes the energy in *all* space; our reality shifts, we become different energetically. Once we dial into another frequency, we can see what exists there and it is very different from what we saw a moment ago. This is nothing short of miraculous. The question is: are we willing to be in charge of our miracles? Or at least collaborate on them?

**Everything happens for a reason**

In life we are driven by our subconscious far more so than by our conscious mind; most of which is established very early in our lives. Otherwise we would just decide something needs to appear and it would, but it does not always happen that way. Early in life we draw conclusions based upon a limited perspective, history and experience that are distortions of the larger picture. We think it was wrong that we were treated as we were or that it should be different in some way. We do not yet know that everything is happening for a perfect reason to reveal our magnificence. We have not yet realized that saying "Even in the face of this, I am ok" reveals our empowerment, our Divine design as co-creators, creating our ok-ness rather than waiting for it to appear. And so we drew conclusions that the happening was simply wrong and it limited the pattern of possibilities in our lives. We also limited our perception that we have any power over our internal experience, subconsciously establishing the belief that the outer world determines it for us.

Until we wake up to the fact that we need to reframe much of what we have subconsciously concluded we tend to be carried through life based upon the perception that we are disempowered and we begin to pray for the miracle. Ironically, the miracle does not happen in the realm of the disempowered—it happens in the realm of Grand Neutrality and Possibility. We must resonate with possibility at the conscious and subconscious levels, vibrationally and internally.

We have access to those realms and we use them all the time, but they are so insidious and subtle that we often do not recognize them as anything significant or substantial. Oftentimes they are not because we are not paying attention to them, honouring them, or regularly honing in on them. So we think of them as coincidences, good luck, or an act of God. Well guess what? You are part of all of that, not separate from it!

We may have a hunch or a gut feeling, which makes no sense to us. For example, we might hear a definitive voice in the back of our minds that says, "Call Joe now." We have not thought of him in six months yet we follow that source vibration registering in our conscious mind only to find that Joe was about to call us regarding a tremendous opportunity he wanted to include us in. It made no sense, but did we listen anyway? Or did we over-ride it with logic? It is time to blur that boundary and listen sooner.

Incidents such as these are often separate from everyday occurrences as they make it through the filter system of our limiting perceptions about ourselves, but something was at play that day that could be at play every day. We can focus on ways to get this to line up to our advantage more often than not by identifying the aspects within that are activated when it all seems to come together, allowing these miraculous moments to occur on a more regular basis, intentionally and on purpose.

We are either vibrating at a frequency where miracles can happen more regularly or we are not. If we are not it is probably not because of our conscious choice, but because of information at the subconscious level that creates a recipe of energies unable to pass through the filter system from the Greater Possibility to register in our physical reality.

**Becoming the vibration of miracle**

There are things we can do in our lives to enhance the information at the subconscious level, such as sitting in meditation—stilling the mind when we are awake and lucid but not thinking. The eastern cultures have been teaching us meditation for thousands of years, but somewhere along the way we lost the truth that when we meditate we are allowing ourselves to dial into an energetic frequency that more closely resembles the radio station in which miracles occur. Instead we think of meditation as a way to escape the chaos and find respite for a blissful moment when we could be doing great work here to change our life experience.

The goal is to become this vibratory frequency of miracle possibility, bliss or stillness even when we are in situations such as driving along the highway, running along the airport concourse to catch a flight or when we are faced with questions like: do I accept the job? Do I stand up for what I want to say in this situation? Do I end the relationship? How do I change my health? These kind of questions must be asked from that place of stillness yet it is difficult to get there if we are bombarded with information stored at the subconscious level saying: "I'm inadequate, I'm unsafe, it's a cold cruel world and I can't trust anyone." When we are operating like that we are definitely not vibrating from the frequency from where the miraculous can manifest in our personal space. Through meditation we can identify with the vibration of peace, joy and deep silence and then learn to bring that vibration back into the space where we ask the most significant questions in life. The ability to do this is developed in the *in between* moments in life, not in the midst of turmoil. A regular practice of consciousness is needed.

## Reprograming

If we can teach ourselves to be focused and present and still with the conscious mind, we can observe what naturally rises from the subconscious and learn to identify what is interfering with our abilities to move toward a greater possibility. The job of the subconscious is to protect us and keep us safe, so it automatically seeks out anything that might be potentially threatening and stores it in memory so we never have to encounter the same danger twice.

That is what is happening when you feel something rise in you that says, "Oh no, I've been in this situation before and I'm not going back there." Your subconscious is kicking in for you and saying, "Don't worry, I've got your back." It records everything that was seen as hurtful or dangerous or wrong so we never have to encounter the same experience again. The problem is it may be confused about what to avoid and what to embrace.

For example, perhaps at the age of four we wanted to show our mother how much we loved her by drawing a lovely picture of the house and the family. So we took great pride in showing her our masterpiece. And just when we unveiled our gift she shrieked with horror instead of singing for joy because we drew it on the dining room wall instead of the preferred paper!

This incident stores in our subconscious mind as, "Mom's reaction to my creative expression of love was upset so every time I share my love someone will get upset or I'm going to get in trouble or I'm going to be a disappointment to someone." This develops an illusion of inadequacy and keeps us encased in an extremely limited, survival-orientated reality. No miracles are likely to occur here!

We must begin to reprogram such incidents and enter into

the realm where lives unfold miraculously in an *everything I touch turns to gold* kind of way. And we can. That happens when we align ourselves with our true nature—and our true nature is not to be stuck in overdrive mode, but to be brimming with creative, ingenious, expressive capacity and a given feeling of belongingness. Yet we cannot get there if somewhere in the system potential danger is registered subconsciously.

It is equally important that we understand how to perceive life from the front side of the model rather than continuing to create things we do not want in order to figure out what we do want. If I ask people what their dreams are they often start talking about what they want to get rid of or away from. That is what I refer to as the *back side of the model* approach. We know what makes us miserable so by a process of elimination we conclude what makes us happy. But that is all merely mental activity and a waste of time. There is a deeper place within us, which allows us to move toward pure joy and inspiration.

Focusing on activating that place in people oftentimes has them making decisions from places they never would have thought were safe to choose from, yet these decisions lead to a miraculously unfolding life; a business that doubles in a miraculous amount of time or relationships of deep connection, love and joy. Think of it this way: your life was meant to be a miracle—why have you been shutting that down? Because you did not know that it was even a choice. By the grand design of things it is a choice and you can shift it. And most importantly it was meant to be a challenge, a discovery and an awakening to your true power. We need the challenge until we do not any more. Once we get the hang of it, we are off and running.

There are specific things we can do to access the information stored at our subconscious level, reframe it and activate our core space where our wisdom resides, such as the following Light Practice:

### ☼ **Light Practice** ☼

This simple technique resets the central nervous system by activating the right and left brain, upper and lower body, the autonomic nervous system and the solar plexus, along with the breath. A focal point in the lower abdomen is also utilized to activate electromagnetic energy centers, where creativity and certainty are cultivated.

When we activate this pattern in the body at the same time it resets the timing of these systems for more perfect function, similar to a car engine that must have perfect timing in order to ignite the fuel to start.

☼ Stand with your feet shoulder width apart, look ahead and take one step forward with your right foot. Bend your right knee and put some weight on it.

☼ Put your left arm up straight in front of you at a forty-five degree angle where the wall meets the ceiling and put your right arm back and down to where the wall meets the floor at a forty-five degree angle.

☼ Turn your head to the left toward the arm that is up in the air and close your right eye. Take a breath in, count to ten and feel the feelings of love, joy and forgiveness. This accumulating, nurturing feeling should be felt low down beneath your belly button.

☼ Breathe in through your nose and draw the air way down low into the abdomen, so when you breathe in your stomach goes out and when you breathe out your stomach contracts—the opposite of how most of the western world breathes. Hold that position for a count of ten or for as long as you can then step back to the center and bring everything back to neutral.

☼ Do the same thing on the opposite side. If you hold

your breath until you cannot hold it any more, the brain starts to evaluate and wanting to conserve the oxygen, it shuts down the circuits which hold tension in the body.

☼ In that moment, if you think and feel loving thoughts in your core you will begin to reframe and correct the patterns held at this subconscious level, even though you do not know what they are. The replacement is of a higher frequency and of massive intensity due to the holding of breath.

☼ Do this exercise two or three times on each side, twice each day, perhaps before you go to bed at night and first thing in the morning. At these times the conscious and subconscious areas of the brain are talking to each other more intimately. If you ever wake up at three or four o'clock in the morning, it is a good idea to do this exercise lying down in bed. By opening that doorway we become more resonate with the greater Truth and Reality and far more likely to manifest miracles.

☼ When you do the exercise, feel a loving feeling for yourself. Think about how you would feel if you were tremendously loved by nature, by God or by yourself, or if you were loving something or someone else and creating the vibration of unconditional love.

This is transformative to the nervous system. And to further the effects, if you have a particular vision, miracle, or dream, have them now. And I do mean have them. Do not wish for them or even simply picture them…not even feeling them in your heart is enough for the transformation you seek. You must manage to *become* the very vibrational frequency they exist in. Just open your body and breathe it at your core. You will begin to establish a way of being that will be transformative to your life. This is the way in which hopes, desires and dreams manifest. Miracles occur by first existing in the core of our being.

Miracles are supposed to be happening in our lives on a regular basis as they are our Divine right. If life is not handing us the things we want to have and be there is a reason for it. We want to learn how to bring it into existence ourselves.

---

A female patient, whom I met three years after a severe incident, went to the hospital to deliver her baby. The nurses were unable to give her an epidural on her side so they turned her over and sat her up to attempt another position. They bent her forward on the examination table and this time the injection worked and she became numb in her entire lower body. Unfortunately both nurses turned their back on her at the same time and she fell off the table, unable to catch herself. She hit the floor, had a spontaneous delivery and was knocked out cold for three days. The baby survived, but when she came to she was unable to move without feeling extreme pain, nausea and dizziness. She was rendered disabled and bedridden for the next three years. There was a swelling on her tailbone the size of a fist, prohibiting her from being able to lean against anything for support. She was in immense pain on every level.

In the consultation I looked into her eyes and I could see she was available to hear whatever I had to say. That in itself I found miraculous as she had seen every doctor in town, none of whom wanted to help her for fear of getting themselves involved in the pending law suit with the hospital. But she was available so I spoke.

I told her she would have to drop the law suit if she wanted to heal prior to its closure or else she would have to *stay sick* to prove her point on a subconscious level. And I told her that her beliefs about her ability to heal were paramount to our success. She agreed.

We worked with the technique outlined in this chapter

and others that I teach in my seminars and I treated her using the BioEnergetic work that I practice at Morter Institute & HealthCenter. She instantly became extremely nauseated. Oftentimes we have to rewire some things before we can progress. She went home with instruction to return the following day.

The next day she walked into the office with no assistance and her husband by her side. "I got it," she said. "I understand. I was vibrating at the frequency of victim and I could never heal there." The next day she was walking on her own. Three months later she played third base on our clinic softball team. This story proves that miracles happen.

## To conclude

Dreaming for a miracle or asking for a miracle is the opposite of what I have tried to express in this chapter. The truth is you are a miracle. Begin to recreate the energy inside your body that resonates as you would if your miracle already existed and align your nervous system to be able to sustain that frequency. Do so by practicing the techniques in this chapter and by researching those subconscious beliefs that continue to hold you as separate from the Divine or the Miraculous. Learn to meditate and breathe in a way that stills the nervous system so you can heal and prosper. The truth is you are not separate from anything. You are Light and Light is what creates miracles on this physical level of reality. It is time to set yourself free and be the Light. All miracles happen when there is freedom in the consciousness, love in the heart and the awareness that *you are* the Light.

Take a look at the miracles we are wishing to manifest in our ongoing efforts to spread the Light, via our Vision and Wish List: **www.spreadthelightcampaign/wishlist**.

# About Don Miguel Ruiz

Don Miguel Ruiz was born into a humble family with ancient traditions in rural Mexico. His parents and grandfather believed he would continue their legacy in the Toltec tradition. Instead he attended medical school and became a surgeon. A near fatal car accident changed the direction of Don Miguel's life when he experienced himself as pure awareness. He realized that the Toltec wisdom of his family contained all of the tools needed to change the human mind and he returned to his mother to finish his training and become a Shaman. Soon after Don Miguel wrote *The Four Agreements,* which was a *New York Times* bestseller for more than seven years. His books now include *The Mastery of Love, The Voice of Knowledge, Prayers, Beyond Fear* and *The Fifth Agreement,* a collaboration with his son, Don Jose. In February 2002, Don Miguel suffered a near-fatal heart attack. The damage from the heart attack and subsequent coma left him with a heart functioning at only sixteen percent of its capacity. In August 2010 Don Miguel successfully received a heart transplant. This was a new beginning for him and with deep gratitude he is eager to share his message with all of humanity. For more information about Don Miguel, log on to **www.miguelruiz.com**.

# The Colors of Love

☼

*By Don Miguel Ruiz*

*Your task is not to seek for love, but merely to seek and find all of the barriers within yourself that you have built against it.*

~ **A Course in Miracles**

I see love as a magnificent spectrum of all the colors of the rainbow. We have hundreds of emotions and each one is an aspect of love; which can be placed somewhere within this beautiful spectrum. By looking at love in this way we can see how we fragment love in order for our mind to understand it.

It is easy to see how we divide love in many different directions by looking at the conditions we impose on love. We love our parents, our friends, our children and our partner. We love songs, places and animals. All of these different relationships are only a part of the totality, which is love, but they are not the whole thing. We distort everything we perceive and because of this we do not clearly see the different aspects of love.

When we merge all the radiant colors of the rainbow together the result is white Light. And in the same way, when all the different aspects of love are combined, the result is Truth. It contains everything. So how can we experience the fullness of love?

We cannot understand or experience what love is until we reveal what love is not. I see this as knowing the difference between conditional and unconditional love. Conditions begin at an early age. When we are children we want to be like the adults and from them we perceive what they believe about love. This is the beginning of our understanding and experience of love being fragmented because of early influences. We witness all the dramas that our parents, our friends and our brothers and sisters create about love. But this is not really love in the highest sense. Children play, pretending to be adults and they can hardly wait to grow older just to be like everyone else. I remember pretending to be a medical doctor. Children usually have such a beautiful smile, but as soon as I pretended to be a medical doctor my face changed right away and became very serious. Back then I was only pretending but when I grew up and became a medical doctor my face really did change that way.

It is the same thing with all that romantic love. We see our brothers or sisters falling in love and dating and we wish to become older so we can do the same thing. However, we also see all the dramas, the broken hearts and the consequences of those broken hearts. They say, "Look at what he did to me?" They tell all their friends and everyone knows how much they are suffering. We learn that romantic love hurts. Then we finally grow up and we start dating and falling in love and because of this limiting belief we become like everyone else, distorting love. We follow the rules we were taught, that love should be this way, a man should be this way, a woman should be that way and we believe that this is love. But it is not true. We try to control the other person but that is not love either; it is exactly the opposite. We try to make our loved one the way we want them to be, we grow jealous, possessive and we create a huge drama. If they are not the way we want them to be we say they have broken our heart because love hurts, doesn't it?

Ninety-nine percent of people love conditionally. Everybody believes the way they feel is the way everyone should feel, however this is a great untruth. In the same way, you defend your truth and you think this is right and everybody else is wrong. But there are seven billion people in this world who all believe they are right. It is the same when it comes to love. We believe that what we feel is really love, but it is not. This form of love is very selfish. We look for love, but in a very conditional way because it has to be the way we want it to be. We have Gods for everything. We have a God of the thunder, a God of the sun, a God of the rivers, the lakes and the oceans. We even have the God and Goddess of love and we really believe they exist. However, that God or Goddess represents human sacrifice. Nowadays, we sacrifice in the name of love. You can probably see how many times you have sacrificed yourself in the name of love or how many times you have sacrificed somebody else in the name of love. This is clearly a tainted version of love.

When we put labels on the pure energy of love this will distort it and once it is distorted it is no longer true love. We distort love as soon as we use words to describe what we feel. All of these words are labels that come from our conditioning. For example, we feel intense emotion, but instead of observing the extraordinary energy force moving within us, we say, "I feel so sad, I feel so angry," and then we get caught up in melodramas and our minds spin out of control, wallowing in memories of the past or fears of the future. We have lost the power of the moment and in the process we have lost the essence of the pure energy, which is always present. In every culture and in every language we have invented words and symbols to describe our moods and to give meaning to love. No matter how rich the language, these labels only serve to limit love. They are labels, not love and they are certainly not the Truth.

Love diffuses in many different ways yet it is all from the same source, just as when we put white Light through a prism all the colors of the rainbow are revealed. We can liken our perspectives on love to how we perceive Light. If we see brown or blue, for example, we are only seeing a partial aspect of the whole picture. What we are actually seeing is a reflection of our own beliefs and limitations and this also colors what we transmit in the name of love. Everything is action and reaction.

When Jesus spoke to the public, only the purest of white Light shone into the crowds. When He spoke with His apprentices He was also emanating that same pure white Light, but the way it was received was a little different. When He spent time with women the reflection was received in a different way again. What is important is that the love He was transmitting was white Light, pure love directly from the Source. The way everyone around Him perceived and received the love was different according to their layers of conditioning. If you meet Jesus Christ and He sends you white Light your ability to receive and reflect His Light will be dependent on your filters, or in other words, your limiting beliefs. Your level of radiance will not be as pure and white as His. But with practice and awareness it may become that way. This is the process of enlightenment. The love you receive from your partner may not be the white Light you receive from Christ. When the Light you receive from those in your life is already distorted you have a choice to either make it a little whiter or distort it even more. It is up to you!

It is a good idea to interact with people who send a better quality of Light to you and that way you will evolve more and more. Many cultures teach us to choose our company with care. The disciples worked with the white Light that came from Christ. When He worked with a big group of people it was difficult to measure the reaction, but when He worked with a little group it was easier to measure the limitations falling away and the pure love growing stronger. To be with someone like Christ or Buddha will increase our ability to receive that pure love. It is not that we do not have it, as we do, but we distort it in our mind with our limited knowledge. As a consequence what comes out of us is not what we really are, because in truth we are all just like the Christ and Buddha. When love goes through the filters of our minds it will emerge completely different and distorted. When we learn from someone like Jesus Christ they will help us to recognize those filters and to dissolve them, but no one can do it for us. The easiest and best way to know love is to be in the presence of pure love. It is written that when the disciple is ready the master will appear.

## In love or not?

To know pure love we need to understand what desire is. Desire is completely normal, neither good nor bad, right nor wrong, even though there are many religions and philosophies that state it must be avoided! It all depends on what we do with that desire. It can become obsession, which is extremely destructive and will destroy everything we create. On the other hand, desire can become passion. When this happens we really begin to love what we are doing. That passion can take us to inspiration and inspiration can take us to real love.

Nevertheless, obsession has the power to destroy everything we create. For example, if we get married and obsession comes into that marriage, sooner or later the marriage will be destroyed. If we create a business and obsession goes into that business, sooner or later that business will be destroyed. In reality our desire shifts both ways, sometimes to obsession, sometimes to passion. When the desire turns into obsession we fail in our relationships, marriages, friendships and businesses, but when the desire turns into passion and inspiration we radiate pure love, which is a reflection of who we really are.

## Expressing love for our world

We express love for our world because we have the desire to. If, for example, we try to save the rainforests and that desire turns into obsession, then in our efforts to save the forest we will burn ourselves out and destroy ourselves. The other option is that we get very passionate about saving the forest and then we really will be doing something to help, but at the same time we will have respect for everything else, not just the forest, or the dolphins, or whatever it is we want to support. When we feel passion, this is an expression of unconditional white Light, pure love. Then, if something is not working the way we would like it to, we will not get upset. We will simply express our desire without attachment to outcomes, putting effort into saving the rainforest without expecting anything in return, including that the forest may not be saved. This is unconditional love.

## Loving our self

Loving our self is the first step to real love because we cannot give what we do not have. If we do not love our self, how can we pretend to love someone else? We may feel the need to be loved, we may be obsessed with the idea of love or whatever, but this is not love. We are so insecure that we become jealous about what our partner is doing or not doing. We try to control them; the way they walk, the way they talk and the relationship becomes a complete nightmare. And with that obsession we destroy what we really want. And all of this is because we do not love our self. We need to love the main character of our story, which is our self, or else we can only pretend to love the secondary characters. The key point is when we become honest and aware that we do not even like our self, we realize we cannot expect anyone else to love us. The turning point happens when we stop looking outside our self for love. If we do not like a person, we can walk away. If we do not like a group of people, we can walk away. But if we do not like our self, wherever we go and whatever we do, we are always going to be trapped with our self. We cannot just walk away.

Most of the people who do not like themselves try to bury their feelings of emptiness either by eating too much, drinking too much or indulging in something in order to forget. They suffer and they hate themselves so much that one way or another many of them end up killing themselves.

If we have awareness and we know all the tricks we use to conceal our self-loathing we realize that these addictions are blocking our Light and love from flowing and do not serve us at all. When we have this awareness then we create reconciliation with our own body, with our self. This is a wonderful step. It begins a profound healing. The word *yoga* means *union*; union of knowledge, body, mind and spirit. The problem is not the body, it is the mind and its limited knowledge. The body is judged by the mind. Therefore, the mind is where we need to place our focus if we really want to heal ourselves. We blame everything around us, we see everything we do not like and we try to change the whole world. However, if we want to change the whole world, we need to change ourselves first. If we change ourselves then we can change the world and the only way to do this is by loving ourselves. When we love ourselves everything else then changes as if by magic and we begin to shine.

**About me**

I can say I am a medical doctor, an author and that I used to play a lot of chess and guitar. I can tell you everything that identifies me, but all that is just my creation. It is not me. I never even chose my name. I have no idea what I am, but I am. I know I am alive, I am here, that is the truth and everything else is just an attempt to describe my identity and I already know that I am not that identity. That identity is the way I wish people would perceive me yet people distort that too and they will not perceive me in the way I want to be perceived. They will qualify me and according to what they believe they will change it. They may believe they know me but they do not. They know the image that they perceive, the image that they judge and vice versa. I really cannot say that I know anyone, not even my own parents or my children. I can hardly say that I know myself. To not have to pretend to be what I am not is a relief. I am what I am and people either love me or not. I do not pretend to be what I am not. And, of course, I accept people the way they are. I have been taught many lessons in my life about love, but none of them are important. They are all irrelevant because in truth they were actually lessons in limitation. What is really important is to enjoy life, to love, to be in the moment and to be happy. No one can make you happy, only you can make yourself happy. In the same way we cannot make anyone else happy either.

Now we are beginning to understand what love is not, perhaps we can put our eye on what love is. The only problem is that it is so difficult to use words to describe it. Because in a book we have to use words, the easiest way for me to define *Love* is to say: *love is the equilibrium between gratitude and generosity.* We are so grateful to receive and once we do we become so generous that out of the fullness of our hearts we start giving and do not expect anything in return. We are being ourselves completely with no conditions attached. We become passionate. We react in that way because of the gratitude we feel for what we receive and then the generosity of who we really are shines forth. We do not have to and we do not need to, it just comes out of us and the reason is because we are love. We know we are made by love. This is real love. This is pure love.

## The agreements and love

*The Five Agreements* all together equal real love.

## Being impeccable with the word

We are impeccable because we love our self. Our story will depend on how we express our word. The word is just a word; it is only true because we agree on the meaning of it. We use the word to create our whole story then if we misuse the word we create all those dramas and we do that because we do not love ourselves. But when we are impeccable with the word we create our own heaven and then everything in our world truly becomes a love story. This is the main one of *The Five Agreements*.

## Don't take anything personally

This supports the first agreement, because everyone around us uses the word to create their own reality. And they are the center of their reality as we are the center of our reality. Then, when they perceive us a certain way, they will distort us because that is what they believe about us. When they get angry with us they really get angry with the image they have created in their minds, which in all probability has nothing to do with us; their projection is not who we really are. By not taking anything personally we are supporting the first agreement and that gives us immunity with any interactions we may have with everybody else. We know and understand that this is their story not our story. It may be true for them, but it is not true for us. We are responsible for our own creation, not for their creation. They are responsible for their creation, not for our creation. It is never personal.

## Don't make assumptions

We create all our knowledge and rules with words. At a certain point of our life, knowledge starts speaking with sounds that nobody can hear except us and we call it thinking. Very soon, in our mind, that voice of knowledge creates a whole dialogue as if one hundred people are talking at the same time. They do not agree with each other and we make the assumption that what we are thinking is the truth. But in our mind there are many truths fighting with each other, all making assumptions. If we do not make assumptions that gives us immunity from the endless conflict going on inside our heads, then our direction becomes clearer and our life purpose becomes intuitively obvious.

**Always do your best**

All of the first three agreements are true as concepts in our head, but it is only with action that we make them real. We can create heaven or hell from the content of our minds. Everything we see around us is the manifestation of human thought. It first existed in their minds and then they made it real. And from this we know that whatever our dream is, whatever we believe, whatever our story is, we can make it real if we take action. Agreement number four is about this action. When we always do our best we have the power to make real what is not real, which is a beautiful gift.

These four agreements are of course an expression of pure love. They take us back from all those distortions that we make to see our self just the way we are and the way we are is pure love. The four agreements are an introduction to this way of life, which I call *the way of life of the artist*. I am from the Toltec tradition. Thousands of years ago the Toltec were known throughout southern Mexico as *women and men of knowledge*. As a group they formed a society to explore, practice and conserve esoteric knowledge. The word *Toltec* means artist in all of the languages of the world. The four agreements are the introduction to the Toltec training, taking us back to our roots, to who we really are. After practicing these four agreements for years the moment arrives when we become an expert and that is the time when we finish our training, by learning and applying the fifth agreement.

**Being skeptical but learning to listen**

We begin to question everything we see and hear because we know that everyone around us creates their own reality. And what they say may be true for them but not for me. But when we really listen to them then we know where they are coming from. By doing that we can respect our friends and at the same time completely respect ourselves. When we respect ourselves that is when we no longer believe our own stories. We simply listen to what we say and then the inner war ends. All that conflict of the mind is finished and we become like Christ or Buddha and begin a brand new reality of unconditional love.

These five agreements will take us all the way to that point, but the only way for that to happen is by practicing until it becomes automatic. We are all artists and we have the ability to arrange each language and every symbol in any way we want. We can express our thoughts in exquisite poetry, prose and dreams because we know that we are the Creator. And we know that the highest love lies beyond all of these creations, no matter how delicious they are. Light and Love is the same thing. The Light contains all the information of everything that exists. The only difference is the words that we use to describe the indescribable. The Truth is the same, God is the same; there is no difference. All are synonymous but we usually do not understand it that way. Love, Light, Truth, God exists in the place where all words cease. In that space we find the mystery of Love revealed. In the silence, if we really listen, we will hear Love calling us.

 To do a love deed today and experience loving in action, you might like to check out our online Lightbox, which is full of tools you can download to help us spread the Light. Feel free to go to **www.spreadthelightcampaign/lightbox** and have a rummage around!

# About Michael Hayes

Michael Hayes is a spiritual counselor and seminar leader who works with groups and individuals across the world to transform their lives and awaken them to their spiritual nature. He began his spiritual work with others at the age of twenty-one after receiving a profound spiritual healing for a disabling back condition. He was so moved and inspired by his experience that he offered his life to serving others as he had been served.

Within a year, he met John-Roger, a renowned spiritual teacher. Upon shaking his hand, he had an almost instantaneous out of body experience with Jesus Christ, where the greater purpose of his life was revealed.

Michael began to work closely with John-Roger, assisting him with the greater spiritual work that was being done for many souls and for the planet itself. This accelerated his own spiritual awakening and his ability to assist others in transforming their lives.

For more information about Michael, go to
***www.awake2love.com.***

# Understanding
# the Light

By Michael Hayes

*In the beginning God created the heavens and the
earth. Now the earth was formless and empty, darkness
was over the surface of the deep and the Spirit of God
was hovering over the waters. And God said, "Let there
be Light," and there was Light.*

~ Genesis 1-3

Masters of different paths offer many descriptions of
the Light in the physical and metaphysical levels of
reality. I am happy to offer some of what I have personally
experienced of this Light of God, under the guidance of my
spiritual teacher.

There is an essential stream through which all things
are manifest and it began in the Heart of God; this was an
unconditioned state, which took on conditionality. The
Light, as a totality, is so pure that if we follow the spectrum
up into Spirit it becomes clearer and clearer until we can no
longer see it. At this point it can only be detected by *knowing*
it and by awareness of unearthly, transcendent sounds. These
sounds are so magnificent that mystics have given them
extraordinary descriptions, such as "the sound of a million
violins" or "the humming sound of a million angel wings
flapping."

Watching the Light of God moving down through the
spiritual world towards the material world is like watching
ripples splay out from a rock thrown into water. With
each ripple comes a new level of manifestation. The first
rings are variations of spirit, but as the ripples move away

from the center, the process slows until eventually tangible manifestation occurs.

## Levels of Light

The main levels moving down from Spirit into greater density are:

☼ **Spirit level** - where the Light is clear, moving down into the purest white you could ever imagine.

☼ **Soul level** - this is the boundary between what is created and uncreated. The Soul is individuated God. The Light appears here in varying shades of an extraordinary golden color.

☼ **Etheric level** - also known as the unconscious level, the archetypal level, or the symbolic level. It deals with the collective unconsciousness and is extremely powerful and dynamically creative. The Light appears in different shades of purple and violet.

☼ **Mental level** - here thought predominates and we find the universal mind. The Light appears in shades of blue.

☼ **Causal level** - also called the emotional level. Here emotion predominates. The Light appears as a salmon color and different shades of orange.

☼ **Astral level** - imagination predominates and the Light appears in shades of pink.

☼ **Physical level** - this is the level to which we are used to relating. The Light appears in shades of green.

Obviously, the entire Light spectrum can be found on the earth and in other levels, but the predominate Light frequencies of each level are the colors described.

## The magnetic and spiritual Light

As the Light turns denser and moves into levels of manifestation its color changes and adapts. Though all things were manifested under God's original intention of Light, as Light moves through the levels below the Spirit level it takes on a magnetic quality. We can attract and direct this magnetic Light. Things can be changed, moved and manipulated via our intention. Therefore, the magnetic Light does not always work for our higher good because we can use mind and emotion to manipulate it. The magnetic Light can be used in both positive and negative ways and it adjusts according to our intention and consciousness.

We must learn to take care when working with the Light because we can create negatively with it too. Many great healers work with the magnetic Light. They may simply touch you and your life will change because Light has incredible power. Some of the greatest healers work with the Light of the etheric or unconscious plane, which is closer to the level of the Light of Spirit. It is still magnetic, but as it is purer, it is also more powerful. Healers may do tremendous good work with this Light. However, if they were to enter a state driven by ego or ambition that would be contrary to the highest good of their clients and it might corrupt their service. It is possible for us, if we open up spiritually, to attune to the Light above manifest creation, to the pure Light of Spirit. That Light will not let us corrupt it nor do anything with it which is against the highest good. Nevertheless, the Light in the world can be used however we choose to use it. For example, God has not interceded and stopped us from splitting the atom despite the fact that we could destroy our planet as a result.

One reason people meditate and follow a spiritual path is to get beyond the magnetic Light and access the Spiritual Light. One key to achieving this is to reach a detached, neutral place where we are open to the highest good. Potentially, anyone can reach this state. When we look historically across the different religious traditions and metaphysical paths, many people tapped into that higher Light and were channels and instruments for it. To this day, when we read the poetry of Rumi, for example, his words and the energy behind them take us into that higher Light and give us a sense of inspiration, joy and love. Rumi merged into that higher Light and his subsequent work was radiated. It seems to touch nearly everyone. On the other hand, some people may be moved by a certain piece of music, while it does nothing for many other people. In this case the music is most likely reflecting the magnetic Light from one of the levels of manifest creation. That does not mean it is negative; it can still be beautiful and powerful, but not as universally inspiring.

The higher Light will only work for the highest good. Our prayers go forth into the universe and they are always answered, but the level they are answered from depends on where we pray from and the clarity of our intention. If there is too much emotional demand in our prayer, it will most likely be answered from a lesser level of the Light.

**Keys to working with the higher, spiritual Light**

In the Bible there is a passage about Jesus in the Garden of Gethsemane. It describes Him in great sorrow. Knowing that for God all things are possible, He prays, "My Father, if it is possible, may this cup be taken from me; yet not as I will, but as you will." (NIV, Matthew, Chap 26, verse 40) That is a perfect example of saying, "I really want this, however Father, I trust that you know what's best for me." On this occasion it seems the human side of Jesus emerged and He may have thought, "If there's a way to spread the word without my body being whipped, scourged and crucified then guide me in that direction." Nevertheless, He gave it over to the highest good.

That is an essential step of how to work with the higher

Light; a willingness to accept whatever might happen. In some ways we are able to control the magnetic Light, but not the higher Light, as that Light always serves the greatest good. There are times when people say a really heartfelt prayer, which taps into the Soul and that prayer is always heard as it is so pure.

I once knew a lady, aged thirty-eight, who had not been in a relationship for at least ten years. One day she felt so desperate, she got down on her knees and prayed and wrote a letter to her spiritual teacher. She wrote, "Oh please, please, send me someone I can love." It was an extremely heartfelt prayer. About a week later she met a man at a seminar. She was 5ft 8" and weighed about 250 pounds and this man was 5ft 6" maybe 110 pounds and about fifteen years younger than her. Yet they hit it off. She loved him and he loved her. They married and had two amazing little girls. They are still together now, more than twenty-five years later and it is a dream marriage. She gave away all her preconceptions of the way it should be. When he first showed up she thought, "He's too young, too short, too thin," but she let those thoughts go, accepted him as the answer to her prayer and chose to be thankful.

This story contains another key in how to work with the higher Light because the desperate lady asked for a place to pour her love. God is all about the loving and that brought the power of the spiritual Light forward. We may be held in the magnetic Light when we ask for things which are for our own gratification by saying, "I want someone to give to me, to love me, to care for me." That *me* we are acting from is the false self, the conditioned ego of this level. When we request from that place it may be the magnetic Light which seeks to bring it to us. When this lady asked for someone to love she requested a chance to give and share who she really was and that brought forth the spiritual answer to her prayer.

## Light in medicine

In our time the healing power of the Light is emerging into popular consciousness. Lasers, x-rays, MRIs, radiation therapy and other forms of Light are now used to deal with everything from cataracts to cancers. There are also subtler uses of the Light emerging or perhaps re-emerging. Ancient healing practices were full of ways to use Light as a healing force. Even more recently, in the 1930s and 1940s, Dr. Royal Rife created a microscope so powerful that he could see the Light frequency and color in cells. He could see the exact nature of cancer cells and find the frequency of Light that destroyed them. His success in healing people from cancer was unmatched. However, the world was not ready for such a simple, unprofitable solution to illness at that time and Dr. Rife's work was largely lost.

Recently in Europe, microscopes similar in magnification power to Dr. Rife's have been produced. Perhaps mankind will get a second chance to utilize the power of Light that Dr. Rife revealed. The field of energy medicine, which could also be called Light medicine, is penetrating the mysteries of illness in remarkable ways. Recognizing the elementary truth of Light as the foundation of everything, all of life is being understood differently. Quantum mechanics is opening up even the most reluctant minds to realize that everything comes down to Light and everything can potentially be changed in the Light.

## The Light man, the God-man

One of the oldest names for God is the Sanskrit word, *Hu*, so the word *Hu-man* means *God-man*. The *hue* of Light is how we describe it, so really we are the Light man, the God man. We are collectively reawakening on the planet to truly being *Hu-man*, Light ones connected to *Hu*, the Love, God. Many times people think the Light should give them what they want even at another's expense. Imagine two armies on the battlefield both saying, "We will win because God is on our side. We pray to God so he will give us victory." If the Light does help them in this situation it will be the magnetic Light because the higher Light would not come in and say, "We're in favor of the Iraqis today so let's help them win this battle." The higher Light does not function like that.

## Light and darkness

In reality, darkness is different gradations of Light. In this dualistic world we see it as Light and dark but there is no place where Light does not exist. If the Light is a manifestation of God, how can there be any place where God is not? Because of the magnetic nature of Light in this world, people are able to go into very dark places and the Light they work from is not something of which we want to be part, but it is still there. The God-man is what we are after. We come to that through the higher Light.

## Calling in the Light for the highest good

One of the first things people need to remember is to ask for the Light. There is a saying which goes, "You receive not because you ask not." In the illusion of the ego we often do not ask because we think we can do it alone. People often do not get the support they want from the Light because they refuse to ask for it. It serves to ask for the Light for the highest good. That is important to understand because our idea about what should happen is one thing, but what is the highest good might be another. Maybe we ask for the Light to come in and save the relationship of a couple who are fighting and not getting on. We think they should stay together because we believe in the ideal of love forever, so we ask for the magnetic Light because we have put an agenda on it. We are saying, "Light, save their relationship!" And perhaps our prayers work and they stay together. But what if in separating they would both go on to find somebody who was truly meant for them? Maybe a soul wants to come in and be a child of one of them but not the other. The Soul says, "I wanted that person to be my mother but the right person is not present to be my father." The fighting couple may need to break up in this case or else the family will never get completed. That is why it is important to ask for things for the highest good because the infinite wisdom of God will know the highest action even when we do not.

### Sending the Light for the highest good

We can work with the Light by sending it to people and countries which need it. We just say, "I send the Light to Africa for the highest good." "I want to send the Light to my sister-in-law who has cancer." "I ask for the Light for the highest good." Then it will go out to the relevant places and people. If we try too hard, if we demand, we fuel it with our emotion and that might bring the magnetic Light. Maybe the highest good is for our sister-in-law to pass on, but we can still pour love and Light into the request while respecting and trusting God's perfection. Many people may want a certain person, so they go to their local witch doctor and say, "Do something so they will fall in love with me." That is an example of using magnetic Light in a negative way to control. When people do this they may get the person, but if it is not for the highest good it could interfere with the progression of them both.

It is the same in certain countries, which have feuds dating back thousands of years. Different souls are born into that country as a learning opportunity. We might want it to be a loving, peaceful situation with the people holding hands, hugging and singing songs, but they are here to learn from their conflict. People think we need the Light to come forward and lead us to utopia, the perfect Shangri La.

However, we can understand that earth is a school for souls to grow through experiencing creation in all its aspects; pleasant and unpleasant. We then realize that if earth achieved utopia it would not be much use as a school. There would be no reason for a soul to leave heaven to come to heaven. We are not meant to or able to interfere with the lessons some souls have come to learn, but we can continually ask for the Light so that hopefully learning can take place in easier and faster ways.

Right now the earth is being bathed in extraordinary amounts of Light coming from the spiritual heavens. There is more spiritual Light being poured onto our planet than ever before. It is pushing out a lot of the old energy, resurfacing issues and conflicts. Yet as the old energies are pushed out, the world will operate under a purer Light. The more we cooperate with this process, the easier it will be for everyone. Now is a time to cast off the old skin to make way for the new. It helps to send and visualize the Light as much as possible. We can do this through our intent and there are also techniques such as visualizing columns of Light or seeing a country filled in beautiful Light. We might say, "I want the Light to go to Ethiopia. I see it in my mind full of Light. I see a column of Light going right down through the earth, connecting and expanding until it includes the whole planet."

---

### ☼ Light Practice ☼
### Using Light and the chakras

The human body has a chakra system which steps down Light. The main chakras are at the top of the head, forehead, throat, center of the chest, solar plexus, lower abdomen and pubic bone. We can see Light moving through them in the same way as electricity moving through the power grid; there is a tremendous voltage that is being progressively stepped down. We can visualize Light passing through the chakras in a similar way by moving through the color spectrum. Perhaps we start by asking for God's blessing and protection for the highest good. We then visualize red Light flooding down through each of our chakras and then flooding our body and our aura and then out from us to the whole world. We then repeat the visualization with an orange Light, yellow Light, green Light, blue Light, purple Light and golden Light until we reach a pure white Light. We visualize all these coming down and healing us and our world for the highest good.

## Conclusion

In learning to work with the Light we are accelerating our understanding of creation, the creative process and the creative force most often referenced as God. Scientifically and intuitively we are collectively moving towards the realization that everything is Light. With this awakening awareness, we are starting to change the conceptual boundaries of what life can and cannot be. As individuals and as a collective, as we know that all imbalances of mind and body can be improved upon and perhaps remedied by proper application of Light, we gain great hope for the days ahead. Perhaps we are moving towards a true age of *en-Lightenment*.

For your daily ray of Light, log on to our blog ***www.thelightcolumn.com*** and read the latest inspirational posts.

# About William Arntz

William Arntz began his professional career as a research laser physicist. After a few years he began studying with his first spiritual teacher and the students were given the task of writing a software product/company whereupon William wrote AutoSys—a distributed event processor. He sold the company two years later and retired.

Soon after William began attending the Ramtha School of Enlightenment and became interested in sharing some of the principles gleaned from his decades of spiritual inquiry with the general public. He realized he could use the software proceeds to make a movie. That movie started life as a small documentary about Spirit and Science, but grew in scope and became *What the BLEEP Do We Know!?* which went on to become a global phenomenon, with well over 100 million viewers.

William has recently completed a new film, targeted for a younger crowd, which develops some principles from BLEEP in a sociological, urban setting. The film, *GhettoPhysics*, and its companion book, addresses the question of how a spiritual being navigates through a world obsessed with power, fame and riches.

For further information, log on to ***www.whatthebleep.com***.

# Quantum Light

*By William Arntz*

*Come into my garden and see how all the colors of*
*diversity Blaze in the Light of Unity.*
*If you look closely*
*Lover and Beloved, flower and thorn,*
*Are One!*
~ **Sarmad, 17th century Sufi mystic and poet**

Quantum is the physics of the very, very, very small. When scientists first looked at matter, or Light, they thought it was continuous, like waves. The Quantum theory said that rather than waves, it was actually small packets of energy that became known as Quantum. This all started with the atom. In the classical structure of the atom the proton is in the center, next the nucleus and then the electrons around the outside. Scientists started noticing that when an electron moves from one state to another, for example when orbiting Mercury and moving out to Venus, it can only be at Mercury or Venus, never in between. The idea of Quantum was that it was either at that level or the other level, never in between the two. If you take a spaceship from Mercury to Venus you will go through the space in between. In Quantum it never does. It is in one state and then suddenly it is in the other state; it is discreet. If you go from twenty to thirty miles per hour, you must pass through twenty-five miles per hour on the way. However, Quantum would be like going twenty miles per hour and then going thirty miles per hour in the next instant. When scientists first studied this they thought it was impossible that the universe could work in that way. Nevertheless, they soon discovered that on the electron level that is exactly how it works. *Quantum* is the idea that things come in discreet *quana*—a discreet quantity of energy. But people get all spiritual and start talking about *quantum shifts* and such like, because it is as if you are in one state of awareness and then in the next instant *BOOM*, suddenly the lights go on and you perceive the world in a totally different way. The idea of *quantum shift* is something that does not evolve slowly; in one instant you are at a different level.

Back in the thirties when the scientists were studying this idea of things being discreet, Einstein, the great genius of the 20th century, did not believe Quantum theory because there is a certain randomness built into it. His famous quote was, "God does not play dice." He set out to disprove Quantum theory. Together with two other scientists he discovered that according to Quantum theory if you have two particles bound together and you separate them to the other sides of the universe, then you flip one a certain way, the other one will instantaneously flip the other way faster than the speed of Light. Einstein did not believe there was any force in the known universe to cause the other particle to flip, so he said, "How can an electron across the other side of the universe know what its brother electron is doing?" He turned it over to Heisenberg, one of the big Quantum scientists and said: "Here you go, I've disproved Quantum theory." Heisenberg had a very sleepless night, he did all the necessary equations, and the next morning he met Einstein and said, "You're right, that's exactly what my theory says." Einstein said, "That means I've disproven your theory." However, Heisenberg said, "No, you haven't, you've just brought out an aspect we weren't aware of." This is called the *Quantum Entanglement* and it was argued for years until about a decade ago when scientists finally proved that this is exactly how the universe works. They proved that when particles are entangled they are always connected. At the beginning of the universe, when the Big Bang occurred, all the particles of the universe were entangled, which means that we are all entangled with everything all the time.

The mystics have been saying that we are all One for eternity and now on the level of Quantum theory scientists agree because they know that every time a tiny electron flips over in one part of the universe, elsewhere other electrons flip over too. That is one of the major ways that Quantum has to do with the Light. It is a huge revelation because it proves that everything is connected. Dean Radin, who I interviewed in the movie *What the Bleep—Down the Rabbit Hole* does an experiment where two people get *entangled*. They look into each other's eyes for some time and then he separates them. After, he flashes lights in one person's eye and brain scans are conducted on the other person who is seen to react to the flashes. Most people have had the experience where they are thinking about someone and then the phone rings and there they are. From the Quantum point of view we could say that they are entangled. From a metaphysical perspective we could say, "Well that's only what's happening on the physical level." However, it is a principle that goes through all the layers of the universe." In the higher realms, the entanglement is more obvious and persistent. Mystics go into these states of Oneness; they live in an entangled world where they perceive and feel everything that occurs all of the time. That is why some enlightened people tend to go a little crazy from time to time, because they literally *are* the universe. Some people have mystical experiences and then it takes them three years to figure out how to live back in the world. They quickly realize that they still have to deal with traffic lights and all the mundane attributes of the physical world.

## Light is information

Some theories say that the fundamental building block of the universe is not energy or matter, it is actually information. The interesting thing about information is that it never gets diminished. For example, if you have a bucket of gold and you give a handful to someone else, now they also have some gold but you have less gold in your bucket. The amazing thing about information is that you can give information but you are not diminished by passing it on. You can share it and not only does it not diminish but it actually increases and expands. You can look at everything as information. Even something such as a heavy piece of lead is informing the rest of the universe that if you let it go, it will drop. The way in which information is encoded is complicated because there are lots of different levels of information. There is the physical level, which is the vibration, whereas the subtler vibrations of Light are where a lot of information is encoded. At this level some people have revelations and suddenly they see the world in an entirely different way; all the information comes in at once and they have the whole picture.

*When Mozart was composing symphonies he said that sometimes he would perceive an entire symphony in an instant—as one single note.*

## The world and karma

I think everyone will agree that the world is in a mess right now and it seems to be getting messier. With the advent of technology and the fact that everyone has access to it, we suddenly have the ability to cause even more mayhem. It takes only one little bit of mayhem to cause a catastrophe. This is basically the paradigm that people are living in now; we can look around and realize that the current mindset is creating all this mayhem. I believe there is so much mayhem because the world's perception of the universe is out of balance with the way the universe really works. An example of that is *Karma*, or the *Law of Cause and Effect*. Karma is such that you reap what you sow, but people are generally ignorant about karma. As we are connected, what we do to another, we do to our self. If people realized and understood that, they would probably no longer cheat people or do bad things.

There has been a rise of spiritual materialism that says the other world does not exist and that we only exist on the physical level. In that world there is no karma, so we might as well go and screw someone so we can go and buy a yacht. The lesser evolved mass of people will say, "So what that you've put a thousand people out of work and stolen everyone's pension plans, you have a cool yacht, let's put you on TV." Society thinks that such actions are really cool, whereas an enlightened society would think that person is a crook. I made the *What the Bleep* movies to try and inject a little Light into the world with the idea of looking at a different way to view the universe that we are all pottering around in. The goal was to have one hundred million viewers around the planet and based on DVD sales, theatre ticket sales and the fact that it was a big hit on the pirate market, I think we reached that goal.

## How our actions affect the whole

A topic which is discussed in various spiritual circles is the idea that we create our own reality and manifest our own dreams. For example, when someone is walking down the street and a bus drives through a mud puddle and they get sprayed by dirty water, they will say, "How did I create that?" There is some truth to the idea that we create our own reality. After I made the *What the Bleep* movies I had a conversation with Eckhart Tolle and I asked him what he thought about this concept. He laughed a little and said, "Well, on the one hand it's true, but the idea that we create all of our reality has a fundamental flaw in it." I said, "What's that?" And he said, "We're all connected." So yes, we are creating our own reality but everyone else also has a certain input in our reality. It is similar to when we shine a light. When we are close the light is brighter and the further away we go, the light diminishes. We are creating all of the time. When we get closer to our true Self, we are going to be more aware of our own creations, as well as understanding how they also create waves that ripple out and affect others. If we are far from our self, we are ignorant of our potential as creators and unaware of how our actions and thoughts impact the lives of others. So if there are millions and millions of unhappy, violent people around the planet, that energy will accumulate and join together and it may emerge in a terrorist bombing, or a whacko shooting everyone in a cinema. When the creative impetus of everyone else forms together, this collective vibration creates the reality.

In America now, around half of all families have experienced divorce. We know that on one level for the kids who are involved, divorce is very painful. All of these divorces are creating vast amounts of unhappiness in those who are not taught how to learn and grow from adversity. How does the unhappiness show up in our world? Well, just look around! We do create our own reality and we are all in it together.

> *If we had a world where everyone was thinking*
> *peaceful thoughts there would not be any war*
> *or violence.*

### Repeatedly creating the same realities

We repeatedly create the same realities because we are addicted to our emotions. Emotions are a very powerful psychic and bio-state in the body. Our emotions enlist a biochemical response and then we become addicted to that. The classic situation of someone who is a victim and always thinks *poor me* gets the sympathy they desire from others and that becomes a positive feedback loop for them. As a result they continuously create victimization so that people can say, "Poor you, they shouldn't have done that to you. Let me make you chicken soup." It becomes subconscious. All parts of us are creating reality all of the time. You attract to you those things you are interested in. Personally I like cars and I always notice them around. Someone who is not into cars will never see them. In the same way, if you are addicted to victimization you will always bring that to you in an unconscious way. That is why people get stuck in certain situations; they get something out of being victims. We are all unconscious about a whole lot of issues and part of the enlightenment process is bringing those things to light.

For example, I was making *What the Bleep* and one day I was complaining because many people around me were saying, "Who do you think you are? You're just some software guy and now you want to make movies, but you'll never pull it off." I kept hearing this, so I got on the phone to Betsy, who I made the movie with and I said, "Betsy, I can't believe this, people say I can't do things all the time. Back at college I got in the honors program and my advisor told me I wasn't smart enough to get in, but I showed him...." I went through all the examples in my life where someone had told me I would not be able to do something and then I would prove them wrong. Halfway through my tirade, I stopped suddenly and realized it was an emotional addiction. I got off on people telling me I couldn't do it. That would inspire me to achieve and then I could say I did it and prove them wrong. I started laughing on the phone. Once I realized the truth behind this emotional addiction, it has never happened again. Once it was brought to light, I realized I didn't need it anymore.

**Understanding our connectedness in these times**

It is especially important that we understand we are all One right now because we are destroying the earth, our relationships and each other. Once we understand the connectedness we will no longer pour toxins on the earth, as that would be the same as pouring toxins on our own skin. Unfortunately, the scientific viewpoint is that we are separate. That is *scientific materialism*. If we look at the history of science, which is where the scientific materialism comes in, a lot of it was the reaction to the dogma of Church, which said that from the Bible they had calculated that the world was created in 3000BC along with many other untruths. Then scientists came along and said, "Hang on a minute, that's not right." There was a revulsion against all religious theories and the scientists started inventing steam engines, radios and many other cool household gadgets. The common person looked at the scientists and said, "Wow, these guys are performing miracles and I can't see many of the priests performing miracles." As a result, science became the hero of the industrial revolution and the 20th century. It looked like these scientists had it together, but that was only true on the physical level. All of the spiritual and metaphysical parts were brushed aside as superstition. In certain scientific communities you are considered a relic from the past if you start talking about spiritual topics, never mind that Einstein always spoke about the Divine. Once you go down that path, the law of cause and effect does not exist and there is no life after death and so you might as well eat, drink and be merry and go and screw everyone else. There is a big change happening right now where people are rediscovering a lot of the principles of connectedness, transformation and many of the shamanistic traditions. It is all coming back, but at this point it is a close race whether humanity is going to figure it out in time. Some days it looks like the white hats are going to win, other days it looks like the black hats are going to win!

**What would you say to the people who say there is no God?**

Years ago I heard a great joke and it goes like this: God was eating dinner with a scientist and they were having a conversation. The scientist said, "Hey God, we don't need you anymore. I can modify DNA, I can communicate instantaneously with my electronics, I can even create life now because I know how it's wired together, so we don't really need you anymore." God said, "Hmm, I don't know about that." The scientist said, "Well, let's have a contest creating life and we'll see who wins." "Ok," said God. The scientist said, "Just like you I can take clay and make life." To which God said, "Go and get your own clay!"

Think about why there is anything at all…why does anything exist? If you really think about that then at some point you throw up your hands and say, "What created this?" Can you prove there is a God? There is a hymn about creation in the ancient *Rig Veda* of India. One of the verses asks the rhetorical question, "What was the tree, what was the wood from which He fashioned out the earth and heaven? Ye thoughtful men inquire within your spirit, on what did He stand when He created the universe?"

Someone can have an experience but that does not mean to say anyone else will. But people who have had such experiences say yes, God does exist. For example, when those who are clinically dead come back to life they are utterly transformed. They no longer have any fear and they are very loving people. Even after this someone can still say "Prove it! This could just be a crazy dream you're having." In the end how can we ever prove anything? When someone says there is no Creator, there is no God, simply smile at them and say, "Make your own clay!"

## Science or spirituality?

The thing about science is that you come up with the theory, put it to the test and if it fails the test you throw it out. It is a slow method but it eventually comes around to the truth. In my mind it is still the most effective way of coming to the answer of reality, truth and how the universe really works. If people continue working on scientific methods, a lot of the more spiritual subjects, such as psychic abilities, the role of karma and past lives, will eventually be proven by science. Scientific Method is great but it is used by *people*. There is a very famous line in science: "Progress in science comes about one generation at a time," meaning the previous generation has to die off before the new theory can come in. Scientists go to graduate school and spend their life proving a certain view; it is difficult to shift that theory, so science progresses one generation at a time. Scientists try to fit the data to their theory. There is another great line in science: "Another beautiful theory destroyed by an ugly fact."

## Definition of enlightenment

If and when I get enlightened I will be able to define enlightenment! I do know that enlightenment is a different way of perceiving everything. When I was in my twenties and I first started on the spiritual path, I had a lot of ideas about what it meant, but it is not at all what I initially thought. I thought that the whole point of getting enlightened was to live in bliss all the time, never have any problems and to experience everything as good all of the time, in a state of nirvana, or heaven on earth. From my observation of the few people I have met who are enlightened, the electricity still goes out in their house, the workmen still show up at the wrong time, someone runs into them on the highway, yet they remain in an expanded state of awareness. They are feeling all of the pain in the world. At least in this world, it is not the constant ecstasy I thought it was. Enlightened beings are still human and they still have emotions running through them. I just re-read *Autobiography of a Yogi* and Paramahansa Yogananda certainly seemed enlightened yet he cried like a little boy when his guru died. He still experienced disappointments and emotions.

## Being in the presence of enlightened beings

When we find ourselves in the presence of an enlightened being, it is like the good, the bad and the ugly. On the one hand there is this feeling of the Light and being lifted into higher states, which is quite remarkable. But at the same time, all of the *karmas* are quickened and many of the hidden issues we do not want to deal with come to the surface in order for us to evolve. The spiritual teacher pulls those things out of people. At that point the student must be mature enough to realize this is his or her own unconsciousness and then make the decision to go through the discomfort and get to the other side. On the one hand it is the best of all worlds, on the other hand it is the worst of all worlds. Some people may end up projecting all their ugly parts upon their teacher who revealed these aspects to him or her, showing who they really are in their current state.

As a result of being in the presence of an enlightened person, the vibratory rate becomes quicker, perceptions often get much sharper, everything becomes clearer and brighter. A vibration is like a key in a lock, it opens different worlds. It is not just sound vibration from sacred words or chants, as that is just one form of vibration. It is also about mental vibrations; how we become uplifted in the presence of someone who knows the truth of who they are and our thinking, emotional vibrations and spiritual vibrations resonate at higher frequencies. We may notice the size of the universe and a grain of sand all at once. Sometimes we may see parts of ourselves that we are not happy with. When we go into a meltdown around a spiritual teacher we can be sure it is going to get bad before it gets better. There is a line from the Bible: "For he is like the refiner's fire," which refers to the Messiah that is going to come. That is what being around these folks is like... they are like a refiner's fire and our impurities will burn, so get ready!

**There are no sinners**

Often after healing someone Jesus would say, "Go and sin no more." Originally the term *sin* was translated as *missing the mark*. This is closer to the Buddhist point of view; it is not good or evil, we are just ignorant about the laws of *karma*. Why would we knowingly do something bad when we are going to end up hurting our self and others? The idea of what Jesus said, "Go and sin no more," was about bringing to light persistent emotional and mental patterns. He was really saying, "Whatever you were doing in the past was off the mark, so if you continue doing that, what I just healed you for is going to come back." May we all learn to "hit the mark and stay on it," by delving into the world of Quantum Light and becoming aware of who we really are.

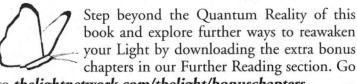

Step beyond the Quantum Reality of this book and explore further ways to reawaken your Light by downloading the extra bonus chapters in our Further Reading section. Go to **thelightnetwork.com/thelight/bonuschapters**.

# About Neale Donald Walsch

Neale Donald Walsch had a variety of professions before retiring to pursue his vision of a world in which people no longer live in fear of God or of each other.

He has written more than twenty-five books on spirituality and its practical application in everyday life, including the multi-million-selling *Conversations with God* series. The titles have been translated into thirty-seven languages and seven of them reached the *New York Times* Bestseller List.

Neale is the creator of several outreach projects: the ReCreation Foundation (CWG Foundation), CWGforParents, Humanity's Team and the Changing Change Network, all revolving around an internet gateway site: ***www.CWGPortal.com***.

He travels extensively throughout the world, speaking to audiences and sharing the messages of *Conversations with God*. His more recent books are *When Everything Changes Change Everything, The Storm Before the Calm* and *The Only Thing That Matters*.

For more information visit ***www.CWGPortal.com***.

# Conversations
# with the Light

*By Neale Donald Walsch*

*You are the light of the world. A city on a hill cannot be hidden. Neither do people light a lamp and put it under a bowl. Instead they put it on its stand and it gives light to everyone in the house. In the same way, let your light shine before men.*
~ Matthew 5:14-16

People ask all the time, "Am I really the Light?" There is nothing in the universe that is not Divine. *Everyone* and *everything* is the Light. Divinity is expressed through life itself at every level and in every way. The Light shines with increasing brightness from beings who have expanded their level of consciousness. If a person knows themself as the Light, they will experience themself as That and others will experience them as That as well. So to move to that place of consciousness, simply take another to that place of consciousness.

When I asked God what it would take for me to get to the place I so deeply yearned for, He chuckled and said, "Neale, I get that you still think your life is about you, but your life has nothing to do with you. It doesn't now, it never did and it never will. On the other hand, if you are clear that I sent you here in a state of utter perfection and it is only you who have imagined yourself not to be in that state, then you will move through the world no longer concerned about yourself at any level. In fact, your only concern will be for all those whose lives you touch. You will, therefore, give to another what you have sought to obtain for yourself."

The fastest way to experience yourself as the Light is to cause another to experience themself as the Light, for what you give to another you give to yourself and that will become eternally true in your experience.

> *Don't go around asking: what are we to eat, what are we to drink, wherewithal will we clothe ourselves? Seek ye first the kingdom of heaven and all these things will be added unto you.*
> ~The Gospel According to Matthew Chapters 31-33

So yes, you are the Light, but the fastest way for you to experience that is to make sure that everyone whose life you touch sees themselves, knows themselves and experiences themselves as the Light and they will know themselves as that depending upon how you interact with them and how you see them. As you give them their own sense of being the Light, so too will you grant that same sense to yourself. And the masters have put this in one sentence: "Do unto others as you would have it done unto you."

When people ask me, "Am I the Light?" I ask them, "Am I? How do you see me?" If they see me as the Light then I say, "Good, now see the next one hundred people you meet as the Light and you will begin seeing yourself as that. But so long as you have judgment about another and see them as less than the Light, you can *never* experience yourself as the Light. You will experience yourself as you experience the world around you and it can be no other way."

**The sages and mystics have said they want to see the world full of saints. They want us all to shine. How can we help the world to shine and not hide our own Light?**

By seeing the Light in others, even when they do not see it in themselves, by judging not and condemning not.

> *Judge not and neither condemn, but be a Light unto the darkness, so that everyone might know who they really are and that you might know who you really are as well.*

The answer is to remove negative judgment from our experiences in all things and at all times. Simply see the perfection. When we see the perfection in all things we immediately step outside of negative judgment. And when we step outside of negative judgment we bring ourselves the experience of the Divine. It is difficult for most human beings to see the world without judgment if they do not understand the true nature of unconditional love.

There is no action, activity, choice or decision made by anybody on the planet that does not spring from love. All actions are acts of love. When I make that statement the question I am immediately asked is: "Well, what about if somebody kills, robs or rapes someone? How can that be an act of love?" They do not understand that all acts spring from deep love. A person who acts violently acts that way because they lack something they would love to have, or because something they love has been taken from them, or because something they love and wish they had is not available to them. And so they reach out in violence in order to obtain the things they wish they had. All acts of violence are wailings of love.

All of the great masters have made this clear to us. There is no spiritual master, therefore, who judges anyone, not even the so-called worst among us, which is why *Conversations with God* made the statement that "Hitler went to heaven." When you understand that, you grasp at the edges of Divinity. If we lived in a world where everyone saw each other as the Light, we would see a remarkably different way of being on this planet. In fact, violence, anger, hatred, vindictiveness and acts of perpetration would no longer exist, because everyone would have what they really wanted, which simply put, is Love.

We are currently moving through stormy times until we reach that place of *one thousand years of peace*, which has been predicted for humankind. This stormy period we are now in is a result of a larger and ever-increasing number of human beings awakening to the truth of who we really are, which is a part of the Divine. We are expressions of the pure Light and all that it will take for all of the human-made problems to go away, literally overnight, is for us to assume our actual identity and to treat others as who they really are. Namely, the Light.

**What would make our Light shine brighter? Many people know there is something inside them, but they do not know how to access it. We agree intellectually, but how do we take that knowing and become the embodiment of Light?**

Share it as if you were already it, spread it as if you knew you did have it, be it as if you already were it and cause yourself to see others as if they were already it. That which you wish to experience, cause another to experience. If you want your Light to shine brighter, then you need to embrace with clarity the fact that your life is not about you. It never was. To the degree that you are looking in a mirror and trying to figure out how to make your life better or make your light shine brighter, you are concerned with you and your experience. My answer is a tough love answer…stop it!

I totally understand, as I spent fifty years doing this, but in my fifty-first year, after half a century of trying to make my Light shine brighter and trying to have a better life, I realized that it is not about me. And so I began to live my life in a whole different way. I turned the *lazy Susan* of life around so that my job was not to receive or somehow get better in some way, but to give everything I had to give, so that others may know the magnificence and wonder of who they truly are. The irony of that is others around me began reflecting that back to me. I simply stopped putting myself in the middle of my own mirror.

A mirror is nothing more than clear glass with lead on

the back. All you have to do is take the mirror in front of you, scrape off the backing and you will see clear glass. Suddenly, instead of seeing yourself in full view in the window of your life, you will see who is on the other side for the first time ever. It is like trying to look at a crowd in a mirror and you have to look around yourself in order to see who is behind you. When you take the backing off the mirror, suddenly you will see everything else and you are not even there, which is exactly the position that the Divine invites. Ironically, in the disappearing of yourself from the full view of your own vision, you will appear as who you really are: one who needs and wants and requires *nothing* except the opportunity to give everything there is to give to all those whose lives you touch. And in this way life becomes everything you have yearned for.

**Why does trying to control the Light not serve us?**

The Light does not have a plan. There is nothing that is supposed to occur. It would be a huge misunderstanding of how the whole process of life works if we think there are things that are supposed to occur or if we think the Light is supposed to be doing things. Each of us as an individuation of the Divine is co-creating on a moment-to-moment basis the reflections from the Light. "My will for you is your will for you," said God. Therefore, it is not about controlling the Light, it is about utilizing it and understanding how it works. The Light—or, if you please, God—responds to you and to all the other souls who are co-creating and collaborating with you in the production of your present moment encounter with life itself. If you try to control the Light it is an indication that you somehow think there is something you need or that you want or that you desire or that you are seeking or yearning for in order to somehow be something. "If I could just have this, then I could be that." So we try to use the Light in order to get a job or find our perfect mate or produce some particular outcome...

better health, more wealth, whatever it is we imagine would make us happier. That whole placement of the small self in relationship to the world is a misplacement. It indicates that we do not understand who we really are. Any effort to control the Light is an announcement to the world that we have no idea who we really are.

Can you imagine God trying to control the Light? Why would God try to control the Light, God *is* the Light. And so are you. Do not seek to control the Light, but rather to *be* the Light. When you are being the Light you seek nothing for yourself, you want nothing for yourself, you yearn for nothing for yourself, you need nothing for yourself, you ask nothing for yourself. Yet you be the Light for all those whose lives you have touched. Astonishingly, when you become that, many of the things you once yearned for come to you automatically, without you having to make any effort.

> *Seek ye first the kingdom of heaven and all else will be added unto you.*

So there is no need to control the Light, just be the Light and then watch what happens. And even if none of your desires are fulfilled, it would not matter, because we are not here seeking to obtain these things. We are here as the Source. We are here so that those lives we touch may experience life more abundantly, more joyfully, more fully through us being exactly who we are. In the moment we recognize who we really are our lives will be transformed overnight.

### What is the difference between an ordinary person and an awakened person?

An awakened person knows who they really are and has surrendered to an entirely different reason for living. This, in turn, has created an entirely new way of moving through the world. Whereas a person who has not awakened, who we will loosely describe as *sleepwalking*, is a person who is not clear who they are or why they are really on the earth, not clear what God wants or even if there even is a God or what the Soul is or even if they even have a soul. They are disconnected from the purpose of life itself. Those who are awakened have made the connection between their soul and their mind.

The mind holds the experience of everything it has encountered from the moment of its activation, which it imagines to be knowledge but which is simply a memory of an experience it has had. Whereas the Soul is the source of all knowledge and all awareness. The awakened person has made the connection between the Soul's awareness and the mind's experience, creating a place in between that we call consciousness. Therefore, an awakened person has become highly conscious of what is true in every moment of life: who they are, why they are here and why things are the way they are. When they apply their soul's awareness to those questions, they respond to what is happening in an entirely different way, as all the masters who have walked this planet have demonstrated.

## How is the Soul in relation to Light?

The Soul is the shining of the Light of God in the individual expression of divinity that we experience as ourselves. If we hide our Light under a bushel, if we do not let the Soul's Light shine, if we do not seek to intentionally and deliberately access the Light that lives within us, we will live in darkness.

That does not mean we will be bad people nor have horrible experiences. It simply means we will walk through our lives as if we are blindfolded or at the very least like a horse with blinders on. We have to put blinders on a horse if we are going to have him move through a crowded village because the horse will get very nervous if he can see everything in his peripheral vision. We put the blinders on the horse not to blind him but to enable him to only see straight ahead. The Soul is revealed when human perceptions are removed. We begin to see everything and unless we understand what we are looking at, we will be frightened.

We tend to move through life wearing blinders because we feel safer, plodding straight ahead, moving toward the next important goal of the small self. Once we take the blinders off we begin to see what being *down to earth* is really about. We are no longer concerned with all of those unimportant, petty little goals, which would take care of themselves automatically if we simply allowed ourselves to move through life for the real reason we are here.

The Soul, the Light within us, informs us that the real reason we are here is to expand the Light so that it can shine on all those whose lives we come in contact with, so that the Divine is expressed and experienced through every living thing. The purpose of human life is to allow God to experience divinity through every thought, action and deed; to make the ordinary into the extraordinary. God experiences God Self through the experience of expressing Itself.

People say to me, "What the hell does that mean?" I say, "You will know what it means when you walk down the street and ask yourself this simple question: 'How does what I am doing in this moment serve the agenda of my soul?'" And people answer, "Well, that's very sweet, but what is the agenda of my soul?" And I say, "The agenda of your soul is to achieve the complete expression of the Divine that lies within you." Is this not what every master has done? Indeed, they have done nothing else.

**In all traditions there is the encoded knowledge of the spiritual energy known as *kundalini, chi, shakti* and by other means. How do we get that energy awakened? And what happens when it does start to move?**

When that energy starts to move, you begin to realize that you truly need nothing to be perfectly happy, require nothing to be totally satisfied with your life and ask for nothing from anyone, at anytime, anywhere. And so you begin to move through the day-to-day of your experience in an entirely different way.

When you feel that *kundalini* energy rising within, you literally become a different person. You become who you really are, or at least have glimpses of who you really are—as opposed to this make-believe person we have all imagined we had to be in order to survive—because a person who sees and feels that energy rising within them understands that survival is no longer the issue. They understand that they cannot *not* survive, that they are, have been and will always be a Forever Being.

Once the need to survive is removed from the Mind's experience, the Soul has the space and freedom to express its true nature. We then start walking through the world in an entirely different way; no longer stressing and straining, no longer competing, no longer looking for the advantage, no longer needing, wanting or asking for anything. We simply stand in the space of life with a single and simple question: "How may I serve you, how may I love you, how may I be here with you in such a way that you know exactly who you really are?"

**This awakening has been hidden and is sacred knowledge so why is it now more available at this time on earth?**

It is available now more than ever before because humanity and technology has evolved to the point where we have means of communication that is faster than any censorship imposed on us by regimes and governments. The children of the young people of today will be the first totally free generation that is able to look at what is true in the world instantly, without being censored through the filters of their elders. Nowadays, the average young person has access to more information than the president of the United States had fifteen years ago. That is a fact. So humanity has undergone a revolution in communication where we have instant access to each other and to the sum total of human knowledge with the click of a mouse.

Some Totalitarian regimes are seeking to find a way to close the Pandora's box again and block access to information, so that they can once again control the masses. The reason this awakening is emerging globally is that we have broken through the communications barrier that once stopped us. Even a guy in Zimbabwe can now get on the internet and access information that opens his awareness in ways that he could not have dreamed of even a few years ago. The pace of change is quite remarkable. Why is this now happening? We have found a means of sidestepping the power structure in such a way that we no longer have to experience life through the filters of those in power.

Light has always been coming to the planet. It is not as if the Light says, "You know what, let's give them more in the year 2012 than they had in 1952, because in 1952 they didn't really deserve as much." Light is a constant, not a variable. What reason would God have to shed more Light on the earth now? It has always been there in its fullness. It is about the ability of the species to recognize and become aware of That which has always been there. God does not proportion Himself out depending on what year it is. Wisdom is not proportioned out depending on the day of the calendar. The Light has been glowing and shining through all eternity and it always will.

If you are standing in deep shade and then step into pure sunlight, would you say, "Why has the sun suddenly decided to shine?" Or would you say, "Ohhh, it has always been shining; I was standing in the shade." It is really quite simple.

In our earliest days of civilization on this planet—in Atlantis for example—we knew all of this. This is not new knowledge. It is a cyclical thing. The Light has always shone and we become aware or unaware of it. We went through a period of time when we did not know even half of what we know now. We call those the Dark Ages. We did not go through the Dark Ages because God was not there shining Her Light. We went through the dark ages because we put on blindfolds. This is not a time when the Light is shining brighter; it is a time when we are opening our eyes to what has been there all along.

**Can you share what the sacred teachings of the Light are?**

These can be found in *Conversations with God*, but I can summarize them here. The first and most important teaching is simply:

### "We are all One."

The second most important teaching is:

### "There is enough."

The third is:

### "There is nothing we have to do."

The opportunity is to be the Light and in the being of it, the body, as a function of physicality, becomes an instrument and performs all actions, knowing we are not the *doer*. Beingness, therefore, produces Doingness. It is not the other way around.

People think that if I do this and that, then I will be enlightened / happy / successful / popular, or whatever they are trying to be. So they use their Doingness as a means of getting to their place of Being, when, in fact, the formula is exactly the reverse. First, assume a State of Being and from that State of Being, what you are doing in the moment-to-moment of your life emerges and demonstrates what you are being. I notice that most people have that formula reversed. The answer is to start out being it and come from that place and then the Doingness will become automatic.

## Can you describe your experience of awakening; your moment of realization?

Awakening is not a one-time experience. It is not like getting your tonsils out. That is not the process of evolution or enlightenment, at least not for me. Enlightenment is an every moment opportunity. Just because one has had the experience of awakening or a flash of enlightenment does not mean it stays there forever. I do not declare myself to be an awakened being. I do declare myself to be someone who has experienced enlightenment from time to time. In the moments when I have experienced enlightenment, the experience has been one of indescribable blissful joy, leading almost to tears. Generally, if I am alone, I do have tears of quiet joy and a sense of fullness and Oneness. I feel at One with the plant across the room, at One with the mountains outside my window and even at One with the spider that is crawling across the countertop. In my old days I would have squashed it and thrown it down the drain, but these days I pick it up gently in my hand, carry it outside and sweetly say, "Go, living creature, on your way. Do what it is that you do to express whatever aspect of divinity flows through you and I shall do the same and we will co-exist together." That is what feeling enlightenment is like for me; a reverence for all of life, including the spider on the counter. It is an indescribable response to an indescribable experience of the indescribable God that each of us is.

In my first fifty years on this planet I was not getting anywhere because I did not know where I was trying to go. Ninety-eight percent of the people are spending ninety-eight percent of their time on things that do not matter, because they have no idea what they are doing here or where they are trying to go. My life fell into that category. I had my series of jobs just as everyone else does, I had my series of lovers just as everyone else does, I had my series of children just as many people do. I had all of these experiences that life is made up of and many of them were happy ones, but at the age of fifty my life looked empty.

I cried out to God, "Is that all there is? Get the guy, girl, get the job, get the house, get the office, get the better job, get the bigger house, get the kids, get the grandkids, get the big promotion, get the title on the door and then get the grey hair, get the sickness, get the retirement watch and get the hell out? What is going on here? Why does my life have to be such a continuing struggle?" And that is when God began talking to me.

Since then the *Conversations with God* books have found their way into fifteen million hands in thirty-seven languages. Perhaps with a new contemporary voice it is possible that even more people may start listening. As a result of reading this book, *The Light*, people might say, "This makes more sense to me than the life I've been living. I *knew* there was something more going on here." This will start to unwrap the gift that life has given us.

And then we ask the fundamental questions:
*Who am I?*
*Where am I?*
*Why am I where I am?*
*And what do I intend to do about that?*

## The Light and God are one and the same—Unity Consciousness—what does this mean?

It means that all things are from the One Source. There is only One thing and everything is a part of the totality. We can experience it by opening our mind to the possibility that everything we look at is an aspect of and an extension of the Self.

I recall walking through a city area a few years ago with a spiritual master and there was a disheveled gentleman sitting on the sidewalk. He did not smell great, he looked terrible and he was drinking a bottle of whiskey. He said, "Can you spare a little loose change, please?" And I turned to my spiritual master friend and said, "There, but for the grace of God, go I." And the spiritual master looked at me and said, "No, there b*ecause* of the grace of God, you go. There you go being a drunk again. There you go being a villain again. There you go being a robber and a rapist again. There you go being a saint again. There you go being a master again. There you go being nice again. When you see anything outside of yourself as not a part of yourself you see nothing at all, because nothing outside of your self is apart from you. Do not deny anything you see but rather embrace it as part of the totality that you are and in that moment you understand all you came here to experience. Then you can walk up to that man and with compassion and love in your heart say to him, 'I am part of what you are. I'm not going to give you some change to go out and buy some more whiskey but if you want to come with me I'll be happy to take you into that diner and buy you the best meal you've had in a week. Come with me, be with me, as I am with you.' And that my lovely friend is how we change the world."

Have a *conversation* with us about anything from *The Light* book to our charity, The Light Worldwide by contacting us via our website. The direct link is: **www.thelightnetwork.com/contact-us.**

# The Supreme Experience

There was once a sincere seeker who understood that in order to know the truth of who he was had to diligently follow the advice of ancient spiritual traditions. Gradually his body became supple and strong, his mind became steady, disciplined and able to remain focused in a positive way. As his knowledge of sacred teachings expanded, his heart became a fountain of compassion and his actions gentle and kind. No matter what happened in his life and in the world he handled each moment with equanimity and good humour. When he spoke people wanted to listen. When he entered a room everything seemed to become brighter. In his radiant presence everyone felt respect, love and the warmth of universal brotherhood. They sensed that when they looked into his eyes, there were no secrets. But even more than that, they felt an inner heat burning away their ailments and misunderstandings. They felt lighter and a whole lot better about themselves. They were inspired and hopeful about the ways of the world and the purpose of humanity. They laughed a lot more.

"What has happened to you?" people asked.

"I have been healed," he replied.

"Were you sick?"

He remained silent for a few moments and then, nodding his head as if acquiescing to an inner command, he looked up and spoke.

"The malaise I suffered caused me endless days and nights of torture. I grew up believing I was alone in a cruel and corrupt universe with no one to understand me, no goodness, no fairness, no hope and no God. I felt small and unworthy and that the world and humanity were doomed.

I blamed others for the mess in my life to the point where it had become unbearable and I was sick of it all. Then one night, when I did not believe it possible to hate myself or the world more, I heard a voice. It said, "It is time for you to follow your highest truth." I had no idea what this meant but the following morning a stranger put a Book of Wisdom into my hands saying it would help me to heal. As I began to read I could feel an excitement growing inside me and a profound longing to know that the words within the book were telling the truth. A truth stating that hidden within me and all of creation is a spark of the Divine and that my highest truth is to kindle and nurture this spark into a blazing Light. If I could serve this quest with devotion, forbearance and humility, the secrets and mysteries of the Universe would be revealed and I would be made whole—I would be healed."

"Did you find the Light?" they whispered?

"I began to follow the instructions in the book and apply the spiritual principles to my life. I experienced many times when I felt I would give up but always that inner voice would quietly encourage me. I made sacrifices and great efforts to seek out those who could teach me more. I even went to an enlightened Master and begged him to give me an experience of the mysterious inner Light. He laughed and gave me a slap on the head but the experience was so intense I begged him to stop—it was clear I was not strong enough! He was very compassionate and told me he would "come to me" when I was ready. I went away and did my very best to follow the guidance in the Book of Wisdom. Life became an adventure. I traveled, met amazing people and even began to teach some of the spiritual principles and practices to others and yet, with all the growing knowledge I still felt an aching emptiness. One evening as I lay in my room watching the moon shadows dancing on the walls, I prayed to the master again, begging to know the truth of who I am. I heard a voice say, "It is time" and then there was a whooshing sound and above my body a pinpoint of brilliant Light hovered over me. I lay motionless as it began to expand and my heart exploded with a love so all-encompassing I thought I would die of joy. My human eyes could not look upon a Light so bright, yet even with them closed the brilliance dazzled me. Somehow my essence was lifted out of my physical form and with a lightness of being I was flying through galaxies and dancing across the heavens until I came to a place of marbled halls and skies with no horizon. There were beings who greeted me with the love of eternity. I had come home and I wept with delight as I saw all of those I thought I had lost. And then I saw the earth as if watching a thousand movie screens simultaneously. In every scene, in every land, in every tree, plant, flower and face, I saw the Light. In every word, thought, deed and intention, I saw the Light. In every song, poem and story, I saw the Light. In every war, wound and atrocity, I saw the Light. And then, I saw all of your beautiful faces and my own, and I saw the Light. And I knew. There is only One."

The people around him sat in silence. A great longing was awakened in their hearts. And in a marbled hall in a far off galaxy all of their guides and guardian angels rejoiced.

*The Light*

*See it, feel it, be it.*

# The Light Poem

By Keidi Keating

The silent voice that whispers softly in unsuspecting ears,
The sea of inner peace that calms our pains and fears.

The spark of illogic giving birth to Love,
The pure and mighty presence pouring from above.

The mysterious force that dwells in the depths of our heart,
The silver chord that guides us when we nobly depart.

The blanket of knowing, protecting us as we sleep,
The invisible arms, comforting us when we weep.

The precious moon shining over dark night skies,
The sights of long-gone relatives returning to say goodbyes.

The Divine white butterfly fluttering amidst the trees,
The powerful feeling within, which brings us to our knees.

The strings of Godly energy that bind us together as One,
The splendid golden rays that spill to earth from the sun.

Now go on your way Light being; the road ahead is bright,
Remembering always the ultimate Truth; that you are the Light!

*The traveler stood in the heart of the luminous cave and gazed at his reflection in the crystal waters. And he laughed.*

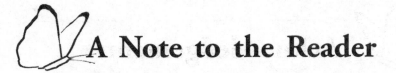# A Note to the Reader

As the saying goes, *Spread the Light!* When you have finished with this book, please pass it onto a friend or relative. The more people who read *The Light*, the greater the chance we have of achieving our goal. It is our sincere wish that every reader will shine even brighter, helping to raise awareness and uplift humanity in these times of great change.

Note that one hundred percent of the profits from every copy of *The Light* sold will be split between seven charities. The goal is to raise at least one million dollars for Alder Hey Charity (**www.alderheycharity.com**), The Forgiveness Project (**www.theforgivenessproject.com**), The Light Worldwide (**www.thelightworldwide.com**), Conversations with God Foundation (**www.cwg.org**), The Heartfelt Foundation (**www.heartfelt.org**), Love a Child Foundation (**www.loveachildfoundation.com**) and Shingirirai Trust (**www.shingirirai.org**).

For news and events about *The Light*, the authors and the beneficiary charities, log on to **www.thelightnetwork.com/thelight**.

# Acknowledgements

May we say a massive thank you to all the contributors of this book.

An extra special thank you goes to Julie Chimes and Richard Laws who spent a lot of their precious time and energy helping to put *The Light* together, enabling it to shine in its splendor. And to Terry Tillman for believing in me, believing in *The Light*, for his support, contacts and simply for being there.

And of course, you the readers deserve the biggest thank you of all; for trusting, believing and having the burning desire to improve your life and shine.

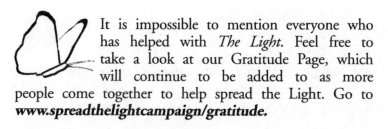

It is impossible to mention everyone who has helped with *The Light*. Feel free to take a look at our Gratitude Page, which will continue to be added to as more people come together to help spread the Light. Go to ***www.spreadthelightcampaign/gratitude.***

# About the Charities

Here is some information about the charities that are benefiting from sales of *The Light* and the amazing work they do.

---

The Forgiveness Project  is a UK-based charitable organization explaining forgiveness, reconciliation and conflict resolution through real-life human experience. The Forgiveness Project staff work in prisons, schools, faith communities and with any group who want to explore the nature of forgiveness, whether in the wider political context or within their own lives. The charity's vision is to build a better future by healing the wounds of the past. Its aims are:

☼ Awareness – to raise the debate about forgiveness by collecting and sharing personal stories.

☼ Education – to encourage and empower people to explore the nature of forgiveness and alternatives to conflict and revenge.

☼ Inspiration – to engage civil society and transform hearts and minds.

Website: ***www.theforgivenessproject.com.***

---

Alder Hey Children's Hospital in Liverpool, in the UK, is the busiest children's hospital in Europe, caring for more than 270,000 young patients each year from all over the north west of England. Founded in 1914, Alder Hey has led the way in the care of sick children and is committed to continue providing the very best pioneering treatment in a friendly and reassuring atmosphere that makes everyone welcome, even at the most difficult of times for the family.

In order to remain at the forefront, Alder Hey depends heavily on charitable funding to provide the things that make a difference. The aim of the charity is to generate substantial funds for the hospital and raise the profile of the appeal and awareness of Alder Hey both locally and internationally. This will help the hospital to continue its pioneering work; to develop facilities; and to offer the very highest standards of care to its young patients. Every donation received helps the hospital to achieve even more in improving the quality of life for children and young people in its care. Funds raised for the charity will be spent broadly in four areas:

☼ Research and Development

☼ Building Environment/Arts

☼ Medical Equipment and Advancement

☼ Patient and Family resources

Registered UK charity number: 1049275

Website: **www.alderheycharity.com**

*Our US supporters can donate online through the American Fund for Charities. Donations from US taxpayers are tax deductible to the extent allowed by US law. Please go to the website on the above link.*

The Light Worldwide is an innovative and exciting new way of raising funds to support those who are committed to uplifting the vibration of the planet through spreading Love and Light. Its first fundraising product is this extraordinary Book of Wisdom, *The Light*. Twenty-two leading luminaries have unconditionally donated their chapters. We aim to raise one million dollars by donating all of the net profit from sales of this book.

Mission Statement: "We have created The Light Worldwide because we have received so much and we want to give something back. We passionately want to help children, especially in the third world, through spiritual education and by supporting other social entrepreneurs who have touched our hearts with their selfless service to humanity."

Founder: Keidi Keating

Trustees: Julie Chimes, Keidi Keating, Terry Tillman

Website: ***www.thelightnetwork.com/about-us/our-charity***

---

The Conversations with God Foundation is a non-profit foundation created by Neale Donald Walsch to address the overwhelming response from people around the world who desire to do something tangible to spread the message of the *Conversations with God* series of books. In order to help people "be the change they wish to see," the Foundation has created retreats, activities and programs that allow people to use this message to change their own lives and the world at large.

In 1993, after receiving the first of the *Conversations with God* material, Neale was deeply inspired by the message that "the purpose of life is to recreate ourselves anew in the highest version of the grandest vision we ever had about ourselves." In order to take action as a result of the messages and guidance of the conversations, Neale wanted to make the truths and lessons from the CWG books not only functional, but also universally available. Therefore, he formed ReCreation, the Foundation for Personal Growth and Spiritual Understanding. The Foundation is known worldwide as The Conversations with God Foundation.

Website: ***www.cwg.org***

*The Light* is also supporting three smaller charities, mentioned below. We encourage you to take a look at their websites and donate to those which resonate with you.

 ***www.heartfelt.org***

 ***www.shingirarai.org***

 ***www.loveachildfoundation.com***

# SPREAD THE LIGHT CAMPAIGN

# Philanthropists Wanted!

You've read the book
You've ignited the spark
Now help us Spread the Light!

Find out ways in which
you can become more
involved...

## Thank you

www.spreadthelightcampaign.com
info@thelightnetwork.com
www.facebook.com/spreadthelightcampaign

# Coming soon in the Light series...

☼

## ✎ *Teachings from the Light*

**From the author, Keidi Keating:**

*"This is the end of an extraordinary journey. As I traveled the mystical road leading to the completion of* **The Light** *book I learned a number of spiritual lessons, sent direct from the Light. Then, one sunny morning from a mountaintop in Spain, I picked up my pen and began to write. All of the lessons I had learned during this adventure shone into my awareness and in those magical minutes, a new book called to my heart:* **Teachings from the Light**. *As my crown chakra tingled with a radiant energy, I received a message: 'Share these teachings with the world and just as you have seen the Light, others will see the Light too.'*
*Now I begin a new journey, delving deeper into the Light of All That Is. Maybe we will see each other on the road that lies ahead. Maybe we will look one another in the eyes as we radiate love from the depth of our hearts. Maybe together, we will see the Light."*

## ✎ *Experiences of the Light*

**Here is a selection of ordinary people's extraordinary experiences of the Light. Read them in full in the book along with a collection of others.**

*"Suddenly the whole room lit up and a beautiful lady appeared. The nearest I can tell you is that she looked like Cinderella, as if the fairy Godmother had waved her wand and made a sparkly, twinkly dress for her to wear."*

**~ Joseph Alexander**

"*I opened my eyes suddenly and there, sitting on the edge of my bed was a translucent figure of Light stroking my forehead as if to comfort me. She looked very beautiful and a sense of peace descended over me. I wondered if it might be a younger version of my Nan, who had recently passed over. She seemed shocked that I had seen her and she quickly stood up then darted in the direction of my bedroom door, before disappearing through it.*"

**~ Keidi Keating**

"*As I sat with her I entered a sort of trance-like state. I found myself in another reality walking with Mom hand in hand towards a bright Light. All around us was pink energy and I could feel immense love pulling us towards this Light.*"

**~ Kimberley Jones**

"*I felt my body speeding upwards towards the sky full of Light then I landed in what I thought was heaven in a room full of white marble with what I thought was Jesus sitting on this white marble throne.*"

**~ Marilyn St-Pierre**

"*It's so bright.*" *His voice was filled with awe and tears.* "*I've never seen Light like this,*" *he whispered.* "*It's so beautiful.*"

**~ Raederle Phoenix West Jacot**

"*As the knife entered my body there was an explosion. Everything before me was filled with a light which shone with a brightness beyond anything I had ever seen. All the images of life were before me and then they blended into a sea of dazzling points of light, trillions of multi-faceted gems reflecting a million suns. The cacophony of earthly sound exploded into one crystal-clear note and reverberated throughout the heavens. It was breathtaking. And I knew I was a part of that magnificence. I was the Light and all was well.*"

**~ Julie Chimes**

If you have an experience of the Light for potential publication in a future *Light* book, or for our website, please go to **www.thelightnetwork.com/storysubmission** and fill in your details.